The Economics of Sports Broadcasting

Chris Gratton and Harry Arne Solberg

Routledge
Taylor & Francis Group

LONDON AND NEW YORK

First published 2007
by Routledge
2 Park Square, Milton Park, Abingdon, Oxon OX14 4RN

Simultaneously published in the USA and Canada
by Routledge
270 Madison Ave, New York, NY 10016

Routledge is an imprint of the Taylor & Francis Group, an informa business

Typeset in Perpetua and Bell Gothic by
HWA Text and Data Management, Tunbridge Wells
Printed and bound in Great Britain by
The Cromwell Press, Trowbridge, Wiltshire

British Library Cataloguing in Publication Data
A catalogue record for this book is available from the British Library

Library of Congress Cataloging-in-Publication Data
Gratton, Chris 1948–
    The economics of sports broadcasting / Chris Gratton and Harry Arne Solberg.
        p.   cm.
    Includes bibliographical references and index.
    1. Television broadcasting of sports – Economic aspects.   I. Solberg, Harry Arne.
    II. Title
GV742.G73 2007
070.4´49796 – dc22

ISBN10: 0–415–35779–9 (hbk)
ISBN10: 0–415–35780–2 (pbk)
ISBN10: 0–203–00385–3 (ebk)

ISBN13: 978–0–415–35779–1 (hbk)
ISBN13: 978–0–415–35780–7 (pbk)
ISBN13: 978–0–203–00385–5 (ebk)

Contents

Case studies

Figures

Tables

Acknowledgements

The authors wish to thank the following individuals and organisations for their support and permission to reproduce material in this book:

David Collis; Frank Dunne, *TV Sport Markets;* Peter Elman, *TV Sport Markets;* Rodney Fort; Terje Gaustad; Sven A. Haugland; Stefan Kesenne; Morten Kringstad; Greg Mailer, Scottish Premier League; Lisa O'Keefe; James Pickles, *TV Sport Markets;* Torger Reve; Miriam Sherlock, *TV Sport Markets;* Boye Skistad, Norsk Toppfotball; Neil Shoebridge; Ben Speight, *TV Sport Markets;* Tommy Theorin, Swedish Football Association; *The Australian Financial Review;* Deloitte (*Annual Football Review*); International Marketing Reports Ltd (*International Journal of Sports Marketing and Sponsorship*) The Norman Chester Centre for Football Research; SportBusiness Group Ltd (*TV Sport Markets*)The University of Queensland (*The Internationational Journal of Event Management Research*); WorldScreen.com.

Every effort has been made to contact and acknowledge copyright owners, but the author and publishers would be pleased to have any errors or omissions brought to their attention so that corrections may be published at a later printing.

Chapter 1

Introduction

The most significant change in the sports industry over the last 20 years has been the increasing importance of broadcast demand for sport which has led to massive escalation in the prices of broadcasting rights for professional team sports and major sports events. At the beginning of the twenty-first century for the major professional team sports in both the USA and Europe income from the sale of broadcasting rights has become more important than the amount of income generated by selling tickets to spectators at the stadia. These developments first emerged in the USA in the 1980s but Europe started to catch up in the 1990s. Although there are close similarities between the price escalation for broadcasting rights for professional team sports in both the USA and Europe, there are important differences between the two continents in the way these rights are distributed over different categories of television channel.

Although live broadcasts of professional team sport games in the USA were established in the 1960s, even by 1980 major league baseball earned only $80 million from local and network television and radio (Fort and Quirk, 1999). By 1990, this had increased by nearly 800 per cent to $612 million. Similarly, the NFL had income from broadcasting rights of $167 million in 1980 but this had increased by close to 600 per cent to $948 million by 1990. By this time revenues from broadcasting rights became the single most important source of income for professional team sports in the USA.

The early years of the relationship between sport and television, however, gave no indication that this was likely to be the case. Quirk and Fort (1999) chronicle the early years of televised professional team sports in the USA which focused on the trade-off between new income from television and lost revenues from reduced attendances. In 1950, the Los Angeles Rams signed a contract involving the televising of six home games to viewers in the Los Angeles area. The contract specified that the sponsor would make up any loss resulting from lower attendances due to the live transmissions. The two home games that were not televised generated an average revenue of $77,000. The six televised games averaged only $42,000, resulting in the sponsor having to pay $198,000 in compensation. The contract was not renewed in 1951.

In these early years of televised professional team sports in the USA, this perceived negative impact on attendances was a major constraint on the development of more television coverage. It was also the case that live attendances at professional team sports, the National Football League (NFL) in particular, were nothing like the levels of today so that any drop off in attendance was a major threat to the leagues.

By the early 1960s, however, the market for televised sport in the USA had begun to change. McChesney (1989) identified four factors responsible for this change. First, for the first time television was available in most American homes. Secondly, the technology for sports broadcasting was changing with videotape allowing slow motion and replays and the advent of colour television substantially increasing the quality of the experience of television viewing of matches. Thirdly, the Sports Broadcasting Act 1961 allowed professional sports teams to negotiate together as a cartel with broadcasters substantially increasing their market power. Fourthly, broadcasters had started to appreciate the potential of using sport to sell advertising slots during the games. In particular, the type of audiences attracted to sports broadcasts were particularly attractive to advertisers who were therefore willing to pay a premium price for these slots.

In the 1960s increased competition amongst the three major networks, CBS, NBC and ABC, led to more television coverage of the four major team sports: American football, baseball, basketball and ice-hockey. Downward and Dawson (2000) and Cashmore (1994) argue that ABC, in particular, led the way with an aggressive attempt to broaden the interest in televised sport beyond the normal male audience introducing technical innovations such as slow motion replays, close-ups, and split screens. Increasing advertising revenues generated through televised sport drove the networks to extend their coverage. ABC was also the first to televise the summer Olympics in the 1960s.

By 1970, the NFL earned $49 million a year from the sale of broadcasting rights and this had increased to $167 million by 1980 (Quirk and Fort 1997). It was in the 1980s, however, that growth in the size of deals for sports broadcasting rights accelerated dramatically. Quirk and Fort (1997) estimated that in 1991 broadcast revenue accounted for 25 per cent of National Hockey League (NHL) revenues, 30 per cent of National Basketball Association (NBA) revenues, 50 per cent of baseball's American League (AL) and National League (NL) revenues, and 60 per cent of NFL revenues.

The escalation in the price of broadcasting rights continued during the 1990s. In early 1998, American broadcasters agreed to pay $17.6 billion for the rights for the NFL for eight years. The previous deal, for 1994–7 was for $1.1 billion. One of the reasons for the bidding up of the broadcasting rights to the NFL in 1998 was that CBS learnt its lesson in 1993 when it allowed Fox, which is owned by Rupert

Murdoch's News Corporation, to outbid it in the previous auction of broadcast rights for football. With the loss of the sport, CBS plunged from first to third in the rankings and this deal projected Fox to be one of the big four broadcasters in the United States together with NBC, CBS and ABC. In the 1998 deal, Fox and CBS shared NFL coverage with ABC and ESPN (both owned by Disney), and left NBC with no football coverage at all.

In America, the major funding for these television deals has come from free-to-air channels. Sport attracts massive audiences. American football is definitely the number one sport. Nine of the all-time top ten television programmes in terms of audience size are Super Bowl finals. The record is the 1996 Super Bowl final which attracted a TV audience of 138.5 million viewers. In recent years, MLB and NBA have competed for the number two status, while NHL is ranked as number four among the professional leagues. This picture is confirmed in Table 1.1 which shows the TV rights for the four major professional leagues. The table shows strong price increases, although one also finds periods with slower growth, for example in the early 1990s. Table 1.1 confirms NFL's dominating position also in monetary terms. However, as the table only includes deals between national channels and

Table 1.1 North American sports rights (only including central deals)

Period	Annual fees ($ 1,000)
NFL	
1998–2005	2,200,000
1994–7	1,097,000
1990–3	900,000
1987–9	468,000
1982–6	378,000
NBA	
1998–2002	660,000
1994–8	276,000
1990–4	219,000
1986–1990	63,000
1983–6	22,000
MLB	
2001–6	570,000
1996–2000	340,000
1990–3	352,000
NHL	
1999–2005	120,000
1994–9	43,000

Source: SportBusinessNews.com

the leagues, it does not convey the complete story. Over the years, MLB, NBA and NHL have received considerable amounts of money from selling TV-rights to local stations.

The motive of the television companies in bidding for such games is the ability to sell advertising slots at hugely inflated prices during such games, which last two or three times longer than the equivalent in Europe, and are broken more frequently by advertising slots than is the case in Europe. However, the benefits of having televised football go beyond the advertising revenues generated during the games. In fact, in most cases, the price of broadcasting rights exceeds considerably the amount of money generated in advertising. Quirk and Fort (1999) estimated that NBC's four-year NFL contract between 1990 and 1994 lost the network $200 million with CBS losing almost twice as much on the deal. Both networks, however, bid for the next contract and CBS lost out considerably by being outbid by Fox.

In contrast to the USA there was little or no competition in the European television market in the early post-war years. Although European countries differ substantially in the development of sport and broadcasting there are common trends and this will be illustrated by looking at the UK position in detail. In the UK, for instance, until 1955 there was only one channel, the BBC, a non-commercial public service broadcaster. Over this period the BBC developed extensive televised sports coverage in Britain, televising most of the major national sporting spectacles. Over this period, however, there was no live television coverage of the matches in the main professional team sports because of fears by these sports that live television coverage would reduce attendances at matches.

Whannel (1992) suggests that there were good economic reasons for the BBC to put so much emphasis on sport. He indicates the inequality of market power between the buyers and sellers of broadcasting rights for sports events that existed in the early part of the post-war period with one buyer, the BBC, faced by a large number of suppliers of sports events, leading to low broadcasting rights fees and cheap programming costs for the BBC's sport coverage.

The arrival of ITV, a commercial public service broadcaster, in 1955 destroyed the BBC's monopoly on the buying side of the market and increased the level of fees. However, the BBC continued to dominate the broadcasting of sport, with ITV only really competing to televise soccer.

Throughout the 1970s, soccer coverage was handled by negotiation between the BBC and ITV, and the Football League and the Football Association. The two TV channels cooperated to share coverage rather than compete against each other. Table 1.2 shows the history of the contracts for televised soccer from 1983, when the first televised live Football League matches were shown, until 2001. Deals for 1983–5 and 1986–8 were joint deals with both the BBC and ITV with the annual rights fee rising slightly from £2.6 million in the 1983–5 period to £3.1 million in the 1986–8 period.

Table 1.2 *The cost of the rights to live league matches from the top division in England, 1983 to 2001*

	1983	1985	1986	1988	1992	1997
Start date of the contract	1983	1985	1986	1988	1992	1997
Length of contract (years)	2	0.5	2	4	5	4
Broadcaster	BBC/ITV	BBC	BBC/ITV	ITV	BSkyB	BSkyB
Rights fee (£m)	5.2	1.3	6.2	44	191.5	670
Annual rights fee (£m)	2.6	2.6	3.1	11	38.3	167.5
Number of live matches per season	10	6	14	18	60	60
Fees per live match (£m)	0.26	0.43	0.22	0.61	0.64	2.79

The major escalation came when ITV pushed up the annual fee to £11 million in 1988–92 for its exclusive coverage with a large increase in the number of live televised matches to 18 per year.

It was not, however, until BSkyB, a pay-service satellite broadcaster, entered the scene, most notably with its bid for soccer's newly formed Premier League matches for the 1992–7 period, that the landscape of sports broadcasting in Britain changed dramatically. BSkyB, with its owners Rupert Murdoch's News Corporation (owners of Fox), used to the much stronger competition for sports broadcasting rights in the USA, simply raised the price for the rights from its artificially depressed level. The 250 per cent increase in the level of fees for televised soccer in 1988 was matched again in 1992 when BSkyB won the rights for 60 live matches of the Premier League at a cost of £38 million per year. When the deal was renegotiated in 1997 there was a further 337 per cent rise in the annual rights (MMC, 1999).

The 2001–4 deal of £1.1 billion was again with BSkyB, as was the 2004–7 deal. Both these deals involved more live matches per season. The fact there was no increase in the price BSkyB paid for the 2004–7 rights to all the live games was seen by many as an indicator that the boom time for broadcasting rights was over. By 2004, for many English Premier League clubs broadcasting income was already the single most important source of income. For Chelsea, for instance, in 2003/4 39 per cent of total revenue (£143.7 million) came from the sale of broadcasting rights compared to 37 per cent from matchday income, and 24 per cent from commercial income. Manchester United, with by far the largest capacity stadium in the Premier League (at 67,500), had the same proportion of revenue (36 per cent) for both broadcasting income and commercial income. Arsenal, on the other hand, with a stadium capacity of only 38,500 had 52 per cent of its total revenue coming from broadcasting income in 2003/4 with only 29 per cent coming from matchday income (Deloitte, 2005).

During the life of the 2004–7 contract the European Commission intervened on the grounds that BSkyB was in a monopoly position in relation to the control of broadcasting rights for live Premier League games. It insisted that when the rights for the 2007–10 period were auctioned that at least one of the packages offered went to a different broadcaster. As a consequence, of the six packages offered by the Premier League for the 2007–10 period, BSkyB only secured four of them consisting in total of 92 live matches. BSkyB paid £1.3 billion for these games at a cost of £4.76 million per game compared with an average cost per game over the 2004–7 period of £2.47 million per game, a 93 per cent increase in the cost to BSkyB. The other two packages went to an Irish television station, Setanta. Their packages consisted of 46 live games per year at a total cost of £392 million, or £2.8 million per game, considerably less than the cost to BSkyB but more than BSkyB paid for each game over the 2004–7 period. The total income to the Premier League from the new deal was £1.7 billion over three years, a massive 67 per cent increase compared to 2004–7. The intervention by the European Commission resulted in a considerable escalation in the price of the broadcasting rights.

Britain has followed America in the escalation in the fees for broadcasting rights for the major professional team sports. There is a clear difference, however, between the motives of the American broadcasters competing for the rights to the NFL and the motives of BSkyB, also 40 per cent owned by Rupert Murdoch's News Corporation, for acquiring the rights to Premiership soccer. American broadcasters bid up the rights to the NFL because of its importance in winning them market share, and also because of the ability to increase advertising revenues for advertisements during soccer games. BSkyB bids for Premiership rights to increase revenue from subscriptions to its pay-per-view channels.

For BSkyB, however, sport has become much more important economically than it ever was for the BBC. The BBC receives its revenue from the licence fee and has a responsibility to provide a breadth of programmes to satisfy 'the national interest'. This included prominence for sport because of the historically important role of sport in British culture. However, the BBC could never dedicate the share of its income (over 50 per cent) that BSkyB dedicates to sport, as this would be regarded as unbalanced for a public service provider.

Whereas in the American scenario, there is correspondence between the objectives of clubs, broadcasters, the league, advertisers and major sponsors since they all get maximum exposure to the country's largest television audiences, in the British case there is conflict between the objectives of the broadcaster (maximum subscriptions) and those of the league, clubs, advertisers and major sponsors (maximum exposure). To some extent, this conflict is reduced in British soccer by the fact that there is major soccer coverage on the BBC with the 'Match of the Day' highlights programmes and on ITV with the European Champions' League coverage, matches which achieved the highest television audiences of any sports programmes in the 1998/9 season. Whereas audiences for BSkyB's live Premiership matches vary between 1 million to 2 million with the odd key match getting slightly more than 2 million, 'Match of the Day' viewing figures often exceed 10 million although average viewing figures are around 6 million. ITV's live coverage of Manchester United versus Bayern Munich in May 1999 attracted an audience of 15.6 million in Britain (with a peak of 18.8 million).

Although soccer has managed to avoid the negative effects of reduced exposure on BSkyB, other professional team sports in Britain, in particular rugby league and rugby union, have not fared as well. Both these sports, encouraged by the success of the Premier League, signed exclusive contracts with BSkyB in 1996. Rugby League made the biggest change to its structure with the formation of Super League, playing in summer rather than winter, to fit in with Rupert Murdoch's Super League World Club Challenge involving Australian and New Zealand teams. However, in the case of rugby league, their normal television audience of 2.5–3.5 million that they achieved on BBC's Grandstand dropped to 100,000–200,000 on BSkyB. This represents a serious reduction in exposure and marketing of the sport.

Similarly, rugby union internationals in the Five Nations Championship involving England used to attract 4 million on the BBC, but dropped to below 500,000 on BSkyB. England were the least watched of all the Five Nations teams over this period despite a highlights programme on ITV following the live coverage on BSkyB. This is particularly a problem for the impact these sports have through their exposure to younger generations with potentially serious implications for the future economic health of these sports. As a consequence, England went back to the BBC Six Nations coverage when its BSkyB contract ran out.

These UK developments were mirrored in other European countries. The result has been that soccer has become the dominant TV-sport in Europe, both in terms of rating figures and rights fees. In 1998, a World Cup year, a soccer match topped the television programme popularity ranking lists in 75 per cent out of 50 European countries. In Germany and France, 86 per cent and 73 per cent respectively of the top 100 programmes were soccer-related. Six of the top ten TV programmes in the UK were soccer matches from the World Cup finals.

In the rest of Europe, as in the UK, the price escalation took off during the 1990s. This growth, however, did not correspond with the rate of growth in the rest of the economy. In each of the big-five soccer nations, the UK, Spain, Italy, Germany and France, the value of sports rights increased considerably faster than the Gross Domestic Product. For example, the Italian soccer rights increased by almost 250 per cent, in a period where the activity in the overall economy decreased by 4 per cent. In Italy, soccer absorbed 64 per cent of the total amount spent on sport rights in 2000. This proportion was 51 per cent in the UK and Spain, 41 per cent in Germany and 3 per cent in France.

In the Italian and Spanish leagues the top clubs negotiate individual broadcast rights contracts. Both AC Milan and Juventus had broadcast income close to £90 million in 2003/4, the highest of any soccer club in the world. In both cases it accounts for over 60 per cent of total revenue. At the other end of the scale, Celtic and Rangers received £16.1 million and £7.5 million respectively (the difference largely stemming from Celtic's longer run in European competitions) from broadcasting income in 2003/4 accounting for only 23 per cent and 13 per cent of their total income. These two clubs are big clubs from a small league and the collective broadcast rights deal for the Scottish Premier League disadvantages these two major clubs in income terms.

We can therefore see major differences between the European situation and the situation in the USA with regard to sports broadcasting over the post-war period. In Europe, professional team sports programmes were mainly broadcast on public service broadcasting channels until late in the 1980s. In recent years this pattern has changed. Pay channels have acquired a large slice of the most attractive soccer rights, while public service broadcasting channels and other channels with maximum penetration have been restricted to highlights programmes. As an example, live matches from the domestic premier leagues in the 'big-five' European soccer nations are only screened on pay channels.

The discussion above indicates that European prices were significantly cheaper than American prices for sports broadcasting rights until the 1990s. The main reason for this was a lack of competition, combined with the strict regulation of European broadcasting which made it impossible for the channels to spend the same amount on sports rights as the US networks. This pattern changed late in the 1980s when European broadcasting was commercialised. Over the years, a large number of profit-maximising TV channels entered the scene and acquired sports rights in order to strengthen their market position. Advertising channels have given priority to programmes which are able to achieve high rating figures. Pay-service channels have concentrated on acquiring sports rights which attract a sufficient number of viewers willing to pay to watch. The latter channels have been especially successful in acquiring the rights to live matches from the domestic soccer leagues pushing soccer way ahead of the other sports in terms of income from broadcasting rights. The main reason for the price escalation in Europe was the deregulation in the broadcasting market in the 1980s creating much greater competition for sports broadcasting rights, turning a buyers' market into a sellers' market.

In addition to the escalation of boadcasting rights fees for domestic leagues, we have also seen a similar escalation for the two major global international sporting events, the summer Olympics and soccer's World Cup. Table 1.3 shows the escalation in the broadcast rights fees for the summer Olympics in Australia, Europe and the USA between 1992 and 2008. Fees increased by 88 per cent for Australia, 122 per cent for the USA and a massive 366 per cent for Europe over this period. However, when the fees are put on a per capita basis, Australia pays the most per head of population at just over $3 per head for the 2008 Olympic Games. The USA pays a similar amount per head but Europe only pays around $0.5 per head. A similar escalation occurred in the rights for soccer's World Cup. The three competitions,

■ **Table 1.3** *Summer Olympic rights (US $million)*

	Australia	Europe	US	Total
1980	1.4	7.2	72.3	100.0
1984	10.6	22.0	225.0	287.0
1988	7.4	30.2	300.0	403.0
1992	34.0	95.0	401.0	636.0
1996	30.0	248.0	456.0	898.2
2000	45.0	350.0	705.0	1331.5
2004	51.0	394.0	793.0	1498.0
2008	64.0	443.0	894.0	1715.0

Source: Multimedia.olympic.org/pdf/en_report_344.pdf; 2002 LOC Salt Lake City, US Olympic Committee

Note: US and Europe do not include profit-sharing

1990, 1994 and 1998 sold to a consortium of mainly public broadcasters for a total of $344 million. The two competitions in 2002 and 2006 were sold to Kirch of Germany for $2.36 billion.

Why has sport been seen such an escalation in the price of broadcasting rights?

Todreas (1999) provides a possible explanation that relates more to the development of the television industry than that of the sports industry. His explanation is mainly in the context of the US market. Todreas points to the supply chain of television programmes which consists of 'content' and 'conduit'. 'Conduit' refers to the distribution of programmes to consumers by the television companies. He refers to this as the downstream end of the supply chain. 'Content' consists of the upstream suppliers, in our case the teams and leagues that produce sports contests. As television markets have developed, he argues that value 'migrates upsteam', that is profitability switches from the owners of the conduit to the owners of the content.

To explain this, he identifies three eras in the history of television: the broadcast era (for the USA, late 1940s to early 1970s); the cable era (early 1970s to early 1990s); and the digital era (early 1990s to the present). He argues that in the broadcast era, it was the television stations that owned the conduit that were highly profitable because of their monopoly power. There were few suppliers and these tended not to compete directly with each other but rather operate more as a cartel. The cable era saw some expansion of operators at the conduit end of the supply chain, but cable licences were restricted with often only one granted for each municipality.

The digital era, however, brought in new competitors in the distribution of programmes and new ways (e.g. telephone, internet) of distributing content. This new competition reduced margins and profits, and destroyed value in the conduit and increased value in the content. The new technology changed the methods of distribution but it did not change the process of content creation. Sports teams and leagues supplying content were in a strong bargaining position. There was increased competition for the limited supply of sport content.

If this was the situation in the USA, the situation was even more favourable for sports content owners in new markets targeted by the new generation of broadcasters. Sports programmes almost uniquely had this ability to attract the size and characteristics of audiences most attractive to distributors, sponsors and advertisers. These audiences were also willing to pay a premium price to broadcasters to receive more of the sports content than had been previously supplied by the old free-to-air networks. As these developments were taking place, in Europe in particular, governments were stepping back from the old regulatory distribution systems and liberalising television in order to encourage the development of the new digital technology. However, it was not long before these same governments stepped in to regulate what they perceived to be the adverse effects on sports broadcasting from the new television landscape.

Although the escalation in the price of broadcasting rights for sports events and leagues is the single largest development in the sports broadcasting market, it is not the only one. In 1964, CBS bought the New York Yankees for $14 million. In 1965, Jack Kent Cooke, a cable TV operator, bought the Los Angeles Lakers and a year later the Los Angeles Kings. Although CBS and Cooke resold these franchises in the 1970s, these episodes signalled the beginnings of a closer relationship between television companies and professional sports teams in the USA that was to become more common both in the USA and globally in later years.

In more recent times, we have seen the growth in what has been called the 'global mass media oligopoly' (Law, Harvey and Kemp 2002) including AOL-Time Warner, Bertelsmann, Disney Corporation, News Corporation, Viacom and Vivendi-Universal. In many of these global media giants sport has played an important role. AOL-Time Warner owns the Atlantic Hawks of the NBA and the Atlanta Braves of the NL. Disney Corporation, which owns ABC and ESPN, also owns the NHL team, the Anaheim Ducks.

Perhaps the strongest relationship between sport and global media expansion, however, is that of Rupert Murdoch's News Corporation. Andrews (2003) analysed how News Corporation used sport as an instrument for successfully penetrating national television markets within the USA, the UK, Asia and Australasia. We have already discussed how Fox did this by using sports broadcasting rights in the USA and BSkyB did the same in the UK. Similar tactics were achieved by Foxtel in Australia, JSkyB in Japan, Zee TV in India and Sky in New Zealand. In most of these cases (the main exception being Fox in the USA), the News Corporation channel was introduced as a pay-per-view channel, with sports prominent, into markets conventionally used to free-to-air public service broadcasting.

We will return to analyse in more detail these trends and themes identified in this chapter in later chapters of this book. Most chapters of the book concentrate on the interrelationship between broadcasting and sport on the supply side of the market. Before we move on to that though the next chapter considers the demand for broadcast sport.

Chapter 2

The demand for sports broadcasting

The demand for sports broadcasting is inextricably linked to the demand to watch major sports events. Fans of sport have a choice: they can pay to watch the match live, where the total cost will include the price of entry to the stadium, the cost of travel to and from the stadium, and the costs of food, drink and sometimes accommodation associated with the trip. In the case of major sports events such as the World Cup in soccer or the Olympics, such costs can be exceedingly high. Even in the case of a fan supporting a local professional team to an away fixture, such costs are significant and have risen steeply over the last decade in many sports. If the event is broadcast live, watching the event on television may provide a substantially cheaper substitute. In many cases, the marginal cost of watching a sporting contest on television (e.g. the Olympics or the World Cup) is zero. Increasingly, watching sport on television will require the fan to pay for the privilege through a pay-per-view channel. Even then, the total cost of watching on television will normally be substantially cheaper than attending the game live.

To understand the demand for broadcast sport then it is important to look at the parent demand function, the demand to watch live sport. We then need to analyse the derived demand to watch broadcast sport and the relationship between the two demand functions. In analysing these demand functions we will concentrate on the main area of broadcast sport, professional team sports. Finally, in this chapter we look at three case studies of the demand for broadcast sport, a major European swimming championship, rugby league in Britain and the World Snooker Championship.

DEMAND FOR PROFESSIONAL TEAM SPORTS

The analysis of demand for professional team sports follows the standard consumer choice model. The quantity demanded of the product (i.e. the game) depends on the price of the activity, the prices of other activities that may have a substitute or complementary relationship with live spectating at the game and the income of the consumer. The price variable is more complicated than simply the price of admission since it needs to take into account the cost of travel to and from the venue and also other costs associated with going to the game such as expenditure on food, drink and maybe the match programme.

One possible substitute relationship that has been discussed in the literature is whether a live broadcast of a match has a negative effect on attendances at the game. We saw in Chapter 1 that early experiments in broadcasting sport did have a significant negative effect on attendance demand. Later studies, however, have been less conclusive. American studies have found a negative impact in baseball (Thomas and Jolson, 1979), college football (Fizel and Bennett, 1989) and basketball (Zhang and Smith, 1997). In Europe, Bainbridge et al. (1995) found a negative effect for rugby league but the loss in revenue by the club in gate receipts was more than compensated for by the facility fee paid to the club by the broadcaster.

One of the key features that makes the economics of professional team sports 'peculiar' is that demand for the product is positively related to the uncertainty of outcome as El-Hodiri and Quirk (1971) state:

> the essential economic fact concerning professional team sports is that gate receipts depend crucially on the uncertainty of the outcome of the games played within the league. As the probability of either team winning approaches one, gate receipts fall substantially, consequently, every team has an economic motive for not becoming too superior in playing talent compared to other teams in the league.

Economists have highlighted this as the crucial feature of the professional team sport industry that distinguishes it from all other industries. The conventional textbook firm in economic theory has an interest in increasing its market power and ultimately it maximises its own interest (and profit) when it achieves maximum market power as a monopolist. In professional team sport once a team becomes a monopolist, revenue would disappear altogether; output would be zero since it would be impossible to stage a match.

One major function of the league is to ensure that no team achieves too much market power, or excessive dominance. The league therefore aims to restrict competition. This explains why price competition between clubs is effectively prevented. Other non-competitive characteristics of professional team sports' leagues include labour market restrictions giving clubs property rights in players and the pooling of revenues so that poorer clubs are cross-subsidised by the richer ones. As Noll (1974) points out:

> Nearly every phase of a team or league is influenced by practices and rules that limit economic competition within the industry. In most

cases government has either sanctioned or failed to attack effectively these anti-competitive practices. Consequently professional team sports provide economists with a unique opportunity to study the operation and performance of an effective and well-organised control.

Despite almost universal acceptance by economists writing in this area that uncertainty of outcome is the key to demand analysis in professional team sports, Cairns *et al.* (1986) point out the lack of conclusive empirical evidence in support of this contention:

> Given the importance of uncertainty of outcome to professional team sports research, it is unfortunate that not only has empirical testing of the key relationship between demand and uncertainty of outcome been limited, but also that the discussion of this central concept has been unmethodical, if not confused. Inadequate attention has been paid to determining the appropriate empirical specifications of the underlying theoretical notions.

They go on to point out that at least three distinct versions of the uncertainty of outcome hypothesis have appeared in the literature: uncertainty of match outcome, uncertainty of seasonal outcome and uncertainty of outcome in the sense of the absence of long-run domination by one club.

Quirk and Fort (1997) incorporate all three aspects of the uncertainty of outcome hypothesis in their measure of competitive balance in American professional sports leagues:

> Our primary emphasis, however, is in the dispersion ('spread') of W/L percentages in a league and the concentration of championships and high W/L percentages among league teams. A league in which team W/L percentages are bunched together around .500 displays more competitive balance than does a league in which team W/L percentages are widely dispersed; and the more concentrated is the winning of championships and high W/L percentage among a few teams, the less competitive balance there is in a league.

The approach Quirk and Fort (1997) take is based on the work of Noll (1988). This approach is effectively comparing the actual performance of a league to the performance that would have occurred if the league had the maximum degree of competitive balance in the sense that all teams had equal playing strengths. The degree of competitive balance is greater the smaller the deviation of actual league performance from that of the ideal league where all teams have equal playing strengths. They carried out this analysis for all the five major American professional team sports leagues (National Football League (NFL), National Basketball Association (NBA), National Hockey League (NHL) and the two baseball leagues, the American League (AL) and the National League (NL)) for each decade from 1901 to 1990.

Quirk and Fort (1997) found that all five leagues operated with a significant degree of competitive imbalance. The NFL had the most competitive balance, and the NBA the least, but even the NFL fell a long way short of the ideal league. They concluded:

> One obvious conclusion from our extended look at historical data on competitive balance in the five major team sports leagues is that none of the leagues comes close to achieving the ideal of equal playing strengths. There is ample evidence of long-term competitive imbalance in each league, despite the league rules that are supposedly designed to equalise team strengths. On the other hand, with all their flaws, the leagues have not only survived but have flourished, with growth in numbers of teams, in geographic coverage, in attendance and public interest, and in profitability.

One interpretation of their conclusion would be that uncertainty of outcome and maintenance of competitive balance are not as important to the success of professional team sports leagues as the previous economic literature has suggested. Another interpretation would be that the various restrictions on competition imposed by American sports leagues have achieved sufficient competitive balance to make the leagues successful.

Although uncertainty of outcome may be a major determinant of attendances at a whole league over a season, each individual club is mainly concerned about its own home gates. One major determinant of this is the size of the local market, in terms of population. Also the number of clubs competing in the local catchment area will influence the size of each club's attendances.

A major determinant, however, of any one club's demand will be playing success. In general, other things being equal, the more successful the club, the higher the attendance. This is an obvious conflict with the uncertainty of outcome hypothesis discussed above. Whereas each club can maximise its attendances by maximising the number of wins, the league as a whole may suffer by a reduced uncertainty of outcome. This conflict is a major feature of professional team sports.

Despite this conflict, it is generally accepted that the role of the league is to operate as a cartel to restrict open competition between clubs in both the product and labour markets so that no one club becomes too dominant (Cairns et al., 1986). The cartel model as a representation of the sports league is based on the assumption of profit maximisation of both the club and the league. In order for the league to secure profit maximisation for the group of clubs that make up the league, it is necessary for the league to impose restrictions on the profit maximisation of individual clubs.

The role of the league in managing the collective interests of all clubs is in direct conflict with the individual profit maximisation interests of the most successful clubs, who would be more profitable without the restrictions imposed by the league. The league has the objective of ensuring uncertainty of outcome and competitive balance. Each individual club has the objective of maximising sporting success and the consequent economic benefits of television, sponsorship and gate money revenue. This conflict of interest between the objectives of the cartel and those of individual members of it is the classic scenario of the economics of cartels. Normally, the cartel's role is not only to impose product and labour market restrictions on members, but also to restrict output in order to keep the price high. In American team sports, in the NFL for instance, this restriction of output is exhibited by no team playing more than one game a week and the length of the season is restricted to one-third of the year. The number of teams in the league is also strictly controlled.

DEMAND FOR BROADCASTS OF PROFESSIONAL TEAM SPORTS

Although there are a large number of studies of attendance demand at professional team sports, the demand to watch live broadcasts of matches has received little attention by economists. Two American studies (Hausman and Leonard, 1997 and Kanazawa and Funk, 2001) looked at the demand for televised basketball matches in the USA. The first concentrated on the effect of having a 'superstar' in the game and the second on having a high proportion of white players in the game. A more comprehensive modelling of television demand is the study by Forrest et al. (2004). They argue that there are particular advantages in modelling television demand rather than attendance demand for Premier League soccer matches in England, in particular because it avoids various problems that undermine estimation of models of attendance demand.

The first problem is caused by the fact that most of the tickets to Premier League grounds are allocated to season ticket holders. Since most season ticket holders attend every home game, the variance in attendances between games is therefore wholly due to variance in the number of people paying for tickets on a game by game basis. However, no data is normally available on this element of demand. Normally studies use total attendance figures which will lead to underestimation of the elasticity of demand with respect to any match characteristic included in the regression equation. Another problem is due to the common situation for many Premier League clubs that home games are a sell out and therefore actual demand cannot be observed. Neither of these problems is applicable to the measurement of television demand. There is no capacity constraint and no equivalent to the season ticket effect and the variance in the observed television demand is therefore more likely to reflect the attractiveness of the matches to the viewers.

Forrest, Simmonds and Buraimo (2004) model not only the determinants of the television audience but also the determinants of the broadcaster's choice of which game to show. Over the period studied, 1993–2002, BSkyB had exclusive rights to live broadcasts of Premier League games. The choices of matches broadcast before Boxing Day were made pre-season therefore no account could be taken of actual league performance during that season. Matches after Boxing Day could be selected on the basis of which matches were likely to be most interesting given the relative positions of the team in the league. Consequently, independent variables used to explain BSkyB's choice of matches to broadcast fall into three categories: season-long variables, pre-Boxing Day variables and post-Boxing Day variables.

The current strength of teams was a major factor in determining BSkyB's choice on screening a match. The strength of a team post-Boxing day can be represented by current season performance. However, pre-Boxing Day matches are selected before this information is available and Forrest *et al.* use the size of the wage bill for the two clubs (combined wages) as a proxy for the quality of the players in the match. This variable proved to be significant in the determination of match choice pre-Boxing Day. Uncertainty of outcome also cannot be measured directly pre-Boxing Day since normally relative league position would be used to measure this but this is not available to the broadcaster at the time match choice is made. Instead, difference in relative wages is used to represent matches where the teams are likely to be relatively closely matched and those where they are not. This variable was significant with a negative sign suggesting that matches were most likely to be selected where the playing strengths of the two sides were perceived as similar and less likely to be selected where there was a large difference in the perceived quality of the two sides as reflected in the cost of the players' wages at each club prior to the season.

Post-Boxing Day match selection could take account of performances in the current season and match significance (whether the match involved a team that were likely to be either champions of take a European qualification place) and uncertainty of outcome were both significant in the post-Boxing Day match selections.

In the estimation of the model for audience demand, the combined wages variable was significant with a positive sign indicating that viewers were more inclined to watch matches involving the highest paid players. Audiences increased by more than a quarter in matches where the wage bill was twice the average. Again, audiences were higher when the match involved one of the top two teams in the league but there was no significant effect for matches involving teams in the European qualification places.

Uncertainty of outcome was significant for post-Boxing Day matches but not for the pre-Boxing Day period. However, the quantitative significance of the outcome uncertainty variable is limited even in the post-Boxing Day period leading Forrest *et al.* to conclude 'that even radical measures to change the degree of competitive balance in the Premier League would have limited impact on the incomes of the member clubs'. Thus they argue that unlike some studies of attendance demand it is possible to show a significant effect for uncertainty of outcome on the size of the audience for televised matches although the effect is modest.

The Forrest *et al.* study shows it feasible to model the demand for broadcast sport and that some of the variables that influence the demand for live attendance, such as uncertainty of outcome, also have an influence in determining the demand for broadcast sport. In the rest of this chapter we concentrate on three specific case studies of demand for broadcast sport. The first looks at how the timing of the broadcast can have an important impact on the size of the audience in the case of a major swimming championship. The second examines how the switch from a terrestrial channel to a satellite channel can have a dramatic effect on audiences even when the amount of coverage increases substantially. The third concentrates on how audience size can be used by sponsors and host cities to put a valuation on the place marketing benefits an event can generate.

■ *Case study 2.1* *Assessing the public profile of major sports events: a case study of the European Short Course Swimming Championships*

Simon Shibli and Chris Gratton (1999)

This case study examines the 'public profile' of the European Short Course Swimming Championships (ESCSC), held in Sheffield in 1998, achieved via dedicated television coverage of the event. Although the main objective of the research was an assessment of the public profile of the event, the results are also relevant for two other key parties. First, it allows the main sponsor of the event, adidas, to make an assessment of how much their investment cost compared with the return achieved. Secondly, the governing body (ASFGB) is able to have a greater appreciation of the value of their television rights and also the price at which it can realistically sell sponsorship packages. Obviously, the greater the public profile of the event, then the greater the exposure will be for the sponsor's name and the more the governing body can command for sponsorship rights.

The ESCSC were held in Sheffield between 11 and 13 December 1998 and were hosted by the Amateur Swimming Federation of Great Britain (ASFGB). The event was only the second major short course championships held in Europe. In 1996, Rostock had hosted the first European Sprint Championships, but these had failed to establish themselves in the swimming calendar and were viewed as having been only a modest success.

The ESCSC were televised in the UK and in mainland Europe. In total six countries took live feed during the European Broadcast Union's 'offer times'. The 'offer time' is the time slot offered by the host broadcaster to affiliated members of the European Broadcast Union (EBU). In the case of this event, the BBC was the host broadcaster and was able to offer its 'feed' to EBU affiliates. This means that people buying the 'feed' only have to add their own commentary to the images produced by the host broadcaster. This enables considerable economies to be achieved as well as avoiding numerous camera crews from different nations competing for the same images.

The offer times for ESCSC were as follows:

1   11 December 1998 16.00–18.10 GMT
2   12 December 1998 16.00–17.55 GMT
3   13 December 1998 15.00–17.15 GMT

A total of six broadcasters were taking live feed, however no data are available for the Greek broadcaster 'ERT Greece' and thus the results are based upon the five broadcasters for whom data were available. Although the broadcasters featured in this report subscribed to the offer times above, it does not necessarily mean that they actually showed the event live. In a number of cases, broadcasters take the live feed and record their own commentary over the pictures. Full coverage or edited highlights may then be shown at some other time, for example in the case of Italy, at one o'clock in the morning.

All audience figures used here were collated from official sources. For the UK the figures are supplied by the Broadcasters' Audience Research Board (BARB) and the European figures are supplied by Eurodata. The sources of data serve two important and complementary purposes. First, BARB and Eurodata confirm independently that the broadcasts actually took place. Secondly, having confirmed that broadcasts actually took place, it is then possible to deduce that the viewing figures, market share and other performance indicators actually relate to the event concerned.

The method used by BARB to arrive at audience figures is the largest piece of ongoing research of its type in the world. A total of 12,000 people in 4,500 homes across the UK have been recruited to report on their viewing habits. Each household is provided with an electronic device that relays to BARB the programmes people in a given house are watching. From this sample, the proportions of the sample watching given programmes are aggregated upwards for the population as a whole.

Glossary of terms

In order to understand fully the data shown in the tables in this section, it is worth clarifying some of the terminology that is used.

Audience

The actual number of people watching a given programme at a given time. For example, on Saturday 12 December 1998, during the 16.10 to 16.40 slot shown on Grandstand (BBC1), the size of the audience watching the swimming was 2,677,000.

Percentage share

The proportion of people watching a given programme expressed as a function of the total number of people watching television at that time. Thus, if 2,677,000 people were watching the swimming between 16.10 and 16.40 on 12 December 1998, and the percentage share for the swimming coverage was 23 per cent, then during the times in question 12,420,000 people in total were watching television in the UK.

Television rating (TVR)

The TVR of a programme is the key performance indicator of the size of an audience for any given programme. TVR is expressed as the percentage of all the people in a country with access to a television actually watching the programme or programme segment in question. In the case of the UK, there are approximately 54 million people with access to a television. Thus if a programme has an audience of 2.6 million (e.g. the swimming on 12 December 1998) then it would achieve a TVR of $((2.6/54) \times 100) = 4.9$ per cent. That is to say, on average 4.9 per cent of the UK population with access to television watched the programme.

Programme segment

A programme segment is a part of a composite programme (e.g. Grandstand) that is made up of a number of different sections. In the case of Grandstand the programme segments might be: Football Focus, horse racing, a featured sport such as rugby union, half-time soccer scores and Final Score. The audience figures for each segment are provided by BARB and can be used to make comparisons between the viewing figures for the various sports being covered in the programme.

Results

The results of this research are discussed in three parts:

1   the absolute audience size and market share in countries taking live feed;
2   an analysis of the audiences for the different segments of the Grandstand programmes in the UK which showed the swimming championships on Saturday 12 December 1998 (BBC1) and Sunday 13 December 1998 (BBC2);

3   an analysis of the audience for the prime swimming broadcast (12 December 1998 16.10–16.40) compared with the best performing segments on Grandstand over the previous month.

The audience size and market share in countries taking live feed

From the five countries where the broadcast and audience data were available, the ESCSC attracted a cumulative audience of 7,973,000 of which 5,451,000 were UK viewers. The UK broadcasts and their key performance indicators are shown in Table 2.1.

Table 2.1 shows that, in total, coverage of the ESCSC in the UK totalled 369 minutes (6 hours 9 minutes) on BBC and Eurosport channels. The highest share (percentage of those actually watching television) achieved was 23 per cent which equates to 4.9 per cent of the UK's television watching public. BBC coverage accounted for 98 per cent of the audience figures with Eurosport claiming the remaining 2 per cent. The most popular slot was on Saturday 12 December 1998 during the Grandstand programme. This slot is arguably the most prestigious non-soccer segment in Grandstand as it falls between the regular half-time soccer scores round-up and Final Score, the most watched part of Grandstand. An important feature of the 16.10 to 16.40 time slot is that updates of latest scores in both English and Scottish soccer matches are provided on screen on a continual basis which act as an additional incentive for viewers to watch the sport being featured in that time slot.

In mainland Europe the data for the broadcasts shown in Germany, Italy and Finland are shown in Tables 2.2–2.4.

A total of 229 minutes (3 hours 49 minutes) of the ESCSC were broadcast in Germany to a total audience of 789,000 viewers. The highest share achieved was 1.7 per cent of those people watching television which in turn equates to 0.4

■ **Table 2.1** UK broadcasts' data

Date	Channel	Programme	Duration (mins)	Start time	Audience (000s)	Share (%)	TVR (%)
11/12/98	Eurosport	ESCSC	72	16:35	41	0.9	0.2
12/12/98	Eurosport	ESCSC	97	16:00	47	1.0	0.2
12/12/98	BBC1	Grandstand	10	14:55	1,186	14.0	2.2
12/12/98	BBC1	Grandstand	30	16:10	2,677	23.0	4.9
13/12/98	Eurosport	ESCSC	85	16:05	10	0.2	0.1
13/12/98	BBC2	Grandstand	75	15:45	1,490	10.7	2.7
Totals		6	369		5,451		

Source: BARB

Note: ESCSC = European Short Course Swimming Championships

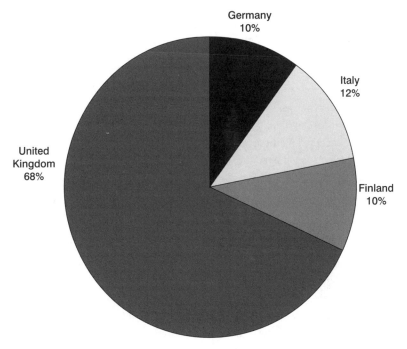

■ **Figure 2.1** *Country share of total European audience*
Source: BARB, Eurodata

■ **Table 2.5** *Summary of ESCSC television coverage*

Indicator	United Kingdom	Other European	Total
Number of programmes	6	12	18
Total duration (minutes)	369	718	1,087
Cumulative audience (000s)	5,451	2,522	7,973
Highest share achieved	23.0%	9.8%	23.0%
Highest TVR achieved	4.9%	9.0%	9.0%

Source: BARB, Eurodata

them in the past. Commercial revenues can make a significant contribution to the operating costs of an event and thus it is important that value for money is achieved when advertising and sponsorship sales are being made. As UK Sport increases its understanding of sponsorship, it may enjoy downward pressure on the proportion of an event which it is asked to fund (currently up to 35 per cent) as governing bodies become more able to secure an economic rate for their sponsorship rights.

Second, host venues, advertisers and sponsors can evaluate the return on their investment. For example, the total value of the Sheffield City Council support of the event was £25,000. This can be traded off against the value of the place marketing achieved. Using the data in Table 2.5, a degree of quantitative evaluation of place marketing can be made. A 'Sheffield National City of Sport' advertising board was on display at pool deck level alongside the main sponsor's (adidas) advertising board. The number of minutes a board was on display for, linked to the size of the audience, can be converted into a cash equivalent. Regardless of the methods used to value sponsorship exposure the basic points are clear, that is, sponsorship exposure does have a commercial value and that there are methods of valuing this exposure using industry accepted methods.

Third, for events supported by National Lottery funds via the World Class Events Programme, the broadcast data has an important role in evaluating the public profile achieved by an event. As governing bodies become more familiar with research reports such as this, more precise answers may be given on the bidding forms about the likely public profile an event will achieve. In the applications made to the World Class Events Programme thus far, a major characteristic has been the misguided assumption that television coverage *per se* can be assumed to confer a positive 'public profile' on an event. To date, there is no evidence of governing bodies contextualising their anticipated television coverage by making estimates of audience sizes, market share or TVR ratings. Perhaps the most significant contribution of this case-study is to air in the public domain the notion that the benefits of television coverage are not homogenous and that different qualities and values of television coverage exist. Thus not only should governing bodies submit estimates of the amount of television coverage their event will achieve, they should also be able to set targets for the 'quality' of that coverage in terms of audience size, market share and TVR rating. This in turn will provide the UK Sport with further information with which to evaluate bids pre-event and to justify its own investment in an event.

Having analysed the audience for the event in broad terms and discussed the implications, we now focus on a more contextual and micro-scale analysis of the UK findings.

An analysis of Grandstand by segment for 12 and 13 December 1998

Figure 2.2 shows clearly that the main coverage of the swimming on 12 December 1998 was the second most watched segment of the Grandstand programme on that day. A total of 4.9 per cent of the television-watching public (some 2.6 million people) watched live coverage of the event between 16.10 and 16.40. The only segment which enjoyed a higher rating was Final Score which focuses mainly on soccer results in England and Scotland. Final Score has the added attraction of being the first opportunity many people have to check their football pools coupons and thus it is not surprising that this is consistently the most popular slot of the programme.

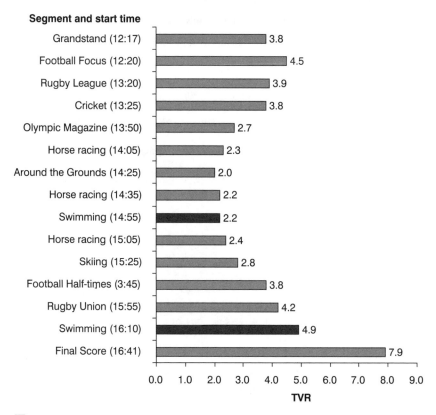

Segment and start time

Grandstand (12:17)	3.8
Football Focus (12:20)	4.5
Rugby League (13:20)	3.9
Cricket (13:25)	3.8
Olympic Magazine (13:50)	2.7
Horse racing (14:05)	2.3
Around the Grounds (14:25)	2.0
Horse racing (14:35)	2.2
Swimming (14:55)	2.2
Horse racing (15:05)	2.4
Skiing (15:25)	2.8
Football Half-times (3:45)	3.8
Rugby Union (15:55)	4.2
Swimming (16:10)	4.9
Final Score (16:41)	7.9

TVR

Figure 2.2 *TVR BBC1 Grandstand 12 December 1998*
Source: BARB

It is notable that the swimming achieved a higher rating than the weekly soccer magazine programme Football Focus, rugby league, Ashes cricket highlights, skiing and rugby union. This finding endorses the notion of the 'quality' of television coverage. The ESCSC achieved a TVR of 2.2 per cent at 14.55, i.e. five minutes before kick off in the various soccer leagues, yet 75 minutes later i.e. after half time in the soccer, the TVR had more than doubled to 4.9 per cent. Thus in terms of the valuation of sponsorship rights it is not the mere fact that a minority sport will be featured on television that is important but also the precise timing of the coverage. Obviously any governing body who can secure BBC coverage in the 16.10 to 16.40 slot during the soccer season is in a particularly strong negotiating position with potential sponsors.

A similar pattern of TVR ratings emerged on Sunday 13 December 1998 when the final day of the championships was shown on BBC2's Sunday Grandstand programme, as shown in Figure 2.3.

The audience on BBC2 for the final day of the event was 1,490,000 viewers which was only 56 per cent of the total who had watched coverage the previous day

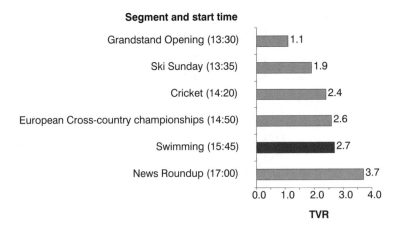

Segment and start time

Figure 2.3 *TVR BBC2 Grandstand 13 December 1998*
Source: BARB

on BBC1. The TVR rating also fell from 4.9 per cent to 2.7 per cent. This may seem to be a surprising figure given that the final day of a championship is arguably the most prestigious.

The explanation for this finding may be that many sports shown on BBC1 enjoy artificially high viewing figures because of the beneficial effects of intermittent soccer coverage. That is to say, some viewers who would otherwise not watch swimming do so because they are also being constantly updated with soccer scores. The only difference between Saturday 12 December and Sunday 13 December was that on the Saturday there was a full programme of league soccer in England and Scotland, whereas on the Sunday only a few soccer matches were played, primarily for the benefit of Sky TV subscribers. The contrast between the Saturday and Sunday viewing figures for the ESCSC suggests that television coverage *per se* does not guarantee a high public profile. For a sport such as swimming featured on a multi-sports programme such as Grandstand, the key determinant of the value of sponsorship rights is the timing and the context of the coverage rather than the sport itself.

Regardless of the relative strengths of Grandstand and Sunday Grandstand and the 'propping up' effect of the swimming being featured between half time and full time in the soccer, the coverage of the ESCSC achieved the second highest TVR ratings during each Grandstand programme. These are highly valuable benefits to be able to offer to sponsors. For a company such as adidas the event represented an ideal opportunity to place its message in the living rooms of both swimming and soccer enthusiasts at a rate indirectly subsidised by National Lottery funding.

Segment and date of broadcast

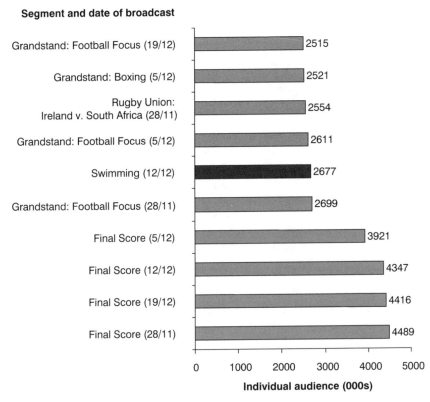

Figure 2.4 *Top ten Grandstand segments 28 November 1998–19 December 1998*
Source: BARB

The ESCSC in context

To put the viewing figures for the ESCSC into a broader context, we examined the 10 highest rating segments of the BBC1 Grandstand programme shown on the Saturdays of 28 November 1998, 5 December 1998, 12 December 1998 and 19 December 1998. The audience figures for these 10 top segments are shown in Figure 2.4.

Figure 2.4 shows that for the month under investigation, the swimming coverage was second only to four Final Score segments and one Football Focus segment. Notably, the swimming achieved a higher audience (2,677,000 v 2,554,000) than a rugby union international match (Ireland v South Africa) screened the previous week and featuring the current rugby World Cup champions.

To enhance the context of the event further, an analysis was compiled of the top 100 most watched sports programmes or programme segments in the UK for the four-month period September to December 1998. A digest of the findings of this analysis is shown in Table 2.6.

Table 2.6 *A digest of the top 100 sports programmes September–December 1998*

Rank	Date	Programme	Channel	Audience (000s)	Share (%)	TVR (%)
1	09/12/98	Champions' League (Football)	ITV	9,870	42.3	18.0
10	24/11/98	Match of the Day Live	BBC1	6,105	24.4	11.1
20	15/09/98	Match of the Day Live	BBC1	4,654	20.6	8.5
30	12/12/98	Final Score	BBC1	4,347	29.5	7.9
40	05/12/98	Match of the Day	BBC1	3,965	26.7	7.2
50	12/09/98	Match of the Day	BBC1	3,512	33.2	6.4
60	21/11/98	Scotland v South Africa (Rugby Union)	BBC1	3,137	29.4	5.7
70	17/10/98	Football Focus	BBC1	2,798	42.8	5.1
75	**12/12/98**	**European Short Course Swimming Championships**	**BBC1**	**2,677**	**23.0**	**4.9**
80	24/11/98	Top Gear Rally Report	BBC2	2,536	16.3	4.6
90	14/10/98	Match of the Day	BBC1	2,476	23.0	4.5
100	10/10/98	Football Focus	BBC1	2,378	39.5	3.8

Source: BARB

Over the four months of viewing figures under consideration, the ESCSC ranks as being the 75th most watched sports programme or programme segment. Given that soccer dominates much of Table 2.6, a rating of 75th out of 100 programmes should be looked upon as a positive endorsement of interest in the event. From a sponsorship perspective, some of the events featured in the top 100 most watched sports programmes give encouragement to other relatively minor sports. Most notably, showjumping, rugby league and saloon car racing all achieved audiences of around 2.5 million in the 16.10 to 16.40 slot during the soccer season.

Conclusions

In broad terms this initial monitoring of an event's television coverage has revealed some interesting and perhaps unexpected findings. The key finding is that the event achieved television audiences that were greater than some sports generally perceived as having larger audiences than swimming. Most notably, audiences for the ESCSC

Table 2.10 *Performance indicators for Premier League matches shown on BBC and Sky Sports, 1997*

		BBC audience (millions)	BBC share (%)	BSkyB audience (millions)	BSkyB share (%)
Wednesday 1 January	Everton v Blackburn	3.9	30.2	1.4	8.5
	Man Utd v Aston Villa			2.0	12.7
Saturday 5 April	Chelsea v Arsenal	4.5	39.9	0.9	5.6
Saturday 19 April	Liverpool v Man Utd.	4.5	33.9	1.9	11.2
Saturday 3 May	Leicester v Man Utd.	3.5	24.2	0.9	5.3
	Liverpool v Tottenham	3.2	34.6	1.3	7.9
Monday 5 May	Man Utd. v Middlesbrough	4.1	33.4	1.9	11.5
Tuesday 6 May	West Ham v Newcastle	3.1	24.2	1.4	8.3
Sunday 11 May	Leeds v Middlesbrough	6.0	27.4	1.4	8.2
	Man Utd. v West Ham			0.7	4.1

Source: BBC Information and Analysis Department and BSkyB Research Department

If this is the case in soccer, then we must examine rugby league to try to identify whether the scenario is the same. Have audience figures fallen due to the change to a satellite broadcaster or because demand for televised rugby league has actually declined?

The following section compares like-for-like games on BBC in order to demonstrate whether the fall in audience figures has more to do with the switch to satellite television, than a reduction in broadcast demand for the game of rugby league.

Changes in broadcasting demand, pre- and post-Super League

The fall in broadcast demand for the game of rugby league can be identified by examining in greater detail the broadcasting figures pre- and post-Super League. Although the number of broadcasts and the hours devoted to coverage of the game have increased, the actual audience figures have declined every year. The severity of this problem is highlighted when comparing audience figures for the four years since 1996 on BSkyB with those of the BBC from 1992 to 1995.

Table 2.11 demonstrates the difference in performance indicators between the four years before Super League and the four years after. The indicators are used to show the number of people viewing a certain programme at a certain time. These are expressed as percentages and represent, in the case of share percentage, what proportion of those watching television are actually watching rugby league. TVR is also expressed in percentage form but uses the number of possible viewers, i.e. how many people who have access to a television are watching rugby league.

The four years pre-Super League saw considerably higher average audiences than in the post-Super League years. This is clearly demonstrated by both the share percentage and TVR. The decline in television rating shows that over the years 1992–95, on average nearly 5 per cent of the televised viewing population watched rugby league. However, since the start of Super League, this figure has dropped, with less than 1 per cent of the UK population watching rugby league on BSkyB.

At first glance, the reason for this dramatic decline could be attributed solely to the change to satellite television for the majority of rugby league coverage. As already explained the benefit of satellite coverage for the game of rugby league has been the increase in the game's television coverage in terms of hours covered. BSkyB transmits mainly live matches compared to the BBC's highlights shows and dictates the majority of rugby league televised, now accounting for 96 per cent of all the games broadcast.

Satellite stations have a limited, potential audience when compared to that of terrestrial channels, 16.6 million for BSkyB as opposed to 54 million who have access to the BBC (BARB 1997). Due to this, audience figures are obviously lower due to a smaller audience reach.

The figures on BSkyB are, on average, 2.5 million less than those shown on the BBC, highlighting the difference in coverage for the game on the two stations. Similarly, in terms of percentage share, the figures for BSkyB are minimal compared to those of the BBC.

A clearer view of whether there has been a decline in interest for televised rugby league can be obtained by making like-for-like comparisons. This is carried out using data from pre- and post-Super League Challenge Cup Final audiences, presented in Table 2.12. The BBC continued to show the Challenge Cup Final even after the introduction of Super League in 1996 and therefore this provides a good indicator of interest in the sport. From the Challenge Cup Final viewing figures between 1992

Table 2.11 Performance indicators, pre- and post-Super League

	Average audience (millions)	Share (%)	TVR (%)
BBC coverage pre-Super League	2.630	26.7	4.9
BSkyB coverage post-Super League	0.067	2.1	0.4

Source: BBC Information and Analysis Department and BSkyB Research Department

Table 2.12 Challenge Cup Final audience figures, 1992–9

	1992	1993	1994	1995	1996	1997	1998	1999
Average audience (millions)	4.4	3.3	3.2	3.3	2.8	2.7	2.7	2.1
Share (%)	47.2	45.4	47.6	42.0	35.1	33.1	36.0	31.0
TVR (%)	8.1	6.1	5.9	6.1	5.2	5.0	5.0	3.9

Source: BBC Information and Analysis Department
Note: Audience figures per game

and 1999 it appears that broadcasting demand has still fallen since the introduction of the Super League, regardless of the switch to predominantly satellite exposure for the game.

There has been a dramatic drop in average audience figures since the start of the Super League era in 1996 and the accompanying shift to predominantly satellite coverage. More worryingly for the game is the reduction in TVR from 8.1 per cent in 1992 to 3.9 per cent in 1999. The Challenge Cup Final has always been the highlight of the rugby league calendar and the fall in audiences means that in 1999 just under 4 per cent of the population watched this blue riband event compared to 8.1 per cent in 1992.

There are also numerous individual examples of declining demand for the game on television. Two million viewers watched the fifth-round match between Bradford Bulls and Castleford Tigers in 1998 on BBC. For the equivalent match the previous year, over 3 million watched, further emphasising the serious fall in interest for the game. If we examine the data from Table 2.13 of the average audience figures for the BBC in 1992–5 (previously shown in Table 2.8) and the corresponding data from the first two years since the start of the Super League, this problem is further demonstrated.

As presented in Table 2.13, the amount of coverage in terms of number and duration of broadcasts has declined since 1995. Audiences have also dropped due

Table 2.13 Rugby league broadcasts on BBC, 1992–7

Year	Average audience (millions)	Average share (%)	TVR (%)	Duration (mins)	Number of broadcasts	Cumulative audience (millions)
1992	2.1	22.3	3.8	610	5	10.3
1993	3.1	29.9	5.8	763	10	31.0
1994	2.7	29.3	5.15	1225	14	38.7
1995	2.5	25.2	4.6	1959	20	49.1
1996	2.38	24.7	4.4	995	9	21.6
1997	2.1	24.5	3.9	645	6	12.7

Source: BBC Information and Analysis Department

to a fall in accumulative audience, from a peak of 49.1 million in 1995 to only 12.7 million in 1997. This mainly reflects the drop in BBC coverage since the average audience in 1997 was equal to that in 1992, though lower than the average for 1993–5 when the number of broadcasts increased considerably.

Since the start of the Super League, BBC's broadcasts of rugby league have only covered the Challenge Cup competition, with no other competitions shown. Previously, the BBC had on certain occasions broadcast rugby league only on its regional channels, in the north, although this type of transmission had not taken place since 1995. The game's authorities were concerned about the reduction in broadcasting demand and that this decline may be a possible contributory factor in the decline in attendance. Due to this, the Super League negotiated a deal with the BBC to begin coverage of the game on a regular basis, starting in June 1999, the middle of the fourth summer season.

This saw the start of a new, specialist, rugby league programme, which the BBC named, the 'Super League Show'. It is broadcast on Monday nights for half-an-hour, starting at 7.30pm, covering highlights from the weekend matches. This is only shown on the BBC2's North, North East and North West regional channels, where the majority of rugby league clubs and hence supporters are based. The programme began in June 1999 and was shown once a week until the end of the season, with the last transmission on 9 October 1999.

Table 2.14 gives examples of the key performance indicators relating to the regional broadcasts of rugby league prior to 1996, and gives equivalent data for the Super League show, in order for comparisons to be made. When comparing the figures, a clear decrease in the number of viewers watching the game can be seen, a decline of 16 per cent since 1995. Although the game has been re-scheduled on a regular basis on BBC, fewer people are now watching the game than did four years ago. The highest average audience figures for any given year was 0.5 million in 1992, with 0.1 million the lowest for a regional broadcast of rugby league.

Apart from 1993, season 1999 demonstrates that fewer people in the northern regions, where rugby league is most popular, were watching the game. One of the problems may be the timing of the programme, which is shown on BBC2 during peak

Table 2.14 Rugby league regional broadcasts on BBC, 1992–9

Year	Average audience (millions)	Average share (%)	TVR (%)
1992	0.45	5.5	0.85
1993	0.1	0.6	0.2
1994	0.3	2.4	0.5
1995	0.25	2.2	0.45
1999	0.21	3.1	0.3

Source: BBC Information and Analysis Department

viewing times on a Monday night, sharing the time slot with Coronation Street on ITV and The Holiday Programme on BBC1. For sports fans with satellite television, there is also a live Premier League match shown at this time every week, which may detract from those tuning in to watch a highlights show on rugby league. On average 212,000 watch every week, a significant drop from previous figures gained from BBC coverage. The share percentage has slightly increased from the previous three seasons when rugby league was televised on the BBC's regional channels. This may also be due to the timing of the segment, with more people in general watching television at this time than during a Saturday afternoon.

Overall, BSkyB dominated coverage of the game, accounting for 96 per cent of the total rugby league transmissions. However, despite the increase in number of hours broadcast, the actual number of people watching the sport was reduced, which has potentially serious repercussions for the game in the future. The final section of this case-study addresses the implications of the BSkyB investment in the game. It examines the impact of reduced exposure on network externalities, demand for the game in terms of both broadcasting and live attendance and the long-term consequences of the shift to predominately satellite coverage.

Implications of the shift to satellite television coverage on rugby league

This section examines the possible consequences for rugby league of the change to satellite coverage. Although the sport has remained on terrestrial television, the BBC in 1999 only accounted for 19 per cent of the game's coverage, with the remaining 81 per cent broadcast by BSkyB's Sky Sports channels. The amount of coverage has increased since 1992, with more hours of rugby league shown. However, due to the limited audience reach of satellite television, rugby league is actually receiving less exposure, in terms of the numbers watching, than in previous years.

Although by 1999 there has only been three years of live Super League on Sky Sports, the lack of exposure was already having a detrimental impact on the game. As discussed by Boardman and Hargreaves-Heap (1999) the effect of lack of national coverage may impact on network externalities. If a game is removed from the national audience reach, then fewer people can view the game, which can result in a lack of interest in the sport. People will no longer discuss the game and its personalities, leading to attendances and interest in the game to fall further.

Not only has the demand for the game declined but also coverage on national television is still the lowest for the four professional team sports in Britain. The number of hours rugby league is broadcast by the BBC declined from 5 per cent in 1990 (Figure 2.5) to 2 per cent by 1998 (Figure 2.6). The lack of national coverage highlighted by Figure 2.6 can lead to a lack of interest in the game and have possible effects on future levels of both audiences and support at live matches.

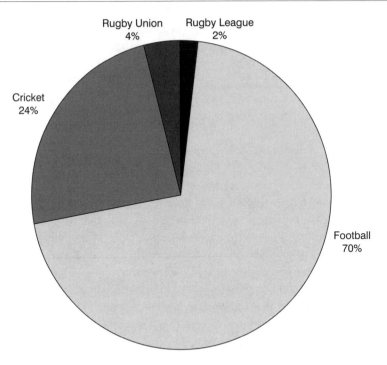

Figure 2.6 *BBC coverage devoted to the four main professional team sports during 1998*
Source: BBC Information Analysis Department and BSkyB Research

The removal of rugby league from the BBC and the loss of regular national coverage can also have long-term detrimental effects of failing to attract new or young supporters and players to the game. It is firmly acknowledged that television can raise levels of interest and extend games to people previously unaware of the sport. The loss therefore of sport from national television can result in adverse effects on a game. Audience profile data for those watching the new 'Super League Show' screened on the BBC's northern, regional channels highlights a potential problem area for the future of the game.

The main area of concern is the ageing supporter base that rugby league attracts. There is a clear distinction in terms of the age of supporters watching the specialised rugby league show on the BBC. The majority of viewers are over 55 years of age in two of the northern regions, and in the Northern region 49 per cent were over 55 years of age. This compares with only 2 per cent to 9 per cent of viewers aged between 4–24 years of age, which suggests that very few teenagers or young adults are interested in watching rugby league. The long-term implications are that if the game fails to attract young supporters, its supporter base could be substantially weakened and eventually crowds will be further reduced.

This can also be linked to the network externalities argument put forward by Boardman and Hargreaves-Heap (1999) that if sports are taken off terrestrial channels, less people will be involved in conversational networks, talking about the sport, and this could also lead to a decline in interest for the game.

The worry for rugby league regarding its lack of appeal is compounded by age-range figures of viewers for other professional sports. Audience demographics for the Premiership in soccer reveal that 39 per cent of the viewers were under the age of 34, suggesting a much stronger younger following. Rugby union also has more support from the younger age groups than rugby league, which is demonstrated by Figure 2.7. Rugby union attracts substantially more viewers (58 per cent) under the age of 34 than rugby league (19 per cent) and so has a much more sustainable audience following.

This is emphasised further by the report from the Monopolies and Mergers Commission (1999) into BSkyB's take-over of Manchester United. The report included data from the NOP Survey (1996), which found that although rugby league was rated as the fourth most regularly watched sport behind soccer, cricket and boxing, less than 5 per cent of respondents indicated it was their favourite sport. The top three plus wrestling, tennis, skiing, golf, motor sports and athletics all gained more votes than rugby league. This clearly shows that interest for rugby league, although high, is not the preferred option for many supporters, which is clearly demonstrated by both attendance and audience figures.

The small television audiences on Sky for rugby league eventually led them to renegotiate the contact for the television rights in 1998. The original contract was

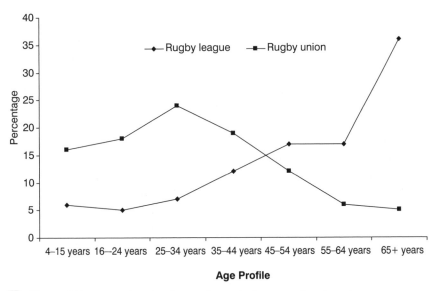

Figure 2.7 *Age profile of audiences for rugby league and rugby union*

■ *Table 2.15* BBC audience profile data for the 'Super League Show', 1999

Age	Northern region (%)	Northeast region (%)	Northwest region (%)
4–15 years	7	5	7
16–24 years	4	2	9
25–34 years	6	4	13
35–44 years	15	11	9
45–54 years	20	14	16
55–64 years	12	11	28
65+ years	37	52	20

Source: BBC Information and Analysis Department

signed in 1995 and was worth £87 million to rugby league as a whole (including first and second division clubs). It covered the five-year period from January 1996 to December 2000 and each Super League club received £900,000 per season. The contract was renegotiated during the 1998 season with separate contacts for Super League and the First and Second Division clubs. The Super League contract was reduced to £45 million for the five years 1999 to 2003, giving each club around £500,000 per season, a substantial reduction from the initial contract.

■ *Case study 2.3* Place marketing evaluation: a case-study of the World Snooker Championship

Simon Shibli and Richard Coleman (2005)

The Crucible Theatre Sheffield has been the host venue for the World Snooker Championship since 1977. During this period it has generally been accepted that the event is something which is positive for Sheffield. However, until 2002 no research had been conducted on the event to quantify how much it might be worth to the city. The overall purpose of this research was to establish a reliable and valid estimate of the value of the 2002 World Snooker Championship to the City of Sheffield. This included an economic impact analysis involving a substantial market survey of spectators and other visitors to the event to establish the additional expenditure in Sheffield that the event generated. Full details of the economic impact study appear in Shibli and Coleman (2005). In this case-study, however, we concentrate on the benefits associated with the value attributable to UK terrestrial television coverage over the 17 days of the event and the associated place marketing effects for Sheffield from such coverage. Having identified the potential benefits of hosting the event, reference is made to how such information may be used by the hosts (City of Sheffield) and the organisers (World Snooker).

There appears to be a general consensus that increased public profile (awareness) and associated place marketing effects are potential benefits for those hosting events. Indeed, public profile is one of the prioritisation criteria used by UK Sport when deciding whether to use National Lottery funding to support an event (Shibli and Gratton 1999). Therefore, not surprisingly recent evaluations undertaken for UK Sport have investigated the public profile of events using primary research and television monitoring (see, for example, the European Short Course Swimming Championships, Sheffield (Shibli and Gratton, 1999).

While clearly it is more difficult to ask people watching on television whether they are likely to visit an area in the future, it is possible to put a notional value on the coverage which gives some indication of the extent of the profile achieved. This measure is based on methods employed in the sponsorship industry and the value is derived from the cost per thousand viewers of a 30-second commercial for the equivalent amount of exposure. Hence, the value of place marketing effects derived from television coverage is dependent upon the amount of coverage received and the size of the audience. Therefore, as a fundamental part of valuing place marketing effects, television audience data must be monitored. All of the television data featured in this report was acquired from the official source, i.e. the Broadcasters' Audience Research Board (BARB).

This section now concentrates on the methodology employed to develop the appraisal of the 2002 World Snooker Championship by examining the public profile of the event achieved via UK terrestrial television coverage. This has been done by evaluating the place marketing and media effects associated with the event on the basis that to date both have been largely under-researched. The methodology detailed herein has developed from the research undertaken into the public profile of the 1998 European Short Course Swimming Championships (see Shibli and Gratton, 1999).

Place marketing effects can occur when a host city receives direct or indirect media coverage resulting from its association with an event. Direct coverage might be a feature such as a behind the scenes tour of the Crucible Theatre, whilst indirect coverage might occur when facilities in Sheffield appear as background to a feature involving an interview with a snooker player. For this research, place marketing was confined to monitoring of verbal mentions of Sheffield and the Crucible Theatre on BBC1 and BBC2 as well as monitoring the content and duration of 'postcards' featured in the televised coverage of the event. In the UK, the figures were supplied by BARB. The source of the data serves two important and complementary purposes. First, BARB confirms independently that the broadcasts actually took place. Second, having confirmed that broadcasts actually took place, it is then possible to deduce that the viewing figures, market share and other performance indicators actually relate to the event in question.

The method used by BARB to arrive at audience figures is the largest piece of ongoing research of its type in the world. A total of 12,000 people in 4,500 homes across the UK have been recruited to report on their viewing habits. Each household is provided with an electronic device which relays to BARB the programmes people in a given house are watching. The statistics derived from this representative sample of the UK public are then aggregated upwards for the population as a whole.

The logic underpinning place marketing at televised events is that it represents a potentially cost effective way for organisers and host cities to obtain value for a 'brand' (i.e. Sheffield) via their association with the event. There is a generally accepted methodology in the sponsorship industry for measuring the amount of exposure a 'brand' receives during an event and then converting this into a cash equivalent.

The basics of this system are detailed below.

■ The amount of television coverage obtained by the event is established, e.g. in this case 99 hours and 58 minutes on the BBC.
■ Within this coverage, the amount of time that the logos or messages of the sponsors are clearly visible or audible is measured (using specially trained staff and software).
■ The volume of exposure obtained is converted to the cash equivalent of how much that exposure would cost to buy in the form of a 30-second television advertisement. At the time of the Championship, the cost of reaching 1,000 people via a 30-second television advertisement was £7.77. Therefore to reach 1 million people the cost would have been £7.77 × 1,000 = £7,770. In the case of verbal mentions the cost was £2.53 per 1,000 viewers. Therefore, a verbal mention of Sheffield or The Crucible to an audience of 1 million viewers would be worth £2,530 in terms of how much that exposure would cost to buy commercially.

Glossary of terms

In order to understand fully the television data presented herein, it is worth clarifying some of the terminology used. This is consistent with that employed by Shibli and Gratton (1999).

Audience and average audience

The audience is the number of people watching a programme at a given time. For any given programme the number of viewers will fluctuate because of behaviour such as channel 'surfing' during commercial breaks and people watching only part of a programme. Thus every programme will have a minimum audience, a maximum audience and an average audience. It is common practice for the results of media evaluations such as this to be based on the average audience. As an example of what is meant by average audience, during the opening session of the snooker on

Saturday 20 April 2002, the live coverage on BBC2 had an average audience of 788,900 viewers.

Percentage share

The percentage share is the proportion of people watching a given programme expressed as a percentage of the total number of people watching television at that time. Thus, if 788,900 people were watching the opening session at 12pm on Saturday 20 April and the percentage share for snooker was 11.7 per cent, then at this time approximately 6,743,000 people in total were watching television in the UK (i.e. 788,900 / 11.7 per cent).

Television rating (TVR)

The TVR of a programme is the key performance indicator of the size of an audience for any given programme. TVR is expressed as the percentage of all the people in a country with access to a television actually watching the programme or programme segment in question. In the case of the UK, there are approximately 60 million people with access to a television. Thus if a programme has an audience of 788,900 then it would achieve a TVR of 1.3 per cent, i.e. $((0.7889/60) \times 100)$. That is to say, on average 1.3 per cent of the UK population watched the programme.

Postcard

A 'postcard' is a relatively short feature within a programme that is incidental to the main theme of the programme and which has an element of human or place interest. An obvious example for this event was six times world snooker champion Steve Davis starting the 2002 Sheffield Marathon. This feature included images of the Don Valley Stadium and had the potential to reinforce Sheffield's image as a National City of Sport. The key point about postcards featured in the coverage of the snooker is that they were potentially positive ways of achieving place marketing effects. This research monitored the number of 'postcards' featured throughout the coverage of the snooker and their duration.

Results

Audience size and market share in the UK

The event was televised on 17 consecutive days and 60 separate broadcasts, equating to a confirmed 99 hours and 58 minutes of coverage on BBC1 and BBC2. The cumulative audience in the UK was 95 million viewers and an estimated 18 million different people (or 30 per cent of the UK population) watched at least some of the snooker coverage. The percentage market share varied from 5.5 per cent to 27.2 per cent, and the more important TVR from 0.63 per cent of the UK population for a highlights programme on day two of the championship to 8.2 per cent for the decisive last session of the final. Analysis of the TVR also revealed that viewer interest in the event increased as the event progressed.

In addition to the overall amount of coverage and audience sizes, the research also compiled some limited data on the demographics of the viewing audience. The 8.8 million audience for the last two sessions of the final on 6 May 2002 was sub-analysed to obtain an indication of the demographic make up of those watching the event. The results are shown in Figure 2.8. This indicates that the viewers on the final day were most likely to be male (57 per cent), aged 55 or over (57 per cent) and from socio-economic groups C2DE (55 per cent). These are important considerations for assessing the effectiveness of place marketing effects. That is, who are the people being exposed to the images and verbal mentions of Sheffield? The associated place marketing effects are discussed in greater detail in the following section.

Place marketing effects

During the near 100 hours of coverage 'The Crucible' (or 'Crucible Theatre') was mentioned 493 times and 'Sheffield' was mentioned 123 times. The commercial cost of purchasing this exposure would have been £2,197,724 and £525,329 respectively; a total of over £2.7 million. However, although the cost of verbal mentions would

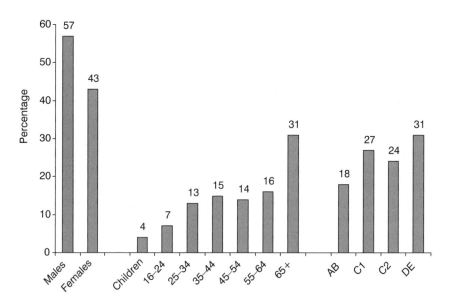

Figure 2.8 *Television audience demographics, 2002 World Snooker Championship final*

have been £2.7 million to buy commercially, it does not necessarily follow that the value of this exposure was actually worth £2.7 million. That is to say, there is no guarantee that exposure by association is necessarily effective. A few practical examples can help to illustrate this point.

1   If the Crucible Theatre had almost £2.2 million to spend, it is highly unlikely that the management would choose to spend it on receiving indirect promotion via an association with a snooker tournament. Thus there is no guarantee that the opportunity cost of such an outlay would ever favour investing in a snooker event. By contrast, Embassy, which is banned from advertising on television, would probably consider an investment of £2.7 million on 616 verbal mentions on BBC television to be money well spent. Thus the true worth of brand exposure is contingent upon the nature and context of the recipient.

2   Marketing is only effective if it is targeted at the correct market. Analysis of the box office records for the 2002 World Snooker Championship cross-referenced with The Crucible's performing arts database revealed an audience overlap of less than 8 per cent. That is, the audience for snooker whether it is live or on television (see Figure 2.8 above) is very different to that for the performing arts. It is highly unlikely that snooker enthusiasts will become converts to, or advocates for, the performing arts simply by virtue of the Crucible Theatre's association with the World Snooker Championship. Thus brand exposure of the Crucible Theatre with a snooker audience is a marketing mismatch and therefore unlikely to be effective, regardless of how much the brand exposure might have cost commercially. Notwithstanding the previous comment, Sheffield City Council might argue that the potential place marketing benefits from the snooker are aimed at tourism in Sheffield as a whole, rather than the performing arts specifically.

3   Most of the verbal mentions of 'Sheffield' or the 'Crucible Theatre' were incidental and occurred in contexts such as: 'and now over to Hazel Irvine at the Crucible Theatre in Sheffield for the second round match between …'; or 'Shaun Murphy in his first World Championship at the Crucible …'.

Thus although the words 'Sheffield' and 'Crucible' were mentioned many times on air, the context in which they were used makes it likely that the only message being reinforced was the association between the event and the venue. It would be difficult to argue that such mentions contribute towards positive images such as Sheffield as a place in which to invest, relocate, visit or to take a holiday.

In short there should be a clear distinction between the 'cost' of exposure and the 'worth' of such exposure and indiscriminate use of such media evaluation data is not recommended.

In addition to the indirect marketing of the Crucible Theatre specifically, and Sheffield generally, through verbal mentions, there was the additional possibility of place marketing effects occurring through the use of 'postcards' (see Glossary of terms above) during the near 100 hours of television coverage. 2002 was the first year that Sheffield City Council had been involved with the promotion of the event and its brief was to contribute to the promotion of Sheffield as a visitor destination. In total 44 postcards totalling 78 minutes and 53 seconds of coverage were featured throughout the 17 days of the event equating to 1.23 per cent of the total televised coverage. Such features were dedicated to human and place interest stories, which included images of Sheffield's facilities and attractions. The commercial cost of purchasing this exposure would have been £488,593 of which 79 per cent was attributable to The Crucible and 21 per cent to other Sheffield attractions. Again, caution should be exercised when interpreting this data as it is unlikely that the coverage of The Crucible in particular will have a direct effect on increasing attendances at theatre performances. However, although by association it may promote Sheffield, in future the Council should seek to transfer some of the value from mentions of the theatre to mentions of the city.

The total commercial cost of the place marketing effects would have been £3.2 million. To maximise the value of such effects, Sheffield City Council were advised to work more closely with the event broadcasters to ensure that future coverage of Sheffield and its facilities is managed so as to be more direct than indirect.

Conclusions

Prior to this research it was generally accepted that the snooker was good for the city, but its benefits had not been quantified. Having conducted a programme of research before, during and after the event it was possible to provide an informed evaluation of the event to Sheffield, using industry recognised techniques underpinned by transparent audit trails of how figures had been derived. A summary of the total value of the economic impact and the place marketing effects attributable to the event is shown in Figure 2.9.

The sum total of the economic impact and place marketing benefits accruing for Sheffield as a result of hosting the 2002 World Snooker Championship was £5.47 million (i.e. the total of the five bars in Figure 2.9). This figure should be treated with caution and should not be used as a glib 'soundbite'. The economic impact figure of £2.26 million (first bar in the figure) is a measure of the net change in the local economy that is directly attributable to the event and which can be measured in cash terms. In contrast, the place marketing effects of £3.21 million are notional figures based on what the same level of exposure would cost to buy commercially, i.e. in the form of advertisements. It is beyond the scope of this research to say how much the place marketing effects actually benefit the city in practice, i.e. how effective they are; this would require longitudinal research involving a variety of agencies with an interest in tourism in the city.

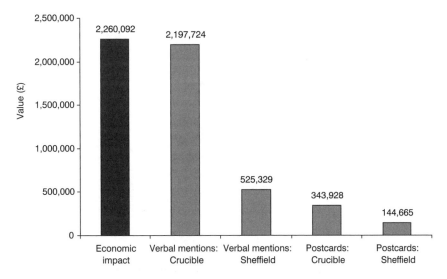

Figure 2.9 Benefits of hosting the 2002 World Snooker Championship

Chapter 3

The structure of supply

This chapter aims to provide an overview of TV channels that are involved in sports broadcasting. It analyses the market behaviour of the various categories of channels, such as public service broadcasters, pure commercial advertising channels and subscription-based channels (pay-TV channels), with special attention on their role in sports broadcasting. The chapter also focuses on regulations, on content as well as advertising, and discusses the consequences for sports broadcasting.

Figure 3.1 gives a broad overview of how TV programmes are transmitted from various categories of TV channels to viewers. Before we analyse it thoroughly, however, it is first necessary to comment on the different use of concepts in different markets. People in North America, Australia and many other continents are familiar with the concept *network*. It can refer to broadcasting networks that are linked to local TV stations (known in the USA as affiliates). However, the concept is also used on cable stations, which transmit their programmes directly to viewers. In Europe, *TV-company* would be the equivalent to *network*. Another difference relates to the concepts *TV-channel* and *TV-station*, which refer to a single channel or a single station. While people in North America are familiar with the concept *station*, people in Europe are more familiar with *channel*.

Network and TV company can include state-owned public-service broadcasters as well as commercial broadcasters. Originally, many networks broadcast their programmes by means of terrestrial transmission, where some were connected to local channels. In these cases, viewers have been offered a mixture of local and central content. This pattern has been altered in recent years as many of them transmit their programmes directly to viewers by cable and satellite.

Examples of networks/TV companies are:

- The North American broadcasting networks such as ABC, CBS, NBC and Fox.
- The UK public service broadcasters: BBC (public) and ITV (private).

- The German public service broadcasters: ARD/ZDF and the private broadcasters: ProSiebenSat. 1 Media and RTL Group.
- The Japanese public service broadcaster: Nippon Hoso Kyoaki (NHK), and the private networks Tokyo Broadcasting System (TBS), Nippon Television Network (NTV) and Fuji Television.
- The Australian public service networks, Australian Broadcasting Corporation (ABC) and Special Broadcasting Service (SBS) and the three commercial networks, Channel Seven, Channel Nine and Channel Ten.

These have all been involved in sports broadcasting, although to different degrees. Some have had to reduce their involvement in recent years because of the escalating cost of securing sports broadcasting rights. This particularly applies to non-commercial European public service broadcasters. Contrary to this, the major North American broadcasting networks still have a strong market position in sports broadcasting.

In addition, a large number of independent TV companies have emerged over the course of the last two decades, many of which are highly involved in sports broadcasting. Some target multinational audiences, such as *Eurosport*, the European-

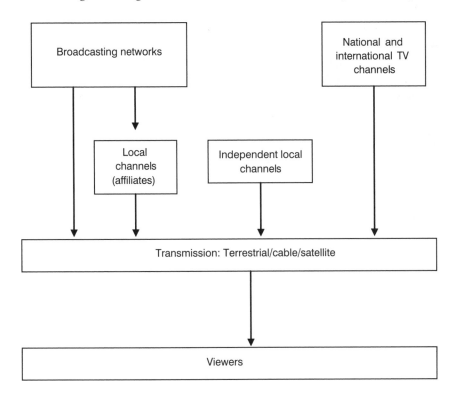

Figure 3.1 The landscape of TV channels and transmission

based sports channel. Others target both national and multinational audiences, such as *ESPN*, the American-based sport network; Canal Plus, the French based pay-TV platform; BSkyB the UK-based pay-TV company which also covers Ireland. There are also a large number of local channels/stations operating in smaller regions, for example across North America where they broadcast matches of local teams in the professional team tournaments.

Figure 3.1 provides a broad overview of the route of TV programmes to the viewers. The major alternatives have been terrestrial, cable and satellite transmission. At the start of the twenty-first century, new technologies such as *broadband* being transmitted by telephone lines have emerged as another alternative. At the time of writing (2007), this alternative still has some way to go to achieve the same capacity as the other three alternatives.

Terrestrial transmission, where airwave signals are sent from a broadcasting channel transmitter to receivers owned by viewers, has been the dominant technology for broadcasting programme delivery during the last decades across most continents. In many nations, the companies involved in terrestrial transmission have been totally or partly owned by the state sector. At the start of the twenty-first century, however, alterations are seen in this pattern as many of these companies have been (at least partly) privatised.

Cable transmission, which uses telephone lines or dedicated separate cable networks where signals are sent along the cables from channels to receivers, represents another alternative. One major advantage with this alternative is that signals are not affected by topographical or geographical obstacles. Moreover, multi-channel capacity is immense and two-way transmission is also possible. A disadvantage, however, is that the cost of establishing a cable network is large relative to terrestrial transmission, which depends only on transmitters and 'translators' that boost signals in large areas or difficult terrain (Withers, 2002).

Satellite transmission became a third alternative for transmission from the early 1990s. With powerful transmitters hovering in orbits above the earth, satellite platforms can distribute signals over a very wide part of the earth's surface. Since distance is no obstacle for satellite, it does not affect costs within the area where the signals are received.

TV channels that are transmitted by cable or satellite are often bundled together as multi-channel packages. Different systems are practised in the construction of such packages. Some cable operators arrange referendums where subscribers can vote on channels to be included in the main packages. Other companies, particularly satellite operators, construct the various alternatives themselves on the basis of the expected attractiveness of the channels.

Table 3.1 reveals great worldwide variations in the penetration of cable and satellite transmission. One reason for this relates to differences in geographical and topographical conditions. As an example, it generally takes less effort to establish a cable network in a small country such as The Netherlands than in a large country

Table 3.1 *Cable and satellite penetration. percentage of TV households and resources spent on advertising and subscription fees, 2004*

	Cable penetration (%)	Satellite penetration (%)	Television advertising per capita (US$)	Multinational subscription per capita (US$)
Europe				
Denmark	60.0	18.0	38.9	n.a.
France	15.1	15.3	43.0	56.1
Germany	56.0	33.0	46.8	49.6
Ireland	49.0	21.0	46.7	159.0
Italy	1.0	10.0	61.9	31.3
Netherlands	94.5	4.5	87.6	39.4
Norway	49.0	25.0	54.7	n.a.
Poland	34.0	20.0	41.5	19.8
Russia	9.7	0.4	6.1	2.2
Spain	4.0	20.0	46.9	32.1
Sweden	63.0	17.0	38.3	n.a.
UK	14.5	25.2	75.3	75.3
Americas				
Argentina	52.0	3.2	6.1	42.3
Brazil	8.6	4.2	15.9	9.7
Canada	66.0	25.0	47.8	89.2
Mexico	13.7	4.5	24.2	16.4
US	72.0	14.3	176.0	149.0
Asia/Pacific				
Australia	12.1	10.1	71.1	31.1
China	29.3	illegal	1.8	1.6
India	54.2	6.0	0.7	1.6
Indonesia	1.5	n.a.	3.4	18.2
Japan	24.2	31.1	150.7	83.2
Malaysia	3.1	27.6	10.6	9.5
New Zealand	3.0	29.0	58.7	27.9
Philippines	10.5	0.8	4.1	1.5
South Korea	27.7	3.3	23.1	16.7
Thailand	0.9	1.9	14.4	2.5

Source: based on information from WorldScreen.com

with varying topography such as Russia. In addition, since transmission can be extremely costly, the differences also have to do with national variations in wealth and standard of living.

Various practices have been applied regarding how to categorise TV channels. A common alternative has been to distinguish between satellite and cable channels. This was based on how the channels originally were transmitted during their infancy period. Nowadays, however, such form of categorisation can be confusing since many TV channels are transmitted by all the three means. The UK-based BSkyB, as an example, is often called a satellite channel. In 2004, however, 51 per cent of its subscribers in the UK and Ireland received the signals from satellites, while 27 per cent received them from cable and 22 per cent received them from terrestrial transmission.[1] For the purpose of our analyses, we will categorise the channels on the basis of revenue sources, which are:

1   Licence fees/public grants (non-commercial public service broadcasters).
2   Advertising.
3   Subscription fees (pay-TV channels/stations).

Although some channels receive their revenues from a mixture of these three sources, many of them will have one main source. Advertising has so far been the most important source globally, with 51 per cent of the total revenues, followed by subscription (35 per cent) and licence fees/public grants (14 per cent), as seen from Table 3.2. In recent years, however, subscription fees have had a large growth.

Table 3.2 Sources of TV revenues, 2005

	Advertising (%)	Subscription fees (%)	Licence/public grant (%)
Canada	53.1	27.2	19.8
USA	57.7	41.8	0.5
Belgium	40.6	40.8	18.6
France	41.6	31.7	26.7
Germany	37.5	23.0	39.5
Italy	61.5	24.7	13.9
Netherlands	35.1	41.2	23.7
Spain	60.0	26.5	13.5
UK	37.5	39.0	23.5
Europe	43.0	30.4	26.5
China	54.1	20.6	25.3
Japan	45.2	28.7	26.0
Global	52.0	35.7	12.3

Source: Datamonitor. Constructed from Broadcasting & Cable, *Country Profiles*, September 2006

Licence fees and public grants have traditionally played a more important role in European broadcasting than in other countries. The difference is particularly notable in comparison to the USA where public service broadcasters have played only a minor role, and no role at all in sports broadcasting.

Another alternative would be to regard public service broadcasters as a category of its own. If so, it is important to bear in mind the differences with respect to revenue sources. Some of them earn their entire revenues from licence fees or public grants, while others are also allowed to earn some revenues from selling advertising. In addition, there are public service broadcasters that earn their entire income only from selling advertising.

LICENCE FEES/PUBLIC GRANTS (NON-COMMERCIAL PUBLIC SERVICE BROADCASTERS)

Non-commercial public service broadcasters (PS broadcasters) receive their revenues from licence fees or public grants. As mentioned above, these channels dominated European broadcasting until the deregulation in the mid-1980s. Since then, however, the situation has altered as a large number of commercial channels have entered the market. PS broadcasters have also had a relatively strong position on other continents, for example in Australia. Examples of non-commercial channels are the British Broadcasting Corporation (BBC) in the UK, Swedish Television (STV), The Norwegian Broadcasting Corporation (NRK), Australian Broadcasting Corporation (ABC) in Australia and the Japanese Nippon Hoso Kyoaki (NHK). There are also a number of PS broadcasters that combine licence fees/public grant and advertising, for example the two German channels, ARD and ZDF; the Italian channel, RAI; and the Canadian channel, Canadian Broadcasting Corporation (CBC). Throughout the 1990s, however, many of them found it difficult to uphold their position in sports broadcasting, mainly due to the strong price increases in sports broadcasting rights. To understand this development we have to investigate the objectives of these channels and analyse how they influence their behaviour.

Direct regulations on sports broadcasting will be discussed thoroughly in Chapter 9, where market interventions such as the European Listed Events and the Australian Anti-Siphoning list are analysed. In this chapter we focus on general regulations of TV broadcasting. Special attention will be given to the role of public service broadcasters, as well as to regulations on TV advertising. It also discusses the consequences these regulations indirectly have on sports broadcasting.

The rationale for PS broadcasters is based on elements from welfare economics, such as *public goods*, *externalities* and *merit goods*. On this basis, they would have to serve objectives other than the entertainment of viewers and the profitability of private broadcasting firms. According to welfare economic theory, their aim should be to maximise the welfare of society, subject to financial restrictions that are set by politicians (Brown, 1996). PS broadcasters with a high penetration enable governments to provide a large audience with programmes that fall in any of these three categories.

Concerns for *externalities* and *merit goods* can be related to programmes that can strengthen national identity and culture; education programmes; catering for the interests and tastes of minority groups; providing programmes that are specially targeting children; a 'local content' provision requiring domestic production of specified proportions and categories of programming. It can also be equity related, for example ambitions to offer broadcasting services of a minimum technical quality to all (or practically all) citizens irrespective of their location and income.

Levin (1980) provides *three reasons* for public financing of *merit programmes* on TV. The first argument reflects the *cultural elitist view*. The idea is that even if people want comedy/variety shows, they should be given *Shakespeare*, which they may never come to like or watch as long as they are offered alternatives, but which will make them 'better people' when they do. The second argument is based on supporting an *infant industry*, where the idea is that merit programmes may eventually become economically viable in their own right after viewers have been exposed to them for some time. The third argument reflects the desire to *uphold diversity* in society. Such programmes would find it difficult to be viable on commercial channels, particularly in smaller markets. Therefore, PS broadcasters are obliged to offer programmes targeting minority groups. This could also include obligations to upholding diversity, for example by broadcasting sports that are popular among minority groups, for instance immigrants.

The footprints of these objectives are seen in the programme policy of PS broadcasters around the world. For example, in the BBC's Annual Report from 2003/4, the chairman declares[2]:

> The BBC (should) deliver value well beyond its programmes and services. ... the BBC is worth keeping because of the immense amount of public value it delivers. Public value means not just the BBC's value to people as individuals, but also its value to people as citizens, and beyond that, its value to broadcasting and creative industries as a whole ...The aims of the BBC are to underpin citizenship, enrich cultural life, contribute to education for all, make the UK a more inclusive society, and support the UK's role in the world.

Similarly, the BBC's 2002/3 report includes statements such as[3]:

> The BBC was founded to *inform, educate and entertain, and education remains central to the BBC's purpose* ... One of the central purposes of the BBC is to be the broadcaster which brings Britain together at times of great joy and celebration. ... We want at least 10 per cent of BBC staff to come from minority ethnic backgrounds by the end of 2003.

As a consequence of this, the BBC had aimed to produce 80 per cent of its programmes in house (Solberg, 2002a).

Similar examples are found in the charter of the Australian PS broadcaster, Special Broadcasting Service (SBS), which declares that:

> its principal function is to provide multilingual and multicultural radio and television services that inform, educate and entertain all Australians, and, in doing so, reflect Australia's multicultural society. [4]

As a consequence of this, its principal function is to:

- contribute to meeting the communications needs of Australia's multicultural society, including ethnic, Aboriginal and Torres Strait Islander communities;
- increase awareness of the contribution of a diversity of cultures to the continuing development of Australian society;
- promote understanding and acceptance of the cultural, linguistic and ethnic diversity of the Australian people;
- contribute to the retention and continuing development of language and other cultural skills;
- as far as practicable, inform, educate and entertain Australians in their preferred languages;
- make use of Australia's diverse creative resources;
- contribute to the overall diversity of Australian television and radio services, particularly taking into account the contribution of the Australian Broadcasting Corporation and the public broadcasting sector;
- contribute to extending the range of Australian television and radio services, and reflect the changing nature of Australian society, by presenting many points of view and using innovative forms of expression.

Such statements, which reflect the objectives of PS broadcasters, do not coincide with the objectives of profit maximising channels.

However, on some continents commercial broadcasters also have to comply with requirements that are similar to the objectives of PS broadcasters. The 'Australian Content Standard', as an example, requires all commercial free-to-air television networks to broadcast an annual minimum transmission quota of 55 per cent Australian programming (which here also includes New-Zealand). [5] There is also a specific minimum annual sub-quota for Australian (adult) drama, documentary and children's programmes. These regulations are based on an objective of:

> Promoting the role of commercial television broadcasting services in developing and reflecting a sense of Australian identity, character and

cultural diversity by supporting the community's continued access to television programmes produced under Australian creative control.[6]

Australian broadcasting also has legislative provisions that require pay TV drama channels to spend 10 per cent of their total programme expenditure on new eligible (Australian and New Zealand) drama programmes.

The element of *public good* also represents a rationale for governmental intervention. Since the reception of a television signal by one person within a broadcast market does not prevent it from being received by another, the marginal cost to a broadcaster of providing the transmission of a programme to an additional viewer within any broadcasting area is literally zero (Brown, 1996). Hence, any charging of the viewers will cause efficiency losses. Thus, PS broadcasters are disallowed from charging viewers any subscription fees or pay-per-view fees beyond the ordinary licence fees.

All these regulations influence the amount of resources that can be spent on sports broadcasting. This particularly applies to programmes where expensive sports rights is a part of the overall cost picture. In contrast to commercial channels, PS broadcasters that receive their entire income from licence fees or public grants do not earn any revenues from sports broadcasting. For them sport programmes only has a cost side, not an income side.

As we will see in Chapter 4, the production of TV programmes is characterised by a high degree of 'first copy' costs. This represents a potential *cost sharing advantage* for channels that can sell programmes beyond their primary market. However, the attractiveness of a programme in foreign markets depends on its content. PS broadcasters are obliged to offer a large number of programmes that mainly are of interest for domestic viewers. Furthermore, some of these are in-house programmes that are quite costly, such as drama (see Chapter 4). In addition are the obligations to supply programmes targeting minority groups. Such programmes will have a high degree of *cultural discount*, which is the reduction in value of a media product when it is sold outside its primary market. Programmes targeting minority groups or other niche markets are unlikely to attract the interest from a mass audience – domestically as well as in other nations. Contrary to this, soaps and other genres that are popular among large audiences have greater potential to generate additional revenues from external markets (see Chapter 4). If successful, this can provide the channel with additional resources that also can be spent on sports broadcasting. In summary, these obligations represent a financial burden that reduces what PS broadcasters have available to spend on sport programming.

In 1988, ITV, the UK commercial PS broadcaster acquired the English First Division rights alone, in a deal which ended their sharing of the rights with the BBC, the non-commercial PS broadcaster. Four years later, however, ITV suffered the same destiny as their former partner when BSkyB acquired the rights for the renamed English Premier League. Due to their obligations as a public service broadcaster, neither the BBC nor ITV could afford to spend the same proportion of their income on sport programming as BSkyB.

In 2004, the Canadian PS broadcaster, CBC, lost the rights for the 2010 and 2012 Olympics to a partnership of two rivals, Bell Globemedia and Rogers Communications. This must have hurt CBC considerably since the 2010 Olympics will be hosted in Vancouver. The Bell Globemedia-Rogers bid of $153 million for the two combined Games was 110 per cent higher than CBC's bid. The price represented a substantial increase from the 2006 and 2008 Games, which CBC acquired for $68 million.[7]

In 1996, the European Broadcasting Union (EBU) lost the TV rights for the World Cup soccer finals (in 2002 and 2006) for the first time ever, and in 2005 they also lost the rights to broadcast Euro 2008 to Sportfive.[8] Most of the EBU's active members are PS broadcasters. In 1999 it included a total of 69 active members in 50 countries, mainly in Europe, but also in the Middle East and North Africa. It also had 49 associate members in 30 countries (Solberg and Gratton, 2000). The EBU has continued to acquire the rights for the Olympic Games, but the competition from commercial rivals has forced it to dig deeper in order to grab these rights than some years ago when they were the sole buyer. The strong price increases have also split the solidarity of the EBU, since the ability to cope with expensive sports rights vary among its members. RAI, the Italian PS broadcaster refused to participate in the joint purchase of the European Olympic rights for 2010 and 2012. RAI also disagreed with the EBU over the valuation for Euro 2008, where RAI was willing to pay only half of the €67 million it paid for Euro 2004.[9]

These examples illustrate the problems of PS broadcasters to continue acquiring attractive sports rights. Furthermore, their ability will get even worse as commercial channels increase their penetration. Commercial free-to-air channels can use their resources entirely on sports programming if they wish, which is not the case for PS broadcasters due to the obligations discussed above.

However, as the gaps in penetration are eliminated, the welfare economic rationale for PS broadcasters to continue broadcasting expensive sport programmes also disappears. These programmes will certainly be taken over by commercial channels, and hence offered to the public. If so, there is no welfare economic rationale for PS broadcasters to spend resources on them. The exception is if the programmes would have migrated to pay-TV channels with a limited penetration. This can, however, be prevented by means of the Listed Events regulations (see Chapter 9).

The profits from the broadcasting of the most attractive programmes are enormous. The extremely expensive rights fees do not reflect the fact that the inputs used in the production process are extremely costly, and the same applies to the transmission process. Hence, the costs of programming and transmission account for a very small proportion of the income that the most attractive events generate. The reason for the expensive broadcasting fee is due to the very high demand for such programmes, combined with how the market power is distributed between the demand side and supply side. These factors are analysed throughout this book. Thus, sport governing bodies of sport such as the IOC, FIFA and UEFA would make a profit from selling their rights even if the fees were reduced to a fraction of the levels we see nowadays. Hence, both sellers and the buyers would lose money if events such as the Olympic Games, the World Cup soccer finals and UEFA's Champions League were not broadcast.

To illustrate the case let us imagine an example where a product has a market value of €1,000. The production requires raw materials worth €50 and contribution from labour costs of €50. This means that the product can generate a profit of €900. However, the programmes would be profitable even if the price of raw materials increased from €50 to €900. Indeed, it is quite understandable that the owner of inputs would try to increase the price and seize a larger proportion of the profit. Why expect someone to sell the inputs extremely cheap and let the producer earn an enormous profit? Indeed, this example illustrates the situation for the most attractive sports events quite well. Thus, any threats from PS broadcasters that events such as the Olympic Games would not be broadcast by other than themselves do not make sense.

Furthermore, live-sport programmes belong to a homogeneous programme category. There will hardly be any differences in the quality of such programmes from one channel to another. For the viewers, it does not matter whether a soccer match is broadcast by ESPN, BSkyB, BBC or RAI. This is similar to when you fill a car with petrol. There is no quality difference between Shell and Texaco. The channels can put different amounts of resources into the programming, which also will influence the quality of the programmes. However, such differences are not evident between PS broadcasters and commercial channels. The only difference is that non-commercial broadcasters do not have advertising. This, however, applies to all sorts of programmes, not only to sport.

There are no reasons to believe that PS broadcasters should deliver live sport programmes that are of better quality than commercial channels. Indeed, the opposite could be true if commercial channels could increase the income from spending more resources on programming. The lack of difference in quality particularly applies to international events where a large proportion of programming is produced by independent companies in the host country. This is different from heterogeneous programmes, for example news programmes where TV channels can cover cases differently and hence provide viewers with a broader perspective than if they only were covered by one channel. This would contribute to pluralism, which in most societies is regarded to be of a value of its own.

The pattern in European broadcasting during the 1990s and onwards, with PS broadcasters spending resources on expensive sports rights, such as Olympic Games, World Cup soccer finals and European Championship in soccer are examples of welfare economic inefficiency. These events would alternatively have been broadcast by commercial channels. Only if the programmes would alternatively be taken up by pay-TV channels is there a welfare economic rationale for PS broadcasters to acquire the rights. Whether they will end up on free-to-air channels or pay-TV channels depends on the demand curve and if governments implement the Listed Events regulation (see discussion in the last section of this chapter).

However, due to the extremely expensive right fees, if PS broadcasters continue broadcasting these events, this will be at the cost of other activities, such as programmes that fall under a *merit good* or *externality argument*. Many of these programmes are unlikely to be taken up by commercial channels, particularly those that target smaller groups of viewers.

This sports broadcasting policy of PS broadcasters has also received attention from the European Commission. In March 2005 the German PS broadcasters ARD and ZDF were investigated for a series of irregularities in the way they had acquired sports rights. The Commission claimed that the behaviour of the broadcasters went beyond their public service remit and constituted a distortion of the market. Therefore, the Commission told the German government to make major changes in the way the broadcasters were acting. It also questioned the need for ARD and ZDF to acquire pay or video-on-demand rights in order to fulfil their public service remit. Furthermore, it argued that licence fee money should not be used to finance the acquisition of pay-rights, given that PS broadcasters were not allowed to operate such a service.[10] This pattern does not only apply to the two German PS broadcasters, but applies in many other European countries.

Theory on bureaucratic behaviour can provide some explanations why PS broadcasters' policy has not corresponded with recommendations from welfare economic theory. Such a perspective regards bureaucrats as individuals who aim to maximize their own personal utility functions. A bureaucrat's utility function may include variables other than the output of the public sector and the welfare of society. According to Weber (1947), a bureaucrat's natural objective was power. Miguè and Bèlanger (1974) emphasise that bureaucrats have positive marginal utility from a budgetary slack. Slack in this case is defined as the difference between appropriated budget and the true minimum cost. Niskanen (1971: 38) lists objectives such as: public reputation, power, patronage and the output of the bureau, as objectives of bureaucrats.

The popularity of sports varies considerably, and representatives of PS broadcasters may find it more exciting to be involved in programmes that attract mass audiences than those targeting minority groups. In addition, such strategies can increase the broadcaster's popularity among the general audience. Ideas that larger audiences can justify increased funding may lead to the production and presentation of more commercialised (non-PSB) programming (Brown, 1996). Representatives from European PS broadcasters have openly admitted that they prioritise programmes which are able to attract large audiences, such as popular sports programmes, in order to legitimise the licence fee. This was confirmed in an interview with

Tor Aune, head of sports rights in the NRK and vice president of the European Broadcasting Union's (EBU) sports group (Helland and Solberg, 2006).

Such a policy is irrational according to welfare economic theory. PSBs are trying to increase their own popularity by spending resources on programmes the public alternatively could have watched on other broadcasters. The Listed Events regulation can guarantee this viewing to be free of charge.

Some PS broadcasters have been willing to give up expensive sports rights quicker than others. BBC, as an example, has not broadcast live football from the English elite division (currently named the Premier League) since 1988. The major reason for this was that price escalation sports rights took off earlier in the UK than in other European nations due to BSkyB's aggressive market policy. Therefore, the BBC had to accept that domestic live football became too expensive before many other European non-commercial PSBs. Their alternative was to compete for a highlights programme (*Match of the Day*).

This was different in Norway, where the Norwegian Broadcasting Corporation (NRK) acquired the rights for domestic Norwegian football (currently called the Tippeliga after its sponsor) much longer, i.e. until the 2005 season. When the rights for the 2006-2008 period were auctioned, NRK finally had to accept that the fees had become too expensive.

However, this has not reduced domestic elite football on Norwegian TV. The rights were acquired by TV2 (NRK's commercial PS rival in Norway), and the TV audience has been offered the same number of matches free of charge as when TV2 and NRK held the former deal together. The same applies to national team matches, which all are being broadcast on TV2's main channel. Hence, that NRK has been forced to give up Norwegian football has not had any negative consequences for the Norwegian TV audience. NRK, on the other hand, now can use the resources they alternatively would have spent on football on other programme activities.

However, both BBC and NRK have continued broadcasting prestigious one-off events such as the Olympic Games, World Cup soccer finals, and BBC also the European football championship for national teams. Since both nations have commercial broadcasters which meet the minimum penetration required by the Listed Events regulation, there is no welfare economic rationale for them to continue prioritising these events.

Similar objectives can characterise the strategies of politicians who are involved in setting up the objectives of these broadcasters, and also the ones to investigate whether they are being followed. Following rational choice considerations (see Friedman and Hechter, 1988) politicians basically aim at being re-elected. This, in turn will influence their policies between the elections (Downs, 1957). This provides a motive to support policies which are popular among the voters and not primarily those that have characteristics of merit goods and externalities.

However, a reduction of such programmes is unlikely to cause any negative reaction from the majority of voters. Musgrave's definition of 'merit goods as goods that ought to be provided even if the members of society do not demand them' also illustrates the reason for why they risk being underprovided (Musgrave, 1958). Individuals do not fully assess the positive impacts of these goods, either for themselves or for others. In economic terms, these variables are not integrated in a consumer's utility functions. Hence, not many people will protest if such programmes are underprovided, neither for the broadcaster nor for politicians. This also makes it easier to sacrifice them in order to afford expensive sports rights acquisitions. Politicians are the ones who should bear the responsibility for motivating public service broadcasters to uphold merit goods programmes, but will not become unpopular among the voters by sacrificing such objectives.

■ **Case study 3.1** *EC says German TV misuses licence fee on sports rights*

TV Sports Markets, vol. 9, no. 5, by Miriam Sherlock

The European Commission last week accused German public service broadcasters ARD and ZDF of a series of irregularities in the way they have acquired and used sports rights. It said that the behaviour of the broadcasters went beyond their public service remit and constituted a distortion of the market. It told the German government to make major changes in the way the broadcasters, and their rights-buying arm, the SportA agency, were acting. A commission letter to the government said that the solution could include a weighting of sports rights according to their importance and/or a restriction on the money made available to the broadcasters for the acquisition of rights. It also recommended that the acquisition of sports rights by ARD and ZDF be subject to a code of principles or governance. The commission was acting after complaints made last year by commercial broadcaster ProSiebenSat.1 and pay-TV company Premiere and an earlier complaint by Germany's association of commercial broadcasters, Verbandes Privater Rundfunk und Telekommunikation. Its preliminary conclusions come at an early stage of a process that could lead to a formal investigation. The commission's concerns form a major part of a wider examination of the role and financing of ARD and ZDF. Other concerns highlight the online activities of the two broadcasters. The commission is also examining the activities of public service broadcasters RTE in Ireland and NOS in the Netherlands.

Commission concerns

The commission said that it is worried ARD and ZDF overpay for rights and go beyond their public service remit:

- It questioned the need for ARD and ZDF to acquire rights such as pay or video-on-demand rights in order to fulfil their public service remit.

- It said that licence fee money should not be used to finance the acquisition of pay-rights, given that the public service broadcasters were not allowed to operate such a service.

- It questioned to what extent ARD and ZDF needed to sign exclusive deals. It said that even where an exclusive deal was signed, it might be beneficial for ARD and ZDF to sub-license some rights so as not to exclude other broadcasters from the market and so as not to pay more than the costs needed to cover their public service duty. It doubted whether the extra costs involved in securing exclusive deals were compatible with the public service remit.

- It said that where ARD and ZDF acquired rights and did not fully exploit them – and this was the case according to information from the private broadcasters – they were overpaying for the rights and this was not a justifiable use of licence fee money. The failure to sub-license unused rights increased public service costs unnecessarily.

- It was concerned that there was no regular or systematic sub-licensing system in place. It was concerned that ARD and ZDF and in some cases SportA have refused sub-licensing requests. It said this behaviour excluded competitors and exceeded the public service remit.

Broadcaster complaints

The German commercial broadcasters have long complained about the public service broadcasters' acquisition of sports rights. ProSiebenSat.1, the Haim Saban broadcast group, made an official complaint to the Commission last July and Premiere in November, backing up their allegations with examples. The main thrust of the complaints was that ARD and ZDF paid over the market rate, putting rights out of the reach of commercial channels which would have to refinance deals from the market. ProSiebenSat.1 claimed that the €180 million ARD-ZDF deal for the 2006 World Cup rights was above the going rate and that the two broadcasters would lose around €84 million on the deal. (The deal cost ARD and ZDF an overall €230 million because there was an earlier agreed €50 million option on the rights.) Both ProSiebenSat.1 and Premiere argued that, in other circumstances, ARD and ZDF are able, through their position in the European Broadcasting Union, to foreclose the market. ProSiebenSat.1 said that it was prevented from securing the rights for the 2010 and 2012 Olympic Games, despite making a higher offer for the German rights. Premiere alleged that it was prevented by the ARD-ZDF deal from acquiring pay-TV rights for the Games despite the public service broadcasters having no means of using the rights. The private broadcasters listed several instances where ARD and ZDF refused sub-licensing requests, despite not fully exploiting their rights. Premiere said that it was refused sub-licensing rights for Euro 2004 matches which

ARD and ZDF were not showing. It was also refused sub-licensing rights for several winter sports properties, even where ARD and ZDF showed only highlights coverage. When ARD and ZDF did offer rights, it was for the most unattractive properties. ProSiebenSat.1 complained that an ARD-ZDF rights deal with the German football association for the German Cup, DFB Pokal, was overvalued. It said that the public service broadcasters did not show all the games but refused to sub-license them. The broadcasters also attacked ARD's and ZDF's use of extra digital channels during the 2004 Olympics to showcase their rights; and the lack of transparency between the activities of ARD and ZDF and SportA.

Government position

The Commission's letter outlines the German government's response to its initial inquiries. The government, defending the public service broadcasters, said that the present level of the German licence fee did not allow ARD and ZDF to pay over the market rate for rights. It claimed that the private broadcasters had, to the detriment of public service broadcasters, driven up rights fees, for example Bundesliga highlights rights. It said that it was often impossible for ARD and ZDF to sub-license rights, such as those for the Olympics, because they did not know in advance what they would want to use. However, it pointed out, the broadcasters did sub-license rights for the Salt Lake Winter Olympics in 2002. Brussels was not satisfied with this response and asked the government to come up with new measures to deal with its concerns. If the Commission is not happy with the government's proposals, or if the government refuses to implement any Commission recommendations, Brussels could launch a formal investigation. This could oblige the government to implement various changes, which it could appeal against by taking the Commission to court. If the government accepted the Commission's proposals but did not implement them, the Commission could take it to court for non-compliance.

Ireland and Netherlands

In Ireland, the Commission's examination of RTE centres on increases in, and the use of, the licence fee. It also cited a complaint by commercial broadcaster TV3 that RTE failed to distinguish between the cost of sports programming within the public service remit and that outside the remit, such as Champions League soccer or Formula One. TV3 pointed out that both events 'take place outside Ireland' and 'neither … has any material Irish content'. RTE said that it was not unduly worried by TV3's complaint. The Irish government had already partially looked into the issue of sports rights as part of a wider report on the effect of the licence fee on the Irish broadcast market. The report, by accountancy firm PricewaterhouseCoopers, published in December 2004, said that RTE had no case to answer. In the Netherlands, the Commission is investigating complaints over NOS's online activities. It is concerned, as in Germany, that online activities such as e-commerce and mobile-telephony constitute the financing of services outside of a public service broadcaster's traditional television activities.

ADVERTISING CHANNELS

This category includes independent profit maximising channels that are free to construct their menu of programmes on the basis of commercial criteria. However, it also includes PS broadcasters that are highly regulated and obliged to follow restrictions that are similar to the non-commercial PS broadcasters. Examples of the latter are broadcasters such as ITV (UK), SBS (Australia), TV4 (Sweden) and TV2 (Norway).

Advertising is the major source of TV revenue worldwide, as seen from Table 3.2. On a global basis it accounts for 51 per cent of the total revenues, and as much as 59 per cent in the USA, 49 per cent in Asia Pacific and 43 per cent in Europe. In 2002, TV advertising amounted to $58.4 billion, which was about one-quarter of the total advertising volume, representing the largest share of any medium.[11] However, enormous national differences exist behind this picture. Nations with a high standard of living spend considerably more on TV advertising than poorer countries. As an example, the amount of money spent on TV advertising in the USA was 251 times more than in India in 2002.[12]

In general, advertising has two basic functions. First, to inform about prices, quality and terms of sale. Secondly, to persuade potential customers to purchase a product. Expressed in microeconomic terms, advertisers seek to shift the demand curve for their product or make it more inelastic, permitting an increase in price. Profit maximising advertisers will continue to supply advertising up to the point where the marginal cost of the inputs equals the marginal revenue from the output (Kaldor, 1950). Since they want to reach as many potential consumers as possible, the amount of revenue received by the broadcaster will broadly be positively correlated to audience size. Thus, profit-maximising, advertiser-financed broadcasters will always have the incentive to provide programmes that attract larger audiences. This explains their eagerness to broadcast attractive sporting events such as the World Cup soccer finals, Olympic Games and the Super Bowl.

Measuring rating figures

The next sections explain the principles for how rating figures are measured. The information is mainly based on how Nielsen Media Research (NMR) measures the national rating figures in the USA.[13] NMR finds out about who is watching what on the basis of a sample that consists of more than 5,000 households, containing over 13,000 people who have agreed to participate. Since there are over 99 million households with TVs in the USA, a sample of 5,000 might seem just not big enough to represent the nation. This, however, does not represent any problem if the sample is representative of the whole population. The *Nielsen TV families* are a cross-section of the households with television sets all across America. They have been selected in a way that gives every household an equal chance of being picked, and all kinds of households are in the sample. This means that there are homes from all 50 states, from cities and towns, suburbs and rural areas included.

In the specially selected sample of homes, NMR technicians install metering equipment on TV sets, VCRs and cable boxes (and even satellite dishes). The TV meters automatically keep track of when the sets are on and what the sets are tuned to. These meters are connected to a central 'black box', which is actually a very small computer and modem. Information from the meters is collected by the black box, and in the middle of the night all the black boxes call in their information to NMR's central computers.

NMR's primary source of information about which programmes are airing for each station or cable channel comes from a very special coded ID number that is part of every TV picture: a series of lines and dots in the top edge of the picture which labels the programme and episode. NMR developed and patented this system, which is called AMOL (Automated Measurement Of Line-ups). All across the country, they have sites where TV stations are monitored and the programme ID codes are detected and collected. Each night, these monitoring sites connect up to NMR's central computer and download the information. The electronic program information is compiled and compared with other sources of information. Keeping track of what is on TV is also done with the help of programme listings provided by networks, stations and cable systems, as well as published TV listings.

NMR track more than 1,700 TV stations and 11,000 cable systems. With this database as a starting point, they can credit tuning and viewing to all of the networks, syndicators, cable networks, TV stations and cable systems involved in providing TV programming to the viewing public.

Identifying commercials

Although there are many TV programmes, there are even more commercials. Using a special passive TV signal identification technology, commercials on TV stations are continuously monitored and converted into a digital 'fingerprint'. These fingerprints are then compared to a computer file of fingerprints from thousands of different commercials and automatically identified whenever possible (which is about 95 per cent of the time). The other 5 per cent of the time, videotapes of unmatched commercials are sent to a central office to be viewed and properly credited. This information is used to produce reports detailing when and where TV commercials actually aired.

Measuring people

This is the main ingredient in the recipe for ratings: who is watching? By combining the measurement of who is watching with what channel is tuned to and what programme is on that channel, NMR can credit viewing to a programme. NMR measures who is watching programmes which reach the entire nation with the *people meter*. In their national sample, NMR installs set meters that have an attachment called a 'people meter', which is a box, about the size of a paperback book, which is placed on or near each TV set. The box has buttons and lights which are assigned to each person who lives in the household (with additional buttons for guests). There is also a remote control to operate the people meter from anywhere in the room.

When viewers begin watching TV, they push their button, changing their indicator light from red to green. When they finish watching, they push their button again and the indicator changes back to red periodically, the lights flash to remind people to check to make sure that the information in the people meter is accurate.

Information from the people meters is combined with set tuning information and relayed to NMR each night. NMR regularly cross-checks the information obtained from different samples and different measurement methods. Remarkably, the ratings produced from more than 100,000 diaries collected from all markets during each sweep month have been similar to the ratings based on 5,000 people meter homes for the same period of time. Different measurement methods, completely separate samples – and a vast difference in sampling size – yet they both produce similar estimates of audience.

The methods that are used by firms that measure the rating figures in other nations follow the same principles that NMR applies in the USA. The size of the samples can vary, depending on how heterogeneous the population is.

Figure 3.2 presents an example that illustrates rating figures in connection to live sport programmes, the broadcasting of UEFA's Champions League matches in Norway. These rating statistics were measured by TNS Gallup, Norway on the basis of a sample that consists of 1,000 Norwegian households, comprising 2,400 people. Their method is based on the same principles as the NMR method described above.

The figure presents the rating figures, both during commercials and the match, from UEFA's Champions League matches in Norway in the period from February 2000 to May 2003 (Solberg and Hammervold, 2004).[14] The matches were broadcast on TV3, which is an advertising channel that is transmitted via cable and satellite. Most programmes started 45 minutes before the match, while some started 15 minutes before it. The programmes in the first category contained seven commercial sections, with the first screened just after the start of the programme. The following three sections were screened before the start of the first half, with intervals of 8 to 10 minutes. Two commercial sections were screened between the first and second half, while the last followed immediately after the match. The rating

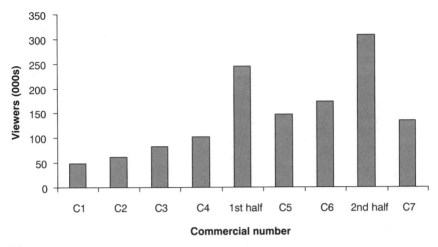

Figure 3.2 *TV rating of UEFA's Champions League in Norway*

statistics were measured regularly during the programmes. As seen, the interest for commercials was quite moderate for the first part of the programme. Indeed, the two first commercials only attracted in the region of 20 per cent of the viewers that followed the matches. The two commercial sections between the first- and second-half were the most popular ones and attracted respectively 52 and 61 per cent of the audience that watched the match.

However, to advertisers, not all viewers are alike. The greater the spending power of viewers and/or the greater their attractiveness to the advertisers, the more the advertiser will pay to reach them. This creates an incentive to discriminate in favour of households with high income and to offer programmes to which they can relate (Dunnet 1990).

Since the values on advertising slots correlate with the number of viewers, any obligations on PS broadcasters to broadcast programmes specially targeting minority groups reduce the revenue potential. Profit maximisation requires resources to be allocated so that their marginal contributions to profit are equal in all alternatives. If not, profit can be increased by reallocating the inputs to other programmes. On the other hand, PS broadcasters have traditionally held the advantage of having the highest penetration in their respective domestic market due to their admittance to terrestrial transmission. This has enabled them to charge higher ad-slots than commercial channels with lower penetration, other things being equal. Furthermore, this superiority in penetration has also made them more popular among sponsors and the governing bodies of sport, particularly in comparison with pay-TV channels that have considerably lower penetration. Over the years, however, this advantage has been reduced as commercial channels have narrowed the gaps in penetration. Some of them have even had the same penetration as PS broadcasters for several years.

As seen from Table 3.2, the US market is heading the list of resources spent on advertising, and this certainly also applies to sports broadcasting. An illustration of this is the amount that has been spent in connection with the broadcasting of the Super Bowl, which is the most attractive sport programme on North American TV, usually with rating figures of around 50 per cent of the US population. For the 2005 Super Bowl, an average 30-second spot cost $2.4 million, that is $80,000 per second.[15] Since 1967, when NBC charged a mere $37,500 per 30-second spot in the Super Bowl, the average cost of a Super Bowl advertisement has soared more than 6,000 per cent, which is 12 times the rate of the average network prime time's inflation in advertising cost over the same period. However, the Super Bowl is not only watched by football fans. During the 2005 final, about 35 million consumers found the commercials to be the most important element.[16] TV advertising also generated enormous revenues to other North American professional team sports, such as the National Basketball Association (NBA), Major League Baseball (MLB) and National Hockey League (NHL), as well as college sport.

Regulations on advertising

TV channels are not 100 per cent free to put on whatever advertising they want. All nations have regulations on TV advertising, but with great variations, as seen from Table 3.3. Many countries prohibit TV advertising for goods such as tobacco and alcohol, or at least have restrictions on it. Furthermore, some countries do not allow commercials connected to programmes aimed at children, while others have restrictions that control such commercials.

In addition, regulations that oblige TV channels to uphold a minimum level of advertising of domestic products also exist. As an example, the Australian Broadcasting Authority (ABA) requires at least 80 per cent of advertising time broadcast each year by commercial free-to-air television licensees, between the hours of 6am and midnight, to be used for Australian produced advertisements.[17]

Similar regulations exist in Europe.

The US TV market has traditionally had the most liberal regulations worldwide. Except for programmes targeting children, it is up to the channels to decide how much advertising they will put on. In Europe, however, the maximum limit is considerably lower, as seen from the table. The European regulations are particularly strict on PS broadcasters. Another European speciality is that the channels are obliged to follow the regulations in the country from which the programmes are being broadcast. Thus, some channels broadcast their programmes from nations with more liberal rules than in the country where the targeted viewers live.

◼ *Table 3.3* *Regulations on TV advertising – some examples*

Australia	Australian TV channels are subject to maximum limits that vary between 13 and 16 minutes per hour for general programmes, while programmes targeting children have stricter regulations. In addition, the Australian regulations also require at least 80 per cent of advertising time broadcast each year by commercial television licensees, between the hours of 6 a.m. and midnight, to be used for Australian produced advertisements. Up to 20 per cent of total transmission time is therefore available for the broadcast of foreign-produced advertisements. New Zealand commercials have fully qualified as 'Australian' since 1981 under the current and previous standards relating to Australian content in advertisements and advertising.
USA	No federal law limits the amount of commercial matter that may be broadcast at any given time. The exception is television programmes aimed at children 12 years and below, where advertising may not exceed 10.5 minutes per hour on weekends and 12 minutes per hour on weekdays.
UK	The BBC is not allowed to air advertising. Channels 4 and ITV are limited to 7.5 minutes per hour, while BSkyB is limited to 9 minutes per hour.
Germany	Public service broadcasters are limited to 20 minutes per day, while private channels are limited to 12 minutes of advertising per hour.
Italy	The public service channel, RAI, is restricted to 7.2 minutes per hour (a daily average of 2.4 minutes per hour). Private national channels are limited to 10.8 minutes per hour (a daily average of 9 minutes per hour). Private local channels are limited to 12 minutes per hour.
France	Private TV channels are limited to 12 minutes per hour (a daily average of 6 minutes per hour), while Canal Plus is limited to 9 minutes per hour (a daily average of 6 minutes per hour).
Spain	Private TV channels are limited to 12 minutes per hour, while Canal Plus is restricted to 2.3 minutes per hour.

Sources: Solberg 2002a; http://www.aba.gov.au/tv/content/advertising/index.htm

SUBSCRIPTION-BASED CHANNELS

Subscription-based TV, more commonly known as pay-TV, has had the strongest growth worldwide of the three sources in the course of the start of the twenty-first century. Among the most known pay-TV companies are:

■ DirecTV, which is the main provider of subscription-based TV in the USA and Latin America;

■ the UK-based BSkyB, in financial terms, probably the most successful company in this category in Europe;

■ the French-based Canal Plus, which was the largest European pay-TV company with approximately 16 million subscribers (by 2002) across nations such as Belgium, Italy, the Netherlands, Scandinavia, Poland and Spain;[18]

■ the Australian-based Foxtel; and

■ the Japanese SKY Perfect Communications.

Many of them are embedded with transmission companies via common ownership, and particularly with satellite platforms. Their menu of programmes is often considerably narrower than free-to-air channels. Attractive sports programmes and films have been the engine to attract new subscribers. However, the fact that they are bundled together with other channels can offer subscribers a broader menu.

The revenues come from the consumer surplus that the viewers would have kept if the programmes were broadcast on free-to-air channels. The charges are usually split into a two-tariff system. First, there is a subscription fee, which is often split between a one-time (lump sum) fee paid when signing the subscription and a current fee paid at regular stages. The latter allows for adjustments in case of cost increases or altered market conditions. In addition, they can also charge pay-per-view fees, on single programmes or on packages consisting of multi-programmes. Due to these fees, the penetration tends to be in the region of 20–30 per cent of the TV households in many markets, which is considerably lower than for free-to-air channels.

Boxing has so far been the most typical pay-per-view sport for single programmes in terms of revenue generating. This particularly applies to title matches, and Table 3.4 shows the top-ten list of pay-per-view matches ever in the USA, in terms of number of buys.

Unlike advertiser channels, pay-TV channels can take advantage from the intensity of viewers' preferences expressed in financial terms when they construct the price policy. By doing so, it has the potential to make profit from broadcasting programmes that attract the interest from audiences that are too small to be profitable on advertising channels. This assumes that a sufficient number of viewers are willing to pay for watching the programmes. In addition, this is contingent

Table 3.4 Top twenty pay-per-view boxing list in the USA (by 2003)

Match	Date	Number of purchases	Income (US$ million)
1. Tyson vs. Holyfield II	June 1997	1,990,000	99.0
2. Tyson vs. Lewis	June 2002	1,800,000	103.0
3. Tyson vs. Holyfield I	November 1996	1,590,000	80,0
4. Tyson vs. McNeeley	August 1995	1,580,000	n.a.
5. De la Hoya v Trinidad	September 1999	1,400,000	71.4
6. Tyson vs. Bruno	March 1996	1,390,000	n.a.
7=. Tyson vs. Ruddock II	June 1991	1,360,000	n.a.
7=. Holyfield vs. Foreman	April 1991	1,360,000	53.0
9. Holyfield vs. Lewis I	March 1999	1,200,000	60.0
10. Holyfield vs. Douglas	October 1990	1,060,000	n.a.

Source: Ben Speight

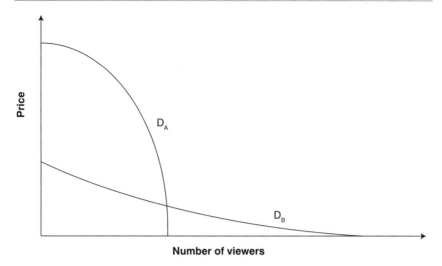

Figure 3.3 *Advertiser versus pay TV*

upon the channel finding a way of extracting a sufficient proportion of the viewer's willingness to pay, to make the programme profitable.

Pay-TV is most effective when a number of viewers are highly interested in some programmes. This of course also assumes they have a high reservation price for watching and that it is possible to charge their willingness to pay. The two demand curves presented in Figure 3.3 illustrate under which circumstances advertising and subscription-based TV broadcasting are most suitable. Let us imagine that a TV channel can broadcast the same programme in two different markets, say market A and B. D_A represents the demand-curve for this programme in market A, while D_B is the demand-curve in market B.

Some viewers in market A have quite a high reservation price. On the other hand the demand curve drops quickly, which indicates that the number of people with a high reservation price is limited. Hence, in this market the programmes will be more profitable on a pay-TV channel than on an advertising channel. In contrast, viewers in market B have different preferences. No viewers have as high reservation prices as in market A. On the other hand, D_B intersects the x-axis further to the right than the D_B-curve, which indicates that there are more people interested in watching the programme than in market A. However, the fact that the D_B-curve starts at quite a low point along the y-axis also indicates that the potential viewers have a limited interest. The channel is unable to earn as much from pay-per-view fees as in market A. Hence, it would be more profitable to broadcast the programme on an advertising channel than on a pay-TV channel in market B. It is also important to bear in mind that shifts in demand can occur. The fact that viewers in market B are quite moderately interested might indicate that this demand-curve is more vulnerable to negative shifts than in market A. Unenthusiastic viewers are likely to drop out if other alternatives appear.

The argument in connection to Figure 3.3 assumes that a relationship exists between the viewers' interest for watching and their reservation prices (willingness to pay). However, such a relationship is not obvious. Some viewers might be interested in watching, but not willing to pay any fees for doing it. Despite this, we nevertheless expect some correlation to exist between the two variables.

Hence, it is no coincidence that pay-TV channels have concentrated most on categories of programmes that are very popular among a niche of viewers, for example people who are extremely interested in soccer. They also have been most successful in acquiring the rights for competitions that have a long season and which take place regularly, such as national premier leagues. This helps to recruit subscribers, rather than in generating pay-per-view revenues.

World Cup soccer finals and the Olympics are extremely popular worldwide and both receive substantial attention from a large number of people. However, such tournaments only take place every four years, which probably is too seldom to make the majority willing to subscribe to a pay-TV platform to watch them. As an example, the North American network NBC spent $500 million on the 1992 Summer Olympics in Barcelona, of which $400 million were on the rights and the additional $100 million on production costs. This also included a pay-per-view project that offered the possibility to watch every single competition in the Games. The network would have needed 5 million subscribers to reach break-even. However, this experiment, which was known as the so-called 'Triplecast' since NBC used three PPV channels to carry the programmes, proved a failure, and NBC lost nearly $100 million on the project.[19] One reason for this was that NBC broadcast many programmes free-to-air, while the pay-per-view alternative was for those who wanted to watch the entire Games. Hence, many viewers were satisfied with the free of charge alternative, at least so much that they were unwilling to pay any extra fees to watch the rest.

Another similar example was Canal Digital's (a Nordic TV and transmission company) acquisition or the Scandinavian rights of the 2002 World Cup soccer finals. In Sweden and Denmark, about 50 per cent of the matches were also broadcast on free-to-air channels with penetration almost on 100 per cent of the TV households. This also included Sweden's and Denmark's national team matches. In addition, a large number of Norwegian viewers were also able to watch the tournament (except for four matches) on the Swedish and Danish broadcasters. As a consequence of this, Canal Digital was unable to attract the number of subscribers that would have been necessary to make the acquisition profitable. Thus the short-term financial loss on the acquisition amounted to NOK48 million (€6.5 million).[20]

Surveys have shown that there are few sports that are able to attract interest from the majority of people (Solberg, 2002b). However, the ability to reach a worldwide audience by means of satellite transmission can make such programmes profitable, even if they receive moderate attention in their primary market. The high degree of first-copy costs, combined with relatively low transaction costs, offers considerable economies of scale advantages when programmes are transmitted to a worldwide audience. These are discussed in more detail in Chapter 4.

Table 3.2 shows that subscriptions to subscription-based TV had become the second most valuable income source for TV by 2004, behind advertising but well above licence fees/public grants. Attractive sport programming has been a major driver behind this development in Europe and Australia, but not to the same degree in the USA, where the majority of attractive sports programmes can be seen on free-to-air channels. In the USA, subscription channels have more been a supplement, rather than a competitor to the free-to-air channels. Although the pay-TV platform DirecTV (which also is involved in satellite transmission) has acquired attractive sports rights, these deals have not been as exclusive and comprehensive as European soccer deals. One reason for this is the mature and solid relationship that has been established between the networks and their advertisers over the years. Indeed, this also includes the relationships to sport governing bodies. It is often claimed that US-sports tournaments are tailor-made to suit advertising channels. As an example, the most popular team sports have short periods of playing time, often broken up by time-outs. Thanks to such breaks, there is ample opportunity to screen commercials, hence allowing advertising channels a comparative edge over pay-TV channels (Solberg, 2002a). Although the original purpose was to allow the coaches and teams to discuss and re-evaluate tactics, time-outs also allow TV channels to screen commercials without interrupting the broadcasting of the game.

■ *Case study 3.2* Ice hockey league hopes pay-TV will boost gates

TV Sports Markets, vol. 9 no. 7, by Ben Speight

Finland's top domestic ice hockey league, the SM-liiga, is to put most of its matches on to pay-TV, dropping its long-term relationship with free-to-air broadcaster MTV3. The league will get a huge increase in rights fees and, it believes, stem the fall in match attendances from the new three-year joint-deal with pan-Nordic pay-channel Canal Plus and free-to-air commercial channel Nelonen. The deal is thought to be worth €3.7 million (£2.5 million) a year, an 85-per-cent increase on the €2 million paid annually by MTV3. Canal Plus will show live regular season matches and Nelonen will show highlights and live coverage of the final and some of the semi-final play-offs – between four and eight matches a season. MTV3 was showing 32 matches a year. The clubs were also unhappy with MTV3's coverage, claiming that too much emphasis was put on analysis and on the personalities of studio experts, rather than the sport itself. Canal Plus, according to one club managing director, will do a better job: it is a renowned broadcaster of ice hockey, having shown Sweden's top league, the Elitserien, since 1996. The Finnish league deal came as a surprise to most industry observers. MTV3, which had held the rights for more than 10 years, had the option of an exclusive negotiation period for a three-year extension and also a matching rights option. But the league's desire to limit the number of games on free-to-air made it difficult for MTV3 to compete. Knowing the league's stance, the channel offered a deal in which it would show only 14 regular season games on its main free-to-air channel and the rest on its digital MTV3 Plus channel on a pay-per-view season ticket basis. Over the last two seasons, it has already been showing one pay-per-view match a week on this basis, with another on the main channel. The league turned down the offer and MTV3 walked away – even though, it said, it could have outbid Canal Plus and Nelonen. The limited number of games it would be able to show on free-to-air did not make a deal commercially viable. The loss of ice hockey is arguably a major blow to MTV3. The league is the third-most popular television sport in the market and was one of the cornerstones of the channel's sports portfolio. But MTV3 said that it was not overly concerned: it still had the top two ranking properties: Formula One and World Cup ski-jumping. Urpo Helkuvaara, the league's managing director, said that he was confident that taking the pay-TV route was right. With the increasing number of digital viewers in Finland, paying to view ice hockey would become the norm in a couple of years. Others are not so sure that ice-hockey will work as a subscription driver for Canal Plus. According to one television executive, 'people in Finland are very conservative and may not pay'. Under the new deal, running from 2005–6 to 2007–8, Canal Plus has the exclusive live rights for two regular season matches each week, on Tuesdays and Thursdays. It will also show the first two ties of the two best of five semi-final play-offs and have second choice of games from the third tie onwards. Nelonen will show the first choice of both semi-final play-offs from the third match onwards and all of the matches of the best-of-five final exclusively. It will also show a highlights programme after every round on Saturday evenings and extended highlights of Canal Plus's live matches.

Canal Plus aggression

The ice hockey deal is another example of Canal Plus Nordic's new aggression in the Finnish market, an area it has targeted for subscription growth. Earlier this year, it paid €4 million in a four-year deal for the rights for all home matches of the Finnish national soccer team, starting in 2006–7 (*TV Sports Markets*, vol. 9, no 3). The fee is 70 per cent up on state broadcaster YLE's existing deal. It has also bought the Finnish rights for the German motorsport series DTM in a two-year deal beginning this season in which former Formula One star Mika Hakkinen, a sporting legend in Finland, will compete. But Canal Plus sees ice hockey as its main Finnish subscription driver, as the sport has proved to be in Sweden. Canal Plus had 768,000 subscribers across the Nordic region at the end of 2004. Canal Plus refuses to give a market-by-market breakdown, but it is thought that 55 per cent of subscribers are in Sweden and 9 per cent in Finland. Formula One, World Cup ski-jumping and soccer's Champions League are also on Canal Plus's Finnish wish list. Some observers say that the cooperation between Canal Plus and Nelonen over the ice hockey could pave the way for a joint bid for the Champions League. Nelonen is the incumbent rights-holder in Finland. Finnish public service broadcaster Y L E extended a four-year deal for ice hockey's annual World Championships for a further four years. The present deal expires after the 2007 tournament in Russia.

Establishing mature relationships between sellers and buyers is often a time consuming exercise, which also applies to sports broadcasting. Advertisers are not qualified to benefit from involvement in sports broadcasting overnight. Thus, it is no coincidence that European pay-TV channels started their successful acquisition of soccer rights when commercial broadcasting in Europe was in its infancy. BSkyB acquired the English Premier League rights for the first time ever in 1992 at a price that tripled the value of the previous deal. The previous holder, ITV, would have needed a huge increase in advertising revenues to challenge BSkyB's bid. This would, however, have been a very risky deal, not only for ITV, but also for their advertisers who were quite inexperienced with how to take advantage from sports broadcasting at that time. Although ITV might have been willing to increase their bid above BSkyB's final bid, it can be questioned whether this would have been profitable at that stage.

As another reason, soccer, which is the most attractive sport in Europe, has periods of 45 minutes and contains no natural breaks such as time-outs. This reduces the opportunities for broadcasting commercials. It is no coincidence, then, that a second break was proposed during the 1994 World Cup soccer finals in the USA. This proposal was strongly opposed by soccer's governing bodies, however, and has not received serous attention since.

The fact that TV advertising is less regulated in the USA than in any other nation represents another reason why it has been more profitable to finance the broadcasting of the most attractive sports programmes by advertising on free-to-air channels than by subscription fees on pay-TV channels

Despite the strong growth, subscription-based TV channels have experienced severe financial problems in several markets, in addition to the failures mentioned above. The German-based Premiere, which was a part of Kirch Media, went bankrupt in 2002, partly as a result of overestimating the value on the German Bundesliga. Likewise, Telepiù and Stream, the two Italian pay-TV channels that shared the rights of Italian Serie A since 1999 both suffered substantial losses after paying too much for these rights. Therefore, Italian competition authorities allowed the channels to merge in 2003. The same year, the Spanish competitive authorities allowed three former rivals to merge into one company, namely Socecable, for the same reason.[21] Sport 7, a Dutch pay-TV channel, acquired the rights for the Dutch Eerste Divisie in 1996 for more than DFL1.04 billion in a deal that collapsed only four months later after incurring losses of DFL100 million – see Chapter 6 for more details..

Chapter 4

The cost structure of sports broadcasting

This chapter will analyse the cost structure of sports broadcasting. However, understanding this also requires an overview of the cost structure for broadcasting in general. The first sections focus on some basic elements from general cost theory, such as the various categories of costs and how they vary with production, with special application to sports broadcasting. It then analyses the relationship between inputs and profit in sport programming in a short-term perspective. Then the existence of *economies of scale* and *economies of scope advantages* in broadcasting is discussed. The last section of the chapter discusses specifically the cost of sports broadcasting rights, which have become a large proportion of sports broadcasting costs in recent years.

FIXED AND VARIABLE COSTS

The distinction between *fixed costs* and *variable costs* is essential in the production of all kinds of goods and services, including broadcasting. Their proportion can vary considerably for the various categories of programmes. In addition, there can also be internal variations within each category. This is particularly the case in sports broadcasting. For example, broadcasting a 100 metre track race will not require the same amount of resources as a marathon race. Another reason relates to sports rights and the enormous differences that exist between various sports and events. While products such as the World Cup soccer finals, the Olympics, the North American Football League (NAFL), UEFA's Champions League and the Australian Football League (AFL) have all become extremely expensive over recent years, the majority of sports find themselves in a position where they can expect very little, if any, income from selling broadcasting rights for their competitions.

Broadly, variable costs are the costs that change as output changes, whilst fixed costs are the costs that do not vary with output. This categorisation, however, also depends on the time perspective. The longer the time perspective is, the better the ability to vary the level of production, and thus the higher the proportion of variable costs. Any company will be more flexible with regards to hiring inputs the longer the time perspective is.

Fixed costs are independent of the level of production. Some of them are dependent on production, but not on the level being produced. When production closes down, these costs disappear. The level of these costs remains constant irrespective of the quantity being produced. In addition, some fixed costs do not depend on whether the firm is producing or not, which can apply to facility costs. It is only when the facilities are closed down that this cost element will vanish (Johnsen, 2001).

Sports broadcasting will generate both categories of costs. Acquiring – and using – cameras, as an example, will cause fixed costs as well as variable costs. In the annual account, some of the fixed costs are measured in terms of depreciation, which expresses the reduction in value from using the inputs. There will also be variable costs, for example electricity costs.

OPPORTUNITY COSTS

Most of the inputs being used on sports broadcasting can alternatively produce other programmes. This applies to resources such as cameras, commentators and other staff. Some of these inputs will be more flexible than others. Cameras and the staff that operate them can be used on a wide range of programmes. A sports commentator on the other hand may not be the best alternative to host a news programme. However, the channel can alternatively employ people with other skills when they initially recruit commentators. Furthermore, there is always an ability to replace its staff with people that have other skills in case it aims to give priority to other genres of programmes than first planned.

Inputs used in sport programming that can be used in other activities will have an *opportunity cost* (also called alternative cost). The term opportunity cost refers to the value the resources could have created in their next best alternative use: the *value forgone* from not allocating the resources differently. The monetary value of the opportunity costs depends on the market value of the programme(s) that the inputs alternatively could have produced. As we will see, this also depends on whether there is a shortage of inputs or not.

To illustrate the nature and consequence of opportunity costs, let us imagine that a TV channel has 100 cameras available, but that it only uses 80 of them. Hence, there will be 20 cameras available for additional programming. We also assume that the inputs that are necessary to use the cameras are also idle. Let us now imagine that the channel wants to make another programme that requires 10 cameras. Doing this will not require any reduction in other programme activities. Hence, the opportunity costs of producing this programme is zero.

This assessment will be different if the circumstances are turned around so that all its 100 cameras and the staff necessary to use them are occupied with other programming. Hence, making the extra programme will now cause opportunity costs as other programme activities have to be reduced. The value of the opportunity costs is the income the inputs could have created in the programmes that will now be displaced. Profit maximising channels will allocate the inputs so that the net contribution in any allocation is equal. If not, profit can be increased simply by a reallocation of inputs. In other words, produce more of some programmes and less of others.

The same principle applies to the transmission process. If a frequency is used to transmit a sports programme, then it is impossible to transmit any other programmes on this frequency simultaneously. Even if the digital technology has enhanced the number of frequencies substantially, it is still impossible to broadcast more than one programme on each of them. On the other hand, the enhancement has made it less likely that such scarcity will occur in transmission.

SUNK COSTS

This picture is completely different for *sunk costs*, which refers to expenditures that have been made but cannot be recovered. Such costs are totally irretrievable and do not disappear, no matter what action the producer takes. In other words, they are 'the water under the bridge'. Whatever decision is being taken with regards to production level, nothing can be done to dispose of sunk costs. Some inputs can be resold, but not all. However, it is the inputs that cannot be resold, or do not have any other usage that are the sunk costs. One reason for this can be that the inputs are very rare and specialised, which limit their field of utilisation. It can also have to do with terms in contracts.

Any presence of sunk costs will influence decision-making processes in production. When sunk costs have been paid, there is no economic regain for the producer even from closing down production and going out of business. Thus, as a rule of thumb, the sunk costs that are paid for should not influence on decisions taken by the firm thereafter (Johnsen, 2001).

Indeed, the difference between sunk costs and fixed costs can sometimes be confusing. Some of the fixed costs can be avoided if the firm stops its production, while all of them will disappear if it goes out of business.

This, however, is different for sunk costs. To illustrate their nature, let us imagine that a TV channel acquires the sports rights for a team tournament that consists of 50 matches. The channel pays a fixed fee of €10 million, which we assume is independent of the income it earns from broadcasting the matches. Thus, the fee does not correlate with the number of matches being broadcast. Hence, the €10 million has to be regarded as sunk costs. Nothing can be done to dispose of them, unless the seller is willing to renegotiate the deal or some other channels are interested in buying the rights. Therefore, the €10 million fee should not influence which and how many matches the channel broadcast. Instead, these decisions should be based on a comparison of the income from broadcasting the matches with the income from alternative programmes.

Table 4.1 shows the TV rating figures from Euro 2004 in all the countries that participated, with the exception of France. As seen, matches involving national teams were the most popular. On average, these matches attracted 220 per cent of the audience of other matches in the respective nations. Such differences influenced the values of advertisement slots. Hence, matches involving national teams were the highest income generators.

Euro 2004 included 31 matches, and in general the channels acquired the rights to broadcast the whole tournament. In some cases, several channels shared the rights. However, the large variations in rating figures indicate that it was not necessarily profitable to broadcast the entire number of matches, even if the channels had the rights for the whole tournament.

Similar incidents have occurred in connection to the broadcasting of UEFA's Champions League matches in Europe. The principle for selecting a club is that each nation is given a quota that varies from one to four clubs. Some nations have not even got one club, but have had to qualify through qualifying rounds before the main tournament starts. The quotas have been decided on the basis of factors such as previous performances by clubs from the specific nations, but also by the size of their home markets. The domestic markets in the big soccer nations, such

Table 4.1 TV rating Euro 2004, average figures

	National team matches		Other matches	
	Nominal figures	TV rating	Nominal figures	TV rating
Czech Republic	1,846,000	18.7	880,000	8.9
Denmark	1,905,000	37.2	786,000	15.3
Germany	22,950,000	31.6	10,653,00	14.7
Greece	2,124,000	23.0	658,000	7.1
Italy	18,454,000	33.0	7,133,000	12.8
Netherlands	7,636,000	51.5	3,220,000	21.7
Portugal	3,333,000	35.4	1,217,000	12.9
Russia	8,218,000	13.6	3,569,000	5.9
Spain	8,053,000	20.2	3,603,000	9.0
Sweden	3,320,000	37.3	1,502,000	17.4
United Kingdom	17,598,000	32.2	6,543,000	12.0
Average		27.3		12.5

Source: *TV Sports Markets*, vol. 8, no. 13

as Germany, England, Italy, France and Spain generate higher revenues than the smaller markets such as Norway, Sweden and Finland. Therefore, the big nations have also been given bigger quotas.

Nevertheless, sooner or later clubs from the big nations are also eliminated from the tournament. History has shown that the performances of teams from these nations have varied. On some occasions the eliminations have taken place earlier than the broadcasters in their respective nations had expected. As a consequence, the rating figures have also declined significantly compared to seasons where their performance was better. To reduce the negative economic effects, broadcasters in the respective nations have downgraded the tournament by broadcasting fewer matches or alternatively showed them on channels with lower penetration, in seasons when the national clubs have underperformed. These incidents are examples of decision-making processes on the basis of the opportunity costs. In other words, channels make a comparison of the income from broadcasting Champions League matches of foreign teams with the potential income from other programmes. When Champions League matches became less attractive, it takes less for alternative programmes to become more profitable. These decisions by the broadcasters have not been appreciated by UEFA, which wants maximum coverage of the tournament.

The number of factors that can influence rating figures at sport programmes is quite long. Knock-out matches tend to attract more interest than ordinary group matches since the effect of loosing is more dramatic. Furthermore, some teams can be extremely popular due to their historical performance, for example Brazil's national soccer team. The same applies to individual sports where some competitors are special popular among TV viewers. The degree of *uncertainty of outcome* and *competitive balance* can influence the attractiveness of matches significantly (see Chapter 7). This aspect can also be influenced by how tournaments are organised. On some occasions, the last matches in a group may not have any importance at all. The reason for this can be that a team has already qualified for the next round or alternatively is already eliminated from the tournament before the final match of the group is played.

Similar factors also prevail for the broadcasting of individual sports. The profitability of broadcasting can drop significantly if national favourites have to withdraw from competitions due to injuries. This particularly applies to nations that only have a few competitors at the highest level.

THE COSTS OF PROGRAMMING

Figure 4.1 presents the costs per hour for some of BBC's programme categories, based on data from 2003/4.[1] Sports broadcasting did not belong to the most expensive genre of programmes. While they only accounted for 30 per cent of the costs for drama, they were 400 per cent more expensive than for news/weather programmes.

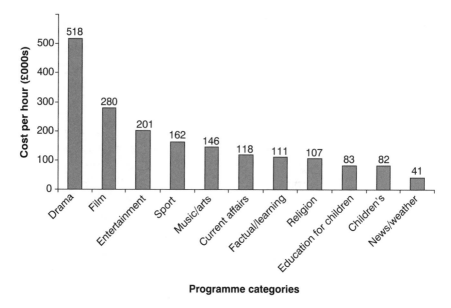

Figure 4.1 *Programming cost per hour BBC, 2003/4 season*

However, great variations exist behind these figures. While some live programmes can be extremely costly due to expensive right fees, the costs on other programmes can be moderate. Furthermore, the programming costs from live sports programmes are influenced by how many resources are being put into their production.

The quality of sport programmes will be influenced by the amount of inputs used on programming. More inputs can improve quality and hence attract more viewers, which in turn can increase income for commercial channels. However, this does not mean that it will always be profitable to spend more on programming. The additional revenues must be balanced against what it costs to create them. It is more difficult to increase revenues in cases when the competition from other channels and programmes is fierce.

Figure 4.2 presents a simplified model that illustrates how much resources a profit maximising channel will use on programming. In this context, inputs can be cameras and various kinds of labour that operate them. We assume the costs per unit of input to be constant. As seen, more inputs will increase revenues (TR). However, it also shows that the growth in revenues decreases the more inputs that are being used. In other words, the additional revenues generated by the first unit of input is greater than the additional revenues from the second input, which in turn is greater from than the third input, and so on.

The gap between TR and TC is maximised at L_1, which also means that profit is maximised at this level. Here, the total profit is $(TR_1 - TC_1)L_1$. Although the total revenues will increase if more inputs are being used on programming, such

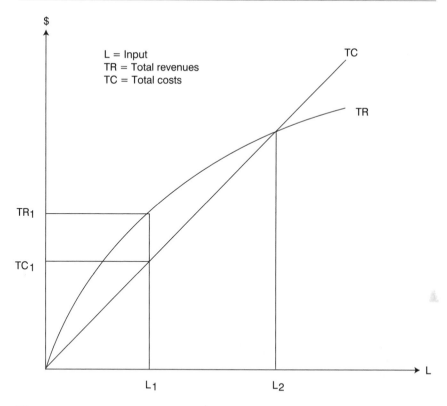

Figure 4.2 *Programming – short term*

an expansion will nevertheless reduce profit, since costs will increase more than revenues. Total revenues are higher at L_2 than L_1, but at this level the costs have increased so much that the channel makes no profit. Hence, L_2 is the break-even level. Increasing L beyond this level gives that channel a deficit on this programme.

The relationship presented in Figure 4.2 is highly relevant for sports programming. The quality of the programmes can be improved by using more resources. By increasing the number of cameras the producer can cover the competition from more angles. As an example, the 2005 UEFA Champions League final between Liverpool and AC Milan in Istanbul was broadcast by means of 19 cameras. In the same season, 25 cameras were used to broadcast a match in the first group stage between Rosenborg (Norway) and Arsenal.[2] Modern technology makes it possible to show several pictures on the TV screen simultaneously. Another example is a camera that only focuses on one player in a team sport or on one competitor in a race. In Formula One races, viewers are offered the choice of watching the race from the car of each of the competitors. Having more resources also improves the ability to show replays of special interesting episodes. Team sport matches have controversial situations, for example dubious offside or penalty decisions. Viewers in general will enjoy watching the replay of such situations, and also repeats of goals from different camera angles. These are examples of increasing inputs in order to attract more viewers, and hence increase the income from broadcasting.

However, at some level the positive relationship between inputs and revenues vanishes. Viewers may have problems following progress of a match if replays are screened too often. Sport contests are not stopped to allow TV producers to show replays of incidents of special interest. There is also a limit on how the quality of a programme will be improved by means of different camera angles. As an example, broadcasting a 100 metre track race will not be of better quality if the producer can use 100 cameras instead of 20. Given its duration is only is ten seconds, this reduces the ability to benefit from multi-camera production. In principle, the same limitation applies to other competitions of longer duration, even though the limits may vary. Although marathon and cycling races will require more cameras than a 100 metre track race, there is nevertheless a limit for how many inputs are needed on such programmes also. A producer cannot keep the overview over a very large number of cameras when he or she decides which picture should be broadcast to the viewers.

THE COSTS OF TRANSMISSION

Some processes in sports broadcasting will have *economies of scale advantages*, for example the transmission of signals to viewers. The principle of economies of scale advantages is illustrated in Figure 4.3. The *marginal cost* (MC) tells us how much it will cost to produce one additional unit. The *average total costs* (ATC) are the total costs divided by total output. The *average variable costs* (AVC) are the total variable costs divided by total output. As Figure 4.3 shows, the average costs declines over the entire range of outputs, which is the definition of economies of scale advantages. Another alternative definition is that output can be doubled for less than a doubling of the costs. Correspondingly, there is also a possibility of *diseconomies of scale*, when a doubling of output requires more than a doubling of cost (Pindyck and Rubinfeld 2004).

As Figure 4.3 shows, the reduction in ATC is lower the more that is produced. Such a cost structure is common in production processes that require huge and expensive initial investments. Hence, companies involved in such production tend to be of a large size. Operating on a large scale can improve the ability to specialise, allowing the staff to concentrate only on jobs where they have expertise. Furthermore, managing large companies can be more effective than small firms, although this can vary from one industry to another. Large companies can also enjoy discounts from buying in bulk.

The production of such goods requires a large base of capital relative to labour. Only a few companies will have sufficient funding to enter markets with such production characteristics. Smaller companies that try to enter the market will often find that they are driven out of business by the large (and more efficient)

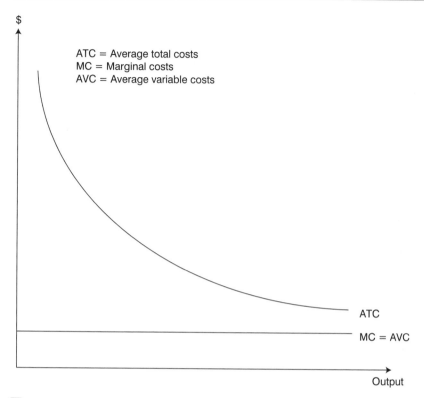

Figure 4.3 Economies of scale in production

companies. The extreme case is when only one company can survive, a situation which is usually referred to as a *natural monopoly*. Where economies of scale are very significant, the few companies that can afford to enter the market will achieve some degree of market power. These will also enjoy economies of scale benefits as illustrated in Figure 4.3. As a consequence of these characteristics, the variable costs will be moderate, at least relatively to the investment costs.

The transmission of TV and radio signals are examples of processes that have economies of scale characteristics. Historically, TV programmes have been transmitted to viewers by means of cable, satellite and terrestrial transmission. These three alternatives all require extremely expensive start-up costs. On the other hand, once facilities and other production equipment have been established, the variable costs from using them are very low relative to the investments costs. The same cost structure applies to new ways of transmission, such as the internet and mobile telephones. Indeed, this pattern has been considerably strengthened by the digital technology, which requires extremely expensive investments.

Even if transmission companies charge expensive fees for transmitting signals (programmes) this does not reflect expensive variable costs. Instead, such a pricing policy often has to do with the distribution of market power between the supply and demand side. Producers operating in a monopoly or oligopoly markets are provided with more market power than those who operate in markets that are characterised by perfect competition. This also improves the ability to construct a price policy that enables them to exploit a high proportion of the profit.

This is seen in Figure 4.4 which illustrates monopoly pricing in a production process that has economies of scale advantages. Profit is maximised at the level where the marginal revenue (MR) curve intercepts the marginal cost (MC) curve. Hence, a price of P_M and quantity of Q_M maximise the profit. However, the figure also shows that at this level the costs of producing an additional unit are lower than what the market (the demand side) is willing to pay. Hence, the solution is inefficient from a welfare economic perspective. The cost of producing one additional unit is lower than its valuation on the demand side of the market. Such a situation is highly relevant for the transmission of TV signals due to the extremely expensive investments that are necessary to enter the market.

It is important to bear in mind that the cost structure will be different for *production* and *consumption* of TV sport programmes. The reception of TV signals is partly a public good. This means that it is non-rival in consumption. Hence,

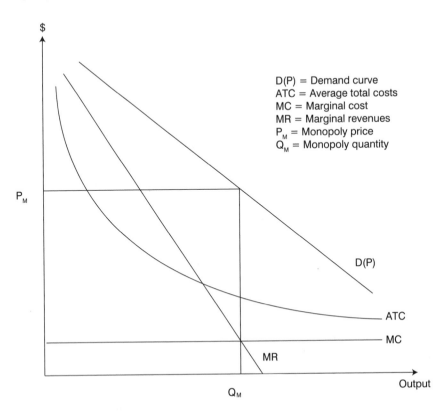

Figure 4.4 *Monopoly pricing*

one viewer's consumption does not reduce the ability of others to watch the same programme. This characteristic applies to the quantity as well as the quality of the programme. No matter how much a person is watching, he or she does not reduce the quality nor the quantity that is available for other viewers. The same applies to the number of viewers. In other words, the marginal cost (MC) of viewing is zero.

Such characteristics, however, only exist within a short-term perspective. It is not cost-free to enhance the transmission to new geographical areas so that more viewers are able to take in the signals. Indeed, in some cases, geographical and topographical factors can make such enhancements extremely expensive. On the other hand, once the enhancement is completed, neither the programming cost nor the transmission costs will be influenced by the numbers of viewers that actually watch or by how much each and every one of them are viewing.

ECONOMIES OF SCOPE

Companies involved in sports broadcasting can also achieve *economies of scope advantages*. The definition of *economies of scope* advantages are traced to the benefits from using a common production factor. More precisely, it refers to the reduction in average cost that occurs when two or more products are produced by a single input. In general, economies of scope are present when the joint output of a single firm is greater than the output that could be achieved by two different firms each producing a single product (with equivalent production inputs allocated between them). If a firm's joint output is less than that which could be achieved by separate firms, then the production process involves *diseconomies of scope*. This possibility occurs if the production of one product somehow conflicted with the production of the second.

Production transformation curves (PTC)

The potential to utilise economies of scope advantages is illustrated in Figure 4.5. In this example, the company produces two programmes, which we call programme X and programme Y. The figure contains two *production transformation curves* (PTC$_1$ and PTC$_2$), also called *production frontiers*. The curves show the maximum combination of the two programmes that it is possible to produce, given the inputs the producer has available. The total production cannot be at a point north-east of the curve that prevails. At a point south-west of a curve, it will be possible to increase the production of one of the programmes without having to reduce the production of the other. The slope of a curve illustrates the trade-off between the two programmes: that is how much has to be given up of one programme to be able to produce more of another good. Hence, the slope also expresses the *opportunity cost*. Inside the curve, the opportunity cost is zero, which indicates that it is possible to produce more of one programme without having to reduce the other. Another alternative, of

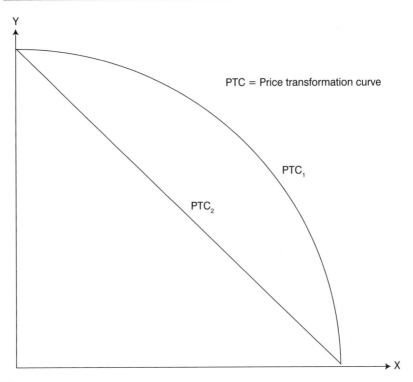

Figure 4.5 *Product transformation curves*

course, is producing more of both programmes. In this context, quantity can refer both to the duration on the programmes or the number of them. It can also refer to the quality dimension.

In principle, the two curves show the same thing, namely how much it is possible to produce of two different programmes given a budget constraint. In other words, what a fixed amount of inputs (labour and capital) allows a company to produce. If the PTC-curve is bowed outward (concave), this indicates that economies of scope advantages exists. This means that joint production will enable a single company to produce more of the two programmes than if the same amount of inputs were put into two production processes separately. The PTC_1 curve refers to a situation where *economies of scope advantages* exist. This means that collaboration between the two production processes makes it possible to produce more than if production is done separately. In other words, collaboration will move the PTC curve eastward. Such an ability do not exist in cases when production is characterised by the PTC_2 curve, which is a straight line. This indicates that joint production entails no gain and would normally apply to products or production processes that are of a different character.

The extent to which economies of scope advantages exist can be determined by studying a firm's cost. If a combination of inputs used by one channel generates more output than two independent channels would produce, then it costs less for a single channel to produce both products than it would cost the independent channels. To measure the degree to which there are economies of scope, one can calculate the percentage of the cost of production that is saved when two (or more) products are produced jointly rather than individually.

The equation below gives the *degree of economies of scope* (SC) that measures this saving in cost:

$$SC = \frac{C(X) + C(Y) \quad C(X,Y)}{C(X,Y)}$$

C(X) represents the cost of producing programme X, C(Y) represents the cost of producing programme Y, and C(X, Y) the joint cost of producing both programmes. With economies of scope, the joint cost is less than the sum of the individual costs. Thus, SC will be greater than 0. With diseconomies of scope, SC is negative. In general, the larger the value of SC, the greater are the economies of scope (Pindyck and Rubinfeld, 2004). We will usually think of X and Y as two different programmes. However, alternatively we also imagine that they are the same programme but are broadcast in two different markets, as in the following example.

Let us imagine that two TV channels broadcast the same event in different markets, which we call market X and market Y. For example, it may be a match between two national teams. Such matches are normally broadcast in both nations. The core programme will be identical for the two channels, and can be produced by either one of them. Alternatively they can hire an independent production company to do the job. Hence the inputs used in this process, the cameras and the staff operating them, will serve both channels. This means that a large proportion of the programming costs are *first-copy costs*. These costs will not be influenced by how many channels that broadcast the programmes. Consequently, they are not influenced by the number of markets to which they are being transmitted.

In addition, the two channels may also want to use some inputs to serve the interests of the viewers in the two markets separately. We can imagine that the programme starts some time before the match starts and finishes some time after it is finished. The pre- and post-match sections can include analyses, interviews with players and coaches, and similar content. This part of the programme will require separate production by the two channels. However, by utilising economies of scope advantages in the core production, the channels will have more resources available to the sections before and after the match.

Broadcasters of international competitions have plenty of opportunities to utilise economies of scope advantages. In case there is a return match, as in the example mentioned above, they can agree to produce one match each. International events, such as the Olympic Games and the most popular international championships, are broadcast to more than 200 nations across the entire world. Table 4.2 shows the number of nations that have broadcast the Olympic Games since the 1936 Berlin Games, which were the first Olympic Games ever to be broadcast. It would be inefficient if all the separate broadcasters that cover such events should produce their own programmes. If so, the programming of the UEFA's Champions League final would require about 5,000 cameras. It would be virtually impossible to find a place for all of them, at least not without reducing the quality of the programmes.

Media companies also have other opportunities to utilise economies of scope advantages. A journalist sent on a mission to cover a sporting event for a TV channel could also be able to serve ordinary news programmes as well as sports news for the same (or other) channels. Furthermore, he or she could also serve other firms that belong to the same parent company, for example radio channels and newspapers. The ability to gain from such multi-firm operations can be the incentive to horizontal integration, which is analysed more thoroughly in Chapter 5.

SPORTS RIGHTS

As highlighted in several places in this book, sports rights have become an expensive part of sports broadcasting in recent years. The most attractive rights have reached levels that were unimaginable some years ago. There are several reasons behind this development, and many of them are analysed throughout this book. The price

Table 4.2 Nations broadcasting the Olympics

Summer Olympics		Winter Olympics	
1936 Berlin:	1		
1948 London:	1		
1952 Helsinki:	2		
1956 Melbourne:	1	1956 Cortina:	22
1960 Rome:	21	1960 Squaw Valley:	27
1964 Tokyo:	40	1964 Innsbruck:	30
1968 Mexico City:	n.a.	1968 Grenoble:	32
1972 Munich:	98	1972 Sapporo:	41
1976 Montreal:	124	1976 Innsbruck:	38
1980 Moscow:	111	1980 Lake Placid:	40
1984 Los Angeles:	156	1984 Sarajevo:	100
1988 Seoul:	160	1988 Calgary:	64
1992 Barcelona:	193	1992 Albertville:	86
1996 Atlanta:	214	1994 Lillehammer:	120
2000 Sydney:	220	1998 Nagano:	160
2004 Athens	220	2002 Salt Lake City:	160+

Source: http://multimedia.olympic.org/pdf/en_report_344.pdf

increases have also brought more attention to the ownership issue than ever before, which also includes controversies when different actors have claimed ownership.

Sports rights are here defined as the rights to broadcast from a specific event, normally within a restricted geographical area. Such rights can apply to a TV transmission, but also to other modes such as radio, internet and mobile phones. The examples in Table 4.1 illustrate that the ownership issue sometimes can be a bit complicated. Due to the joint-product characteristics, it is not the case that a single competitor can be the owner of a contest. In team sports, however, it is quite common that the home team has the ownership. Normally, the ownership is found in one of the two right-hand columns in the table. This can be the local event organiser (for example a club) as well as the governing body of sport, for example a sport federation.

The value of sports rights can be influenced by factors such as:

- the size and the purchasing power of the population in the viewing market;
- the popularity of the sport among the general audience;
- the level of competition on the supply side as well as the demand side;
- whether there is a clear juridical understanding of the ownership issue.

Table 4.3 provides an overview of soccer rights for some domestic European premier leagues. The French league is much more expensive than the Slovakian league. Similar variations exist on other continents, although the names of the expensive and cheap sports will not be the same.

Table 4.3 European soccer TV rights – domestic leagues

Country/ League	Broadcaster	Period	No. of years	Total (€ million)	Per year (€ million)
France/ Ligue 1	Live/highlights: Canal Plus	2005–6 to 2007–8	3	1800.0	600.0
	Highlights: TF1	2004–5 to 2005–7	3	54.0	18.0
Netherlands/ Eredivisie	Live: RTL5	2005–6 to 2007–8	3	10.5	3.5
	Live: Versatel	2005–6 to 2007–8	3	91.5	30.5
	Highlights: TVNL	2005–6 to 2007–8	3	105	35.0
Belgium/ Jupiter	Live: Canal Plus	2002–3 to 2004–5	3	29.4	9.8
	Highlights: VTM	2002–3 to 2004–5	3	7.8	2.6
	Highlights: RTBF	2002–3 to 2004–5	3	7.8	2.6
Slovakia/ Super Liga	Live: Slovak TV	2002–3 to 2005–6	4	19.2	4.8

Source: *TV Sports Markets* – special report 'World Football Leagues and TV Rights'

Chapter 5

Integration

Chapter 3 analysed the market behaviour of different categories of TV channels involved in sports broadcasting. However, to understand their behaviour completely it is also necessary to take into account the relationships that can exist between TV channels since some of them have established forms of horizontal collaboration with each other. Some are members of multi-channel companies, while others have established informal alliances. Some even belong to mother companies that not only include TV channels, but also radio broadcasters, newspapers and other media firms. In addition, TV companies can also have vertical relationships to producers at other levels along the value chain, for example to transmission companies such as cable and satellite operators. Some have also integrated with providers of content, such as clubs (teams), event organisers and sport governing bodies.

There are numerous examples of such relationships between actors that are involved in sports broadcasting. BSkyB, the UK-based TV company, is partly owned by News Corporation, which also has stakes in Foxtel, the Australian-based pay-TV provider, Fox, one of the four national US broadcasting networks, and DirecTV, the leading pay-TV provider in Latin America and the USA. Another and less formal example of horizontal integration is joint purchases of sports rights, which has been quite common in Europe and also in Australia.

BSkyB's attempt to take control over Manchester United some years ago was an example of vertical integration, which also received enormous interest in the media. Although BSkyB was denied the right to acquire full ownership control, they were allowed to acquire 9.9 per cent of the stakes. However, one will find a number of examples where media companies have acquired full ownership of sports clubs. By the end of the 1990s, around 25 per cent of the North American professional teams were partly or totally owned by media groups (Gerrard, 2000).

These forms of relationships will also influence the actors' market behaviour. Two channels that belong to the same mother company will not bid against each other when sports rights are being auctioned. They will also try to avoid offering programmes that target the same viewers simultaneously. Sport governing bodies, sports clubs and event organisers benefit from understanding what consequences such relationships can have for their own activity, for example when selling sports rights. Which buyers are fierce rivals and which are collaborating? How stable are existing collaborations? These questions can be of major importance for sellers that aim at maximising their revenues from selling sports rights as well as other revenues that are influenced by the promotion of the sport and its event in the media.

This chapter aims to provide more insight on these issues. Various forms of integration will be analysed by means of microeconomic theory, with special attention on the consequences for sports broadcasting. What are the potential advantages and disadvantages for the actors involved, on the supply side as well as the demand side? It also discusses the ability to utilize *economies of scale* and *economies of scope* advantages from integration. The final section of the chapter discusses similarities and differences between three alternatives associated with integration, namely: merger/acquisition, alliances, new establishment / internal expansion.

EXPANDING ACTIVITY

Figure 5.1 illustrates how firms can expand their activity. Most firms start the expansion within their own core activity in order to strengthen or protect their market position. However, there are also many firms that expand beyond their core activity and hence become more diversified. The further away the expansion is from a firm's strategic core, the less related is the expansion.

When TV channels merge with one another, this is an expansion within the core activity. When channels buy stakes in a cable or satellite operator or the other way around, this can be regarded as an expansion within its core activity as well as to a related activity, depending on how broad the core activity is defined. In the case of a narrow definition that only includes programming, it will be defined as an expansion into related activities. However, if a wider definition is adapted and production, broadcasting and transmission are regarded to be a part of the same activity, then it is an expansion within the core activity. Such forms of expansion can take place in four different directions, as illustrated in Figure 5.2. *Upward expansion* is when a company establishes a closer connection to its supplier(s), while *downward expansion* when it gets more involved in activities closer to its customers. *Horizontal expansion* is when it establishes closer relationships to its rivals, for instance by merging. *Related* or *unrelated* expansion is when activity is extended into a completely new area. TV channels follow different practises. While some hire external production companies to assist in various kinds of programming tasks, other companies take care of it themselves.

To understand the consequences it can be useful to regard the actors as part of a production process. In this context, TV channels are the producers of sport

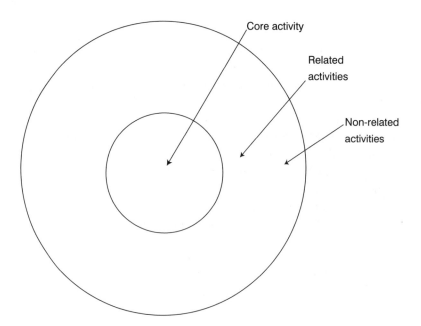

Figure 5.1 *Activity related expansion*
Source: Collis and Montgomery (1997)

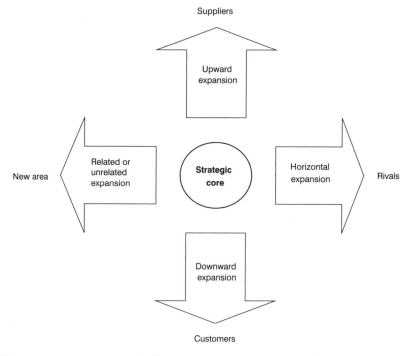

Figure 5.2 *Direction of expansion*
Source: adapted from Reve (1990)

programming, while clubs, event organisers and sport governing bodies are providers of input used in the this production. Transmission companies, such as terrestrial, satellite and cable operators are the distributors of output (programmes) to viewers. Integration between these actors can create economies of scale and economies of scope advantages (see Chapter 4). Integrated firms will have the admittance to complementary resources, for example the sharing of technical and organisational knowledge.

There has been a significant growth in the number of TV channels across the whole world since the early 1990s, partly due to technology improvements from the new digital technology. Many of these new channels are involved in sports broadcasting. There have also been several examples of integration between TV channels and other companies along the sports broadcasting production chain over the years, which both includes mergers as well as forms of alliances. Figure 5.3 illustrates the production chain in sports broadcasting.

One also finds examples of media companies that have expanded their activities to include TV channels, radios and newspapers. Such integration between related enterprises is known as *congeneric integration*. They are examples of integration into related activity, but not between producers of identical products (horizontal integration) or firms along the producer-supplier relationship chain (vertical integration) (Douma and Schreuder, 2002).

A fourth example of integration is between firms of non-related activities and is called *conglomerated integration*. One objective can be to reduce the risk. Thus, such integrations are often between firms operating in businesses where the income there is negative correlation between the core businesses.

HORIZONTAL INTEGRATION

Horizontal integration is when firms in the same line in business combine with one another. This can be TV channels merging with one another, or where a cable operator acquires stakes in another cable operator. It is not uncommon that TV channels join forces in larger broadcasting companies (networks) and such integrations have also taken place in sports broadcasting over the years. In 2003, Telepiú and Stream, the Italian pay-TV platforms that had broadcast the Italian Serie A matches since 1999 merged into Sky-Italy. A similar merger happened in Spain the same year when former rivals merged into one company, called Socecable.[1] Another example is SBS Broadcasting group, a media company with operations in Scandinavia since the early 1990s. Since then their activities have expanded to seven nations (by 2005). This expansion has included pay-TV channels as well as advertising channels in nations such as the Netherlands, Belgium, Hungary and Romania, in addition to the Nordic nations. Many of their channels are involved in sport programming, and some of them operate in the same market. Hence, bringing them together in the same parent company has also influenced the level of competition in the markets.

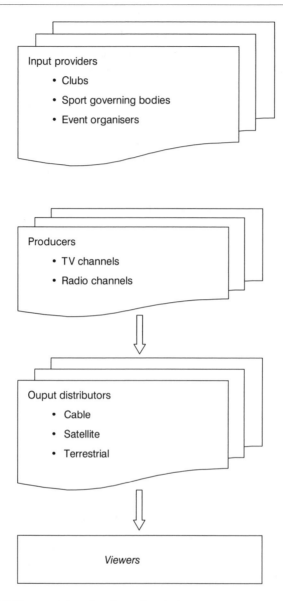

Figure 5.3 *The sports broadcasting value chain*

Horizontal integration will reduce the level of competition and increase the market power of the integrated firms, both towards the remaining companies and towards actors at other levels along the value chain. For any actors that operate on a market, the optimal situation is to be a monopolist at its own level along the value chain, while at the same time there is a fierce competition at the other levels, upwards as well as downwards.

Horizontal integration can take place between companies involved in broadcasting or related areas, but also between actors at another level on the value chain. TV channels can achieve a range of advantages by integrating into multi-channel companies. Together, the integrated channels will be able to provide a more diversified menu of programmes than if they operated alone. This can in turn make them more attractive to viewers and also less vulnerable if they lose out on content, for instance it they cannot afford to acquire attractive sports rights. Such effects can be achieved if complementary relationships exist between the integrated channels.

Having more channels enables a TV company to allocate programmes in a way that maximises profit. Programmes that achieve high rating figures can be put on channels with the highest penetration, while those targeting niche groups can be put on channels with lower penetration, for instance on pay-TV.

Owners of sporting events receive their revenues from different sources, of which the most important are:

- TV rights;
- sponsorship;
- ticket revenues;
- merchandising.

Some of these revenues will be positively correlated with each other. Sponsorship revenues are maximised if events are broadcast on free-to-air channels with maximum penetration. Other media, for instance newspapers, tend to focus less on sports and sporting events that are broadcast entirely on pay-TV channels that are only received by a minority of the population. Thus, event organisers that rely heavily on sponsorship revenues might think twice before selling broadcasting rights exclusively to companies that only include pay-TV channels. This was the major reason why the IOC sold the European Olympic rights for 2000–8 to the EBU, despite the fact that News Corporation submitted a bid that was more than $500 million higher.

Such negative promotion effects were illustrated when English Rugby League sold their TV rights exclusively to BSkyB in 1995. Since BSkyB had considerably lower penetration than BBC (the former broadcaster) the average rating figures dropped dramatically. As a consequence of this, other media also focused less on the sport. Thus, the original £87 million deal which was supposed to cover a five-year period was renegotiated after three years with the result that the value was reduced considerably (O'Keeffe, 2002).

In Norway, handball and skiing (Nordic Games) had similar experiences after selling TV rights exclusively to pay-TV channels in the mid-1990s. The other media, including free-to-air channels as well as newspapers and radio broadcasters, reduced their focusing on these sports, which had negative results on the overall promotion. Therefore, these two deals only lasted a few months (Solberg, 2002a).

Multi-channel companies are able to prevent such problems by giving attention to the sport or the event on more than one channel. In that way, the company can internalise externalities. Indeed, having such abilities can be of importance in case sport governing bodies fear that lower attention can reduce the interest from sponsors. Promotion effects are not only important for sponsorship support, but also for the recruitment of fans to the sport. Thus, owners of sports rights may find it less risky selling to multi-channel companies than to a single pay-TV channel. In the UK, for many years in the 1970s and 1980s, the BBC was the preferred channel for sports such as golf, tennis and snooker. These sports have extended hours of coverage and, since the BBC had two channels while its main terrestrial competitors only had one, the BBC could switch its coverage between the two channels giving continuous coverage of the sport while still showing regular peak-time programmes on its other channel. This advantage disappeared when BSkyB introduced four dedicated sports channels in the 1990s.

Collective sale of sports rights is an example of horizontal integration between suppliers of inputs. Although such a practice is cartel behaviour, and thus would be regarded as illegal in other areas of economic activity, it has nevertheless been accepted in sports broadcasting. The reason for this is its ability to uphold the competitive balance and hence offer consumers products of better quality than if such collaborations were prohibited.

■ *Case study 5.1* Canal Plus and SBS will gain by bidding together

TV Sports Markets, vol. 9, no. 4, by Ben Speight

The takeover of the Nordic Canal Plus subscription channels by SBS Broadcasting will add considerable strength to both parties in the television rights market. By bidding together for top sports rights, SBS's national terrestrial and cable-satellite channels and the pan-Nordic Canal Plus will have far more chance of winning than they do as individual bidders. Industry executives and commentators believe that the two could now realistically bid for rights such as soccer's Champions League, the World Cup or Euro 2008 and compete well against Modern Times Group, which already owns basic cable and satellite channels and the region's Viasat subscription channels. MTG has won pan-Scandinavian rights deals, most notably for soccer's Champions League, sharing the rights between its premium sports channels and basic cable and satellite channel in Denmark, Norway and Sweden. The SBS acquisition comes in what is already turning out to be a year of major change in the Nordic television market. Swedish media group Bonnier has bought MTV3, Finland's most popular channel, and increased its control of Sweden's TV4. Later this year, Denmark's most popular channel, TV2, will be privatised. The eight bidders, which include Bonnier and SBS, will be whittled down to three next month. But, in the short term at least, the SBS acquisition – it is paying private equity companies Nordic Capital and Baker Capital €270 million (£186 million) for Canal Plus – will have greater impact on the sports rights market. Canal Plus, which shows sport on two of its five pan-Nordic channels, has been at a disadvantage when bidding for sports rights because of its restricted penetration, even though it might have had the spending power to financially outbid the opposition. SBS, which owns basic cable and satellite channels in Denmark, Norway and Sweden, has been disadvantaged by not having the spending power and, to a lesser extent, by not having full penetration. A good deal of that will now change. But most commentators believe that the two sides will bid jointly only for the biggest rights, such as the Champions League and World Cup, across the region. Canal Plus will steer away from doing deals with the SBS channels for national sports rights in the individual markets because of the importance of getting exclusive rights in each market. Sharing rights, unless handled very carefully, could drain away its subscribers. Canal Plus is still evaluating whether it is benefiting from sharing rights this season for some English Premier League rights – the Saturday lunchtime match and some highlights – with Kanal 5, an SBS channel in Denmark. But if the two parts of the enlarged SBS can now mount joint sports-rights bids, will they in practice do so? Will the money be made available for big bids? No one is sure. Canal Plus has always boasted strong spending power, but it does not have bottomless pockets. SBS, for its part, has had to pay a lot of money for Canal Plus. Will there be much more for rights? On the other hand, the fact that Canal Plus is owned by a media company rather than private equity companies ought to be an advantage, if only because the main priority should no longer be making a profit. As one commentator put it, 'content can now be the top priority and lower profit can be tolerated'. Nordic Capital and Baker Capital certainly did well out of Canal Plus. They bought the company from Vivendi of France in October 2003 for €70 million. By earlier this month, they were able to sell it for an extra €200 million.

Rights and penetration

Canal Plus owns exclusive pan-Nordic rights for the Premier League, Italian Serie A and North American ice hockey's National Hockey League. In Sweden, it holds exclusive live rights for the soccer and ice hockey leagues; in Finland, exclusive live rights for soccer home internationals; and in Norway, pay-TV rights for the soccer league. The SBS channels have far fewer sports rights properties. Each shows the Scandinavian soccer club competition, the Royal League, and other minor soccer, such as UEFA Cup ties. In Denmark, Kanal 5 has the Spanish Primera Liga as well as the English Premier League on sub-license The SBS channels have varying penetrations. Kanal 5 in Denmark has only 53 per cent, which may not, according to one experienced pay-TV rights executive, help it in winning bids. TV Danmark has 74 per cent, but does not carry sport. In Sweden, Kanal 5 has 65 per cent and Norway's

TV Norge has 89 per cent. As for the opposition, MTG's main cable and satellite channels in penetrations close to 65 per cent.

Bonnier rights power

Bonnier's acquisition of MTV3 and increased control of TV4 can be seen as an important step towards the company becoming the biggest television group in the Nordic region. But observers question whether it can acquire major sports rights across the region without getting a strong footing in Denmark and Norway. Bonnier is one of the bidders for Denmark's TV2, which it would dearly like to have. There is no obvious opportunity to break into the Norwegian market. But pan-regional ownership does not have to be the key to acquiring the top rights. According to one source, 'it is a Scandinavian habit for broadcasters to get together to acquire rights and Bonnier could easily team up with other channels'. The rights for the 2006 soccer World Cup were won by a consortium of broadcasters, all of which had different owners (*TV Sports Markets*, vol. 8, no. 19). Bonnier's acquisitions were made in partnership with private equity company Proventus. They acquired the broadcasting assets of Finnish media company Alma Media for €460 million. It included buying Finland's MTV3 outright and an additional 23.4 per cent stake in Sweden's TV4. Bonnier already had a 26.6 per cent stake in TV4. Proventus recently bought 15.1 per cent. The partners' acquisition followed a hostile bid for Alma Media by Schibsted, the Norwegian media company. Schibsted was mostly interested in TV4.

VERTICAL INTEGRATION

The general definition of *vertical integration* is that firms participate in more than one successive stage of the production or distribution of goods or services. *Upward (backward) integration* is when firms are integrating with suppliers of inputs, for example when a TV channel is buying stakes in a team. *Downward (forward) integration* is when firms integrate in activities on a level closer to the final customer, for example a TV channel buying stakes in a satellite or cable operator.

The history of TV broadcasting (and sports broadcasting) contains several examples of vertical upward integrations. One example that received substantial attention was BSkyB's unsuccessful attempt to acquire full ownership in Manchester United in 1998. Although BSkyB's offer was accepted by the club's board of directors, the merger was blocked by the UK Government on the recommendation of the Monopolies and Mergers Commission (Gerrard 2000). Later, the English Premier League (EPL) introduced a regulation that prevented a single stake in any club to exceed 9.9 per cent. Since then, BSkyB has acquired a minority part of the stakes in clubs such as Manchester United, Chelsea, Leeds and Sunderland. Other broadcasting companies have also acquired stakes in EPL clubs, such as Granada in Arsenal and Liverpool, and NTL in Aston Villa, Newcastle, Middlesbrough and Leicester City.[2]

There are several examples of media companies integrating with professional sports teams in North America. In fact, around 25 per cent of the teams were either partly or wholly owned by media groups at the end of the twentieth century. Companies such as News Corporation, Time Warner and Disney all have ownership stakes in several North American league teams (Gerrard, 2000). Other examples are Canal Plus, the French media company, which had stakes in Paris Saint Germain,[3] one of the major French soccer clubs, and Mediapartner, the Italian media company that had ownership interests in AC Milan, one of the major Italian soccer clubs.

TV companies have also contributed to establishing leagues. NBC, the North American broadcasting network, was highly involved in the Xtreme Football League (XFL), which was launched in the 2001/2 season and invested a total of $50 million dollars in the project.[4] However, the league did not achieve any commercial success and ceased operations after just one season due to astonishingly low television ratings. One NBC broadcast received the lowest ever rating for a major network prime-time television programme. Despite initially agreeing to broadcast XFL games for two years and owning half of the league, NBC announced it would not broadcast a second XFL season when the first season was over. XFL tried to continue, as its television agreements with two other channels were still in place. However, when one of these channels also withdrew, it was the end of the league and its closure was announced in May 2002. The operation of the XFL was estimated to have cost the owners, World Wrestling Entertainment and NBC, a collective deficit of approximately $70 million.[5]

One also finds examples of TV companies that have integrated downward, with cable and satellite operators. The case of News Corporation has been mentioned above. A similar example is Modern Times Group, a Scandinavian-based company that has stakes in TV channels, radio channels and a satellite operator.

The prospect of *reduced transaction costs* is often regarded to be a major advantage from vertical integration (Williamson 1979). A firm may chose to perform activities itself rather than rely on the market when transaction costs are likely to be high. Economies of scale advantages can be internalised within the company from combined operations, sharing of activities and maintenance of a stable throughput in a long stretch of the value chain. One can also reduce any cost penalties in case the firm is unable to pay in time. As we will show in Chapter 6, many TV companies have had severe problems with paying in time after acquiring TV rights.

Firms that integrate upwards will get more control of the supply of inputs. Those that integrate downwards will have more control over its distribution. A broadcasting company that has acquired stakes in a club can influence the sale procedure when TV rights are offered for sale. Indeed, it would not meet any competitor in case the rights are sold individually. Furthermore, it should also have some influence in the case of collective sale. Even if it cannot afford to purchase the entire rights alone, it might be able to block rivals from having total control. Similar options may occur from downward integration, such as acquiring stakes in a cable or satellite operator. This should guarantee that channels will reach viewers, and even be able to block (or at least restrict) rival channels from using the same operator.

The gain from achieving more upward and downward control depends on the ability to substitute inputs and outputs at the other levels along the value chain. If providers of input have many alternatives, then the ability to block these sources by upward integration can be valuable. On the other hand, upward integration may also reduce the ability to tap different suppliers, which can be risky if the commercial values on the input fluctuate. If demand shifts negatively, producers can be left with input that no one wants and thus are difficult to resell. An example could be the acquisition of stakes in a club being relegated. It is well known that relegation can reduce the demand from spectators and TV viewers considerably and hence damage the club owners. This can in turn also affect sponsorship support and other sources of income. Thus, the prospect of reselling the stakes at a good price would not be particularly good under such circumstances.

Vertical integration can reduce the risk of *opportunistic behaviour*, which is when the actors are taking advantage of another when allowed by circumstances (Carlton and Perloff, 1999). If a company becomes extremely dependent of specific products or inputs, this is a situation their partners can take advantage of. Each side will try to interpret the terms of a contract to its advantage, especially when terms are vague or even missing. As an example, a TV channel going through a period with declining rating figures can be in a position where it strongly needs attractive content and thus willing to pay over the market value for sports programmes. This is a situation owners of content such as sports clubs or event organisers can take advantage from. However, by having stakes in input providers, such negative surprises are less likely to occur.

Vertical integration also reduces the risk of being hit by *asymmetric information*. This refers to situations when an actor on the supply side has more or less information than an actor on the demand side, and vice versa. Acquiring sports rights can be risky since rating figures correlate very much with the performance of specific teams and competitors. Revenue sharing clauses (royalty fees) that tie the fee to income generated by the broadcaster can reduce the risk of being hit by unforeseen shifts in demand (see Chapter 8). Such agreements, however, create a monitoring problem known from the principal-agent literature. The agent (TV channel) will have more precise information than the principal (the seller of sports rights) and can take advantage from it by under-reporting the revenues and exaggerating the costs, which in turn will reduce royalty fees. Indeed, this illustrates a *moral hazard* problem where the seller is unable to control the actions of the channel.

Furthermore, the fact that the channel only keeps a proportion of the additional revenues reduces its motives to invest in any post-deal sale efforts, compared to if it received the entire revenues alone. Revenue sharing deals can also motivate the channel to split up the sports broadcasting income from advertisers and/or viewers in a way that reduces the income to be shared (see Chapter 8). Vertical integration, however, will eliminate such incitements since multi-firm companies internalise such externalities. The objective of integrated firms is to maximise the profit of the entire company, not the specific firms.

Upward integration where TV companies acquire stakes in sports clubs can alter the objective of the clubs. This can in turn alter the clubs demand for talent. Profit maximising teams want to hire more talent as long as the marginal revenue exceeds the marginal cost, while win maximising teams want to hire more talent as long as the average income exceeds the marginal costs. This policy may not continue if the club is bought up by a profit maximising TV company.

Indeed, this is another example where externalities can be integrated within the whole company, which is similar to the example above. In the case where the club generates positive externalities in the form of higher rating figures or more subscribers, then the optimal solution can be to hire talent at a sub-optimal level for the club: in other words, beyond the level where the marginal revenue equals the marginal cost. This applies to clubs operating in win maximising regimes or profit maximising regimes. Being integrated in a large profit maximising company can alter the objectives of clubs operating in either of these two regimes.

However, such forms of integration can initiate a conflict between individual and collective rationality. Profit maximising TV companies will spend most on the most attractive teams, the ones that are able to generate the highest revenues. This can threaten competitive balance, which in turn can reduce the commercial value of the league on a long-term basis. Indeed, this is another illustration of the potential conflict between individual and collective rationality that exists in team sports.

Such impacts can also be created by altering the way that sport is performed. Recent history contains several such examples. Skiing (Nordic games), biathlon and skating are examples of sports that have altered competitions in order to become more attractive for the TV audience, for example by introducing joint starts and shorter distances. Some team sports have implemented more breaks in the matches in order to give more room for more commercials. It is often claimed that North American team sports are tailor-made for advertising channels in this respect.

By integrating upwards, match fixtures can be organised so that clashes with other sports programmes the TV company is broadcasting are avoided. Furthermore, they can also move matches to points of time that are able to attract large TV audiences. This was particularly the case when BSkyB acquired the rights to British rugby league and persuaded the sport to move from winter to summer partly to avoid clashes with soccer and rugby union, although the major motivation was to make the British season finish at a similar time to the Australian season so that the champions from both countries could play off in what effectively would be a world club championship.

Integration upwards can also improve the ability to protect valuable assets and know-how from unwanted imitation or diffusion. A broadcasting company which owns stakes in clubs can block them from joining rival leagues. The North American team sport history contains several examples where existing leagues have been challenged, either by new rival leagues or where teams in existing leagues have broken away and joined new leagues. Another example is the plan to launch a European super league for soccer, which challenged UEFA, the European governing body of soccer. TV companies that have acquired sports rights would benefit from preventing any rival leagues being launched.

Integrating with companies where profit or income is negatively related can reduce the level of risk. This certainly applies to sports clubs. If one club is underperforming, the negative effect can be outweighed if the TV company integrates with other clubs that perform better. Indeed, acquiring collective rights for team tournaments instead of individual rights is a way of reducing such risk. Clubs that are underperforming will lose some of their attractiveness among TV viewers. Such effects, however, can be outweighed by the acquisition of collective deals due to the *zero-sum game* nature of sports leagues. If some clubs are unsuccessful, this will automatically be outbalanced by the success of others. Acquiring the broadcasting rights for the entire tournament can eliminate such problems. On the other hand, such a strategy would be more expensive than acquiring the rights for one or a few teams. Hence, the net effect will be uncertain and depend on which of these two effects are strongest. The same principle applies to TV companies' acquisitions of stakes in clubs. Having stakes in only one club may turn out as unprofitable investment in case the club is underperforming. However, similar to the purchase of sports rights, investing in several clubs can be a way of reducing such risk.

Vertical integration will motivate the firm to maintain a balance among the various stages of the value chain. It can make new forms of technology available for the existing business base. In recent years several sports clubs have launched their own TV channels. However, being updated on the innovation in TV technology requires substantial efforts, which can prove too costly for sports clubs. The innovation of the new digital technology represents such an example. Hence, integrating with a TV channel provides sports clubs with a better ability to keep up with technological know-how which otherwise would have been too expensive. It can also enable clubs to enter into new businesses more quickly. Integrating with firms at other parts of the production line can also give clubs the possibility of carrying out a more aggressive strategy to gain market share at another level.

CONGENERIC INTEGRATION

Congeneric integration is between firms that produce goods that are related, but not identical. An example can be a media company that includes TV channels, radio channels as well as newspapers. Such forms of integration can generate cost advantages that are initiated by *economies of scope advantages*. Economies of scope advantages can occur when the same input can be used in more than one production process (see Chapter 4). Joint production of several products in one firm may be the most cost-effective solution, particularly if a common production factor is relatively costly. Such advantages could result from the joint use of inputs or production facilities, joint marketing programmes or possibly the cost savings of a common administration. The benefits of vertical integration may also include cost savings realised through a reduction of redundant services and personnel.

A journalist will be able to serve radio, a TV channel as well as a newspaper within the same company. The same applies to some of the technical equipment and facilities, as well as technological and organisational know-how. A profit maximising media company will alter its inputs so that their net marginal contributions in all allocations are equal. The marginal contribution from using the inputs in a TV channel should equal their contribution in any other allocation, such as radio, newspapers and other firms that belong to the parent company. If not, profit can be increased by simply reallocating inputs. This of course assumes the inputs are mobile between the various firms within the company.

Congeneric integration also enables firms within the same company to promote each other's products. This certainly applies to sports clubs that are integrated in media companies. An article in a newspaper or some minutes of coverage in the news can promote an event much more effectively than ordinary advertising can do.

ALTERNATIVE WAYS OF EXPANSION

So far this chapter has focused on expansion and integration without looking at the alternative ways it can be conducted. This section will look at three alternative ways of expansion and discuss their general advantages and disadvantages. Some of the factors discussed in this section are more relevant for broadcasting companies than for sports clubs and sport governing bodies, at least in terms of the direct consequences. However, indirectly they can also have an important influence on the sports sector. In particular, sports organisations can take advantage from understanding how these relationships work and influence their own situation.

An illustration of this is the stability of the various forms of integration. While a merger of two firms should be expected to endure permanently, an alliance where they agree to buy some TV rights jointly does not contain the same degree of stability. The fact that the channels form such an alliance at one point of time does not guarantee that they will join forces on the next occasion. Indeed, they can become fierce rivals. An example from Australian broadcasting, where different channels formed different alliances for the auctioning of the AFL right deal in 2002 and in 2007, illustrated this quite precisely. In 2002, Channel 9 and Channel 10 formed an alliance which enabled them to bid the rights away from Channel 7. Indeed, this was the first time in 45 years that Channel 7 bowed out of Australian rules football. This alliance seems to have come to an end before the auctioning of the deal for the rights from 2006. At the time of writing, Channel 7 and Channel 10 seem to have joined forces and plan to bid jointly for the AFL rights. If so, this newly established partnership could leave Channel 9 out in the cold.

Another example that illustrates the instability of alliances is the internal disagreements between EBU members regarding the purchasing policy of sports rights. RAI, the Italian public service broadcaster decided not to participate in the joint purchase of the 2010 and 2012 Olympic rights. Likewise, other broadcasters refused to participate in the purchase of the 2008 European soccer championship for national teams, with the result that the rights were acquired by Sportfive, a media investor company. These two examples illustrate that owners of sports rights should not take for granted that actors that operate together on one occasion automatically continue their partnership on the next occasion.

In general, a firm can expand its activity by any of the following three alternatives:

- merger and acquisition;
- alliances;
- new establishment.

Merger and acquisition

The potential advantages from merger and acquisition will be related to the prospect of achieving the synergy effects described in this chapter, for example economies of scale and economies of scope advantages. Synergy occurs if the interaction between two or more forces results in their combined effect being greater than the sum of their individual effects. In the case of a merger, the synergy effects make the value of a merged company greater than the sum of the value of the two individual companies (Brown, 1995).

Financial synergy effects can be achieved if the capital costs are reduced. Firms of a large size can be offered more favourable terms when applying for funding. Larger companies will also have a higher base of funding than smaller firms, and hence be able to take more risk than smaller firms. This can improve the capability of going through a period of deficit. Moreover, increased operating leverage implies a greater fraction of fixed costs and correspondingly greater business risk, which in itself can require higher capital investment. Larger firms also have more funding and thus can afford heavier investments, for instance in new technology, research and development. Indeed, this has been an important element in TV broadcasting where digital technology has required extremely expensive investments. Sports clubs that are integrated with companies with a large financial base will be able to hire more talent than if they operated alone. This can enable clubs to spend more on talent as a safety net and hence become less vulnerable if key players are injured. Smaller clubs that have access to a smaller financial base may benefit from such integration. Indeed, this has been an issue in European soccer where the best clubs are playing more matches than ever before due to the enhancement of international tournaments such as UEFA's Champions League and the UEFA Cup. In order to give players the ability to rest and recover, many clubs have increased their squad of players. However, such strategies have turned out to be extremely costly due to the high wage level among the best soccer players. Being a member of a company with access to large financial base can improve the ability to adopt such a strategy.

Management synergy occurs in the cases when management in one single large firm is more effective than in two firms of a smaller size. However, in the case of vertical integration, merging and acquisition can also reduce the risk of governmental intervention. As an example, there is no price control when one is selling to oneself. Furthermore, it can also be possible to reduce taxes if the integrating firms are operating in regions (or nations) with different tax regimes. The firm can shift profit by charging transfer prices. Indeed, there are many broadcasting companies which operate in more than one country. One reason for this can be differences in tax systems and other regulations. Some European TV channels have taken advantage of such differences by broadcasting from countries that have the most liberal advertising rules, even if the targeted viewers live in other places. On the other hand, if a company becomes too big, management can become inefficient and it can be difficult to obtain a good overview of all its operations.

Operational synergy can be achieved by improved ability to share resources and transfer competence. Sports clubs that integrate with broadcasting companies will have admittance to resources beyond what is available through its normal activity. In addition, by becoming larger a firm can also find new and more effective ways of organising its activity, than two separate firms can. Merger and acquisition can also be based on *non-value maximising motives*. Some leaders (and stock holders) can be interested in building empires. Managing larger firms can be prestigious, since the power and status often is a function of size. TV companies that acquire stakes in sports clubs may achieve goodwill among supporters and the local population in general that can pay off indirectly on a long-term basis.

However, acquisition can be a very costly way of expanding compared to creating informal alliances. Several companies might be interested in acquiring stakes in the most attractive clubs, which in itself can push the stock market prices up further. In addition, buying companies may also have to accept acquiring less attractive divisions. As an example, a broadcasting company that mainly is involved in sports broadcasting may also have to take over non-sport channels as a part of the acquisition. Although such unwanted units can be sold, there is no guarantee that it will achieve a fair price. Hence, having to acquire more than what is necessary can involve more risk.

Merger/acquisition also gives the firms more control than in an alliance where it is easier to walk out from the collaboration. This is illustrated by the internal disagreements within the EBU about the assessments of international sports rights. Hence, such forms of integration are also more stable than alliances. Moreover, it also blocks the possibility for potential competitors to merge with the same firms. Finally, merger/acquisition has tempo advantage compared to new establishment. Hence the company can take advantage of the potential benefits much quicker.

On the other hand, there is also the risk of running into negative shocks, for instance discovering that newly acquired companies are less valuable/effective than expected. Another potential disadvantage relates to increased overhead costs if the new extended organisation becomes too large.

The risk of being hit by the *winners curse* represents another potential disadvantage in case it ends up as an auction where several buyers try to acquire control of the firm. This means that the winner of the auction is worse off as a consequence of overestimating the value of the firm and thereby overbidding. One reason for this can be strategic behaviour from the bidders. The main objective for companies that participate in an auction will be to win the bid. However, similar to the acquisition of sports rights, some companies may enter the auction mainly to push rivals' costs by bidding up the price. Such a strategy could weaken the rivals' ability to acquire stakes in other clubs. The commercial value of sports clubs and competitors vary considerably. Although clubs such as Manchester United, Real Madrid and the New York Yankees are extremely popular and will attract the interest from a wide range of investors, a limit will exist also for the value of such clubs.

Alliances

Companies involved in sport and broadcasting often have several alternatives on how to integrate. Figure 5.4 gives an overview of forms of alliances that exist, and how the dependency between the actors will vary. In the case of *full vertical integration*, the integrated firm(s) will obtain control over all inputs or the supply chain towards the customer. *Full horizontal integration* gives a monopoly on the integrated level. However, there are alternative ways to achieve some of the benefits from horizontal, vertical and congeneric integration than from full integration. In a market solution, the firms are relatively independent of each other. At the same time, the possibility to control and influence one another is restricted. On the other hand, the dependency will be stronger in a hierarchical situation, where the firms also have better possibilities to control and influence on one another (Meyer, 1998).

Alliances, as presented in Figure 5.4 can be an alternative when acquisition is blocked, for example by anti-trust regulations. Competition authorities across the whole world are careful about allowing large companies to merge. These are also subject to more monitoring than smaller firms are. Thus firms that have some degree

Figure 5.4 *Forms of alliances*
Source: Haugland (2004)

of market power will have to apply to competition authorities for being allowed to merge with one another. The application can be rejected in case there are fears of the merged firm becoming too powerful. The BBC and ITV, the two UK public service broadcasters, would not be allowed to merge into one company for many reasons. However, over the years they have been allowed to purchase broadcasting rights jointly on a number of occasions.

Alliances can provide the companies involved admission to many of the *economies of scale* and *economies of scope advantages*, as well as the other synergy effects that are described elsewhere in this book. Companies that are part of an alliance can also transfer competence between each other. Furthermore, the integrated firms can also achieve the same tempo advantages as in the case of merger or acquisition. Hence it is possible to realise the benefits quickly.

Alliances will require lower investment costs than acquisition, and will thus be less risky. Moreover, the firms that form alliances will be more flexible than merged firms, for example if the market conditions change. It will generally be much easier to walk out from an alliance than to resell an acquired firm. This, however, represents a double-edged sword as the allied firms will have less management control over one another. Hence, alliances are less stable than merger and acquisition, which is illustrated by the circumstances in connection to the auction of the AFL rights as discussed above. Thus, alliance partners also have less protection of their core activity, particularly when collaborating with a potential rival. Former partners may take advantage from knowledge they have obtained when collaborating, and hence become a powerful rival once the alliance ceases to exist.

In the case of sports broadcasting, the allied partners will have to uncover important elements that influence their strategic behaviour, for example their assessments of the various sports products. Likewise, the partners will also get insights into each other's cost structure. Having revealed this and other similar information to a potential future rival can turn out to be a major disadvantage. If the companies have serious concerns about such factors, this can in itself reduce their willingness to be involved in the collaboration.

Teams/clubs are unable to merge into a monopoly due to the special character of sports contests. However, less formal alternatives, such as collective sale of TV rights represent a form of alliance that also is an example of horizontal integration.

Such forms of integration also provide the teams with an ability to uphold quality of the products as long as it involves some form of cross-subsidisation. The alliance partners, the clubs, may also find it difficult to agree how income should be distributed. On the one hand, each club wants to keep as much of the income as possible to itself. On the other hand, if the most attractive clubs become too greedy, this can cause an unequal distribution where the competitive balance is reduced so much that the value of the league is undermined.

New establishment/internal expansion

A third way of integrating or expanding is by establishing a new firm or by internal expansion. These forms of expanding a firm's activity are generally more common in cases where the products are in an early stage of their life cycle. The other alternatives, such as merger, acquisition and alliances are more common when the products are more mature and have been in the market for some time, and also have their advantages in cases when there are high barriers to entry. So-called club channels that have emerged in recent years are sport-related examples. An alternative to establishing such channels would be to create an alliance with a TV company. This is likely to be more cost effective than building up a new channel from scratch. The linkage to a mature TV company would improve the club's ability to keeping updated on technology development and hence represent a cost advantage. New establishment and internal expansion require more funding than an alliance, which is the alternative that requires least resources.

Companies that expand gradually will have better ability to prioritise along the way and to influence the situation themselves. Gradual expansion is in itself an advantage in case the market conditions alter or are difficult to predict. Internal expansion also provides an ability to customise products. On the other hand, the gradual development also means that it will take more time before the potential advantages can be exploited. One cannot expect to build up a strong market position overnight by a new establishment.

Contrary to the other two alternatives, establishing a new firm will increase the competition, which in some cases can lead to excess capacity on the supply side. Such a development can represent a major disadvantage for the existing companies in cases where there is already fierce competition in the market, particularly if many new establishments are formed simultaneously. In the sports broadcasting market, such a development can lead to strong price increases on the most attractive rights. This has certainly been the case in many sports rights markets across the world since the early 1990s. Sports fans have limited resources of time and money to spend on watching TV sports. The fact that sports programming is attractive content can stimulate too many TV channels to offer too many similar programmes in the same market. The result of such uncoordinated activity on the supply side can be devastating due to the high degree of sunk costs that characterises sports broadcasting. An excess supply of sports programmes will reduce revenues per programme and per channel, while costs are unchanged.

This has been illustrated in relation to FIFA's plans of making the World Cup soccer finals a biennial tournament, which has provoked other governing bodies within the soccer family that have fears of too fierce competition. Some years ago, FIFA also launched a World Club tournament involving the best clubs from each continent, but without achieving the success it hoped for, mainly due to the large number of tournaments that already exist.

On the other hand, actors at other stages along the supply chain might welcome such a development, as it can increase their own market power. Therefore, clubs in Italian Serie A and Spanish Primera Liga have considered launching their own TV channels in order to avoid the monopoly power of TV companies. These plans emerged after the merger of the former rivals in the pay-TV market.

■ *Case-study 5.2* Spanish football federation may start own channel

TV Sports Markets, vol. 9, no. 2, by James Pickles

The Spanish football federation, the Real Federación Española de Fútbol, is considering launching its own television channel. It believes that it would bring in more money from its own channel, which could be a joint venture with broadcasters. The federation last week renewed a deal for Spain's national team matches with public service broadcaster RTVE. At the same time, in what can be regarded as a first step towards the longer-term own channel idea, it increased the remit of its deal with the Grupo Santa Monica sports agency, which has handled the federation's marketing and image rights since 1996. The agency will now handle the production and international distribution of the television signal for all federation matches, a job previously handled by RTVE. It will also provide images to broadband and mobile phone operators. The move, according to a Santa Monica source, reflected the federation's desire to 'improve the way its rights are handled by adopting an integrated exploitation approach for its commercial rights'. The federation controls the rights for the home matches of all Spanish national soccer and Futsal teams, the final of the domestic cup competition, Copa del Rey, and Supercopa de España matches. The new RTVE deal is for five years, from 2005 to 2009, with an option for a further year. It also covers any of Spain's away friendly matches for which the federation acquires rights, and allows RTVE to show delayed, non-exclusive coverage of matches via its international satellite channel. RTVE's previous four-year deal, which expired last month, was worth between €50 million (£34.8 million) and €60 million. It included international rights, which the new deal does not. With the federation wanting the international rights to go to Santa Monica, RTVE did not make use of an option to extend the last deal. But the federation gave RTVE exclusive first negotiations. The federation said that the new arrangements brought in more money.

Chapter 6

Competition between channels
A game theory approach

In recent years the number of TV channels involved in sports broadcasting has increased substantially. The process started in the 1970s in North America and some years later on other continents such as Europe. This development has paved the way for a fierce competition between channels, which has increased the rights fees on the most attractive sports rights dramatically, as has been documented in several places in this book. On some occasions, however, the competition has increased rights fees so much that the company that acquired the rights has been hit by the *winner's curse*. Over the years, quite a number of sports rights deals have ended up being unprofitable, which is illustrated by the examples below:

- Telepiu and Stream, the leading Italian pay-TV channels lost respectively, $300 million and $200 million each from these deals during the 2001/2 season. Thus, the renewal of the deals before the 2002/3 Serie A season did not go as smoothly as before. The poorest clubs rejected the new offer from the TV channels and therefore the league was delayed by two weeks. The problems were solved when the six wealthiest clubs paid the difference between the offer from the TV channels and what the poorest clubs demanded.[1] As a consequence of these problems the Italian authorities have recently allowed the channels to merge.[2]
- ITV Digital, the UK pay-TV platform, was unable to fulfil its £378 million contract with the Nationwide League, which was supposed to run from 2001 to 2004, but went bankrupt. The league brought the case to court and demanded the owner of ITV Digital to pay the necessary amount, but lost this case. Later on, BSkyB acquired 'the remaining' part of this deal at a price of £95 million, which represented a large discount, compared to the original price.[3]
- Premiere, the German pay-TV channel, was unable to recruit enough subscribers to make the deal with the German Bundesliga, profitable for the

2001 to 2004 period. Thus the deal was renegotiated, with the result that its value dropped by 20–25 per cent.[4]

■ Sport 7, a Dutch pay-TV channel, acquired a seven-year contract with the Dutch Eredivisie in September 1996 (the soccer elite division) for a fee of DFL 1.04 billion for nearly all the soccer matches in the Netherlands. Four months later, in December 1996, the channel collapsed, after incurring losses of DFL 100 million.[5]

■ RAI, the Italian public service broadcaster that acquired the Italian 2002 World Cup soccer rights, lost a considerable amount of money due to the early exit of the Italian team. This reduced the rating figures of the remaining matches, and hence also the value of advertising slots. As a consequence, there were rumours that RAI was considering legal action against FIFA, since TV pictures confirmed that it was a mistake by the referee that sent Italy home from the championship.[6]

■ TF1, the French broadcaster that acquired the French 2002 World Cup soccer rights suffered a similar fate and lost €18 million due to the early exit of the national team.[7]

■ Canal Digital, a Nordic pay-TV platform acquired the Nordic 2002 World Cup soccer rights, but was unable to hire enough subscribers to make the acquisition profitable and lost NOK 48 million.[8]

■ In 2002, News Corporation, the multinational media company, took a write-down of $909 million on unprofitable sports rights deals.

■ The same year, NBC, one of the major US broadcasting networks reported losses on their National Basketball Association (NBA) deal estimated at $300 million over two seasons.[9]

■ Fox, another North-American network, which also belongs to News Corporation acquired the North American Football (NFL) rights for the first time ever in 1994, but almost immediately wrote off more than one-third of the $1.58 billion package (Fort, 2003).

■ CBS, another of the major US networks almost went bankrupt in the early 1990s after paying too much for the Major League Baseball (MLB) rights (Fort, 2003).

These examples should be regarded as paradoxes since the broadcasting of these events generate revenues that exceed the programming costs many times. Examples in earlier chapters have documented the popularity of certain sport programmes and their role as income generator. Many pay-TV platforms have expanded their base of subscribers substantially by means of attractive sport programming. The rating figures on free-to-air channels have also been impressive. The fact that most of these tournaments have been broadcast worldwide have allowed for cost sharing of programming costs. Events such as the Olympics, World Cup soccer finals and other international championships are broadcast to over 200 nations. Such multinational broadcasting represents excellent opportunities to benefit from *economies of scale and scope advantages*. The core programming costs are independent of the number of markets the programmes are broadcast to. Hence, the average costs are lower the more channels that are involved in broadcasting such events. In summary, the many unprofitable deals are caused by how the revenues and costs are distributed, not with the gap between the total revenues and total costs.

The objective of this chapter is to provide more insight on these and other phenomena that at first sight look paradoxical. To achieve this it will use well-known elements from game theory, such as 'prisoner's dilemma', 'chicken' and 'battle of the sexes'. It will analyse issues such as:

■ why the broadcasting of the most popular programmes and sports so often become unprofitable;

■ the problems of distributing sports rights between channels in a way that maximise total profit;

■ why several channels broadcast identical programmes simultaneously in the same market.

THE STRUGGLE FOR THE MOST ATTRACTIVE TV SPORT PROGRAMMES

A pattern where one or more sports achieve a position far above the others on the popularity ladder is common across many markets. Such biases are also reflected in income generation. Soccer has adopted such a position in Europe, as seen from Table 6.1. It is worth noting that this pattern also applies to nations that have been rather unsuccessful on an international level in soccer tournaments. Behind soccer come a few other sports competing for the number two position. Which sports that happens to be varies from one country to another, depending on historical and cultural factors. Rugby and cricket belong to this group in the UK, while skiing, skating and other winter sports have a similar position in the Nordic countries and Austria/Switzerland. In addition, the successes of national competitors on the international arena have also been of importance. Such circumstances, however, can change quickly. As an example, tennis attracted many TV viewers in Sweden and Germany when players like Bjørn Borg, Stefan Edberg, Boris Becker and Steffi Graf were at the top of their careers. Since then the situation has changed dramatically, since neither Sweden nor Germany have come up with any players of the same quality as the former stars. Thus, tennis has fallen down the popularity ladder in both markets. The successes of Michael Schumacher (Germany) and Mika Häkkinen (Finland) and later Kimi Räikkönen (Finland) in Formula One motor racing are other examples where TV rating figures for this sport have increased substantially in Germany and Finland due to the performance of their sportsmen.

Table 6.1 Five top-earning sports, 1998

Germany 732 € million		UK 679 € million		Italy 430 € million		Netherlands 94 € million		Denmark 37 € million		Austria 30 € million	
%	Sport	%	Sport	%	Sport	%	Sport	%	Sport	%	Sport
42	Soccer	52	Soccer	65	Soccer	55	Soccer	45	Soccer	32	Soccer
7	Tennis	12	Rugby	8	Motor racing	9	Motor racing	13	Handball	11	Skiing
6	Motor racing	8	Cricket	5	Basketball	7	Tennis	12	Cycling	6	Motor racing
4	Boxing	4	Motor racing	2	Cycling	4	Cycling	4	Motor racing	4	Tennis
4	Basketball	2	Tennis	1	Skiing	3	Athletics	3	Boxing	3	Ice Hockey

Source: Calculated from Kagan World Media Ltd (1999), *European Media Sports Rights*.

In North America it is the NFL that has the dominant position similar to the dominance of soccer in Europe. As many as 18 of the all-time top 25 list of sports programmes are Super Bowl finals, which is the culmination of the NFL season where the winner is selected. By 2005, the all-time top 40 list of sports programmes only had four non-NFL programmes. The dominance of NFL has also been reflected in the distribution of rights fees. By 2005, the annual NFL rights cost $3.74 billion, which is more than the collective rights to the National Basketball Association, Major League Baseball, Nascar, National Hockey League, PGA Golf, men's college basketball and the US broadcasting rights to the Olympic Games combined.[10] This dominance is somewhat reduced when local TV deals are included, since particularly the MLB and NHL teams have earned substantial revenues from their selling of rights to local TV channels. Nevertheless, NFL is still the leading income generator in North American sports broadcasting.

In Australia, the Australian Football League (AFL) has earned the highest TV sale revenues in recent years, followed by the two rugby tournaments, the National Rugby League (NRL) and rugby union, and cricket. However, the AFL has not been as dominant on a national basis as soccer in Europe and the NFL in North America. While the AFL is the number one sport in the Melbourne area, the picture is different in Sydney and surrounding area where rugby has had the strongest market position.

Profit maximising broadcasting companies will always prefer a product with the highest ability to attract viewers or recruit subscribers. However, when this objective is shared by several others, there is also a risk that too many actors will invest in sports products that are too similar. This can cause a coordination problem where the result is excess supply of one (or a few) sports. In other words, the aggregate profit could have been higher if the companies were able to distribute sports among them instead of going after the same ones.

■ **Case study 6.1** *Tight competition for AFL holy grail*

The Australian Financial Review, 15 August 2003,
by Neil Shoebridge

Television industry executives are calling it Foxtel's folly. The pay-TV operator pays an estimated $50 million a year for the rights to Australian Football League matches, but its two AFL channels are losing millions of dollars a year and missing their subscriber targets.

Fox Footy, which launched in February 2002, and Fox Footy Extra, which started in March this year, have about 120,000 subscribers – well short of Foxtel's target of 250,000 – and are losing an estimated $20 million a year.

Foxtel executives won't discuss the performance of the AFL channels. Neither will they comment on the rumour that the channels will close at the end of 2003 and the AFL rights be moved to Fox Sports. Discussions about shifting AFL coverage from Foxtel – which is 50 per cent owned by Telstra and 25 per cent each by Publishing and Broadcasting Limited and News Limited – to Fox Sports, a joint venture between PBL and News, are believed to have happened recently.

Fox Sports is profitable. Foxtel's chief executive Kim Williams recently said his company would not move into the black until 'around 2005'. PBL and News are believed to be reluctant to take on the full cost of the AFL rights. Fox Sports would need to create a new channel to carry AFL. Jon Marquard, Fox Sports' chief operating officer, would not comment on the AFL rights. If Foxtel is using AFL as a loss leader to drive subscription numbers, the strategy is not working. But the owners of Foxtel – as well as Ten Network and PBL's Nine Network, which share the free-to-air TV rights to AFL – had strategic reasons for grabbing the AFL rights from Seven Network, which had them from 1956 to 2001.

News Limited bought the AFL free-to-air and pay-TV rights for five years in December 2000, paying $500 million. It then sold on the rights to Foxtel, Nine and Ten. The loss of AFL hurt Seven's free-to-air network and effectively killed its C7 pay-TV channel, which closed in May 2002. (Seven is currently suing News, Telstra, Foxtel and PBL, in part, over the AFL rights. It claims they colluded in a bid to destroy C7.) While Foxtel struggles to sign subscribers for the Fox Footy channels, AFL has been a hit for Nine and Ten.

Nine pays an estimated $20 million a year for Friday night and Sunday matches. Ten pays about $30 million a year for Saturday matches and the finals. After a weak start in 2002, when AFL's free-to-air TV audience fell about 5 per cent, both Nine and Ten report higher audiences this year.

Ten's general manager of sport, David White, says its AFL audience is up 12 per cent so far this year compared with 2002. 'AFL fans are now used to matches being spread between Nine and Ten,' he says. 'And the AFL has scheduled stronger matches on Saturday afternoons this year.' Nine's AFL executive producer Cos Cardones says its AFL audience has increased 5.6 per cent, from a weekly average of 2.14 million in 2002 to 2.26 million this year.

Most of that growth has been driven by Friday night matches, which Nine screens live in Melbourne, Adelaide and Perth. Audience numbers this year are up 6 per cent, 12 per cent and 27 per cent respectively. 'Friday night has been a stand out,' Cardones says. 'We deliberately set out to brand it strongly and turn it into the AFL TV event of the week.'

Nine and Ten's advertising revenue from AFL coverage has increased this year, thanks to audience growth and, in Nine's case, the addition of new sponsors such as Crazy John's. Paul Waldren, Nine's Melbourne sales director, will not comment on reports that its advertisement revenue from AFL is $30 million a year.

Both networks say their AFL coverage is profitable, although neither will provide figures. 'AFL was earnings positive from year one and will continue to be,' White says. 'But its margin is lower than Ten's overall earnings margin [31.5 per cent in the nine months to May 31].' The current AFL TV rights contracts expire at the end of 2006. Negotiations for the 2007 to 2011 rights will start in 2005. Seven has the first and last rights to bid.

To illustrate the forces that can lead to these problems, we will now introduce a simplified model that will be used throughout this chapter. In this model there are two TV channels, say Channel A and Channel B. They operate in the same market, and both are highly involved in sports broadcasting. Table 6.2 illustrates the coordination problems that can occur when both prioritise the most attractive sport and neither is willing to compromise. In this example, they can alternatively broadcast two sports, namely soccer and rugby. We assume that soccer is the most popular and hence also the highest income generator of the two. This is a correct situation in many markets across the world, with the exception of Australia and New Zealand where Rugby has been more popular than soccer.

In the first illustration, we assume that they decide which sport to prioritise simultaneously. This means that they are unaware of the rival's decision at the time when they make their own decision. We also assume that each of them only has sufficient resources to broadcast one of the sports. Hence, rugby will not be shown on TV in the case that both of them prioritise soccer, and vice versa.

Table 6.2 presents the pay-off from the various combinations. The numbers to the left in the boxes are Channel A's profit while the numbers to the right are Channel B's profit. The revenues can either come from selling advertising slots, subscription fees or pay-per-view fees. As seen, the total profit will be maximised if one channel concentrates on soccer while the other concentrates on rugby. These solutions are *Pareto efficient*, which means that none of the firms can increase their profit without reducing the rival's profit (Varian, 2002).

The solution where both channels concentrate on the same sport will bring about an abundance of such programmes, in other words an excess supply of the same product. Matches in a league are normally played simultaneously, a pattern which eliminates the ability to watch more than one live match. With both channels concentrating on the same sport, there can also be a lot of programmes promoting

■ **Table 6.2** *Struggling for the most attractive sports (Battle of the sexes)*

		Channel B	
		Soccer	Rugby
Channel A	Soccer	20, 20	50, 30
	Rugby	30, 50	10, 10

the live matches. As an example, two channels may broadcast two foreign leagues in the same domestic market, for example the English Premier League and Italian Serie A. Alternatively, it may be that the competition is between matches in a domestic league and a foreign league. If the matches are played at the same time, it forces the viewers to choose between games from the two leagues. This reduces the number of viewers per match, compared to if only one of the leagues was broadcast. The result of this is that average income per programme is lower than if the channels agreed to concentrate on different sports. Some viewers who are interested in rugby will not be watching soccer and vice versa.

When both channels prefer the same sport, this can initiate bidding wars and hence increase the rights fees compared to if one concentrated on soccer and the other on rugby. The fact that the channels compete for the same audience can increase the variable costs. The prospect of losing viewers to the rival is a motive to increase the quality of the programmes, for example by using more cameras and commentators. However, as seen from Chapter 4, there is also a risk of spending more than the amount that maximises profit. Furthermore, there is also a limit on how many viewers such sports programmes can attract. As this limit comes closer, the competition will approach a *zero-sum game* where any income increase of one channel will be balanced by a corresponding decrease in the income of the rival channel.

As seen from the figure, the optimal solution is when the channels prioritise different sports. However, it will be difficult to agree such a solution since one sport generates higher revenues than the other. Let us imagine that both channels initially only broadcast soccer. Ideally there is a potential for a mutual agreement to alter this solution, so that one concentrates on soccer and the other on rugby in the next period. This will increase both channels' pay-off. The one that concentrates on rugby will increase its income from 20 to 30, while the other that continues concentrating on soccer will increase its income from 20 to 50. Hence, the total increase will be 40, where one receives 30 and the other 10.

An identical improvement can be realised if both channels initially concentrated on rugby, the 'down-right' solution. If they agree that one concentrates on soccer and the other on rugby, the 'soccer channel' will increase its income from 10 to 50 and the rugby channel from 10 to 30, a total increase of 60.

To achieve *pareto-efficiency*, a solution where neither of the channels can increase its income without reducing the income of the other, the channels will have to solve a coordination problem. The problem may well turn out to be a more difficult one than at first sight. The reason for this is that both want soccer, the highest income generator. This can cause fierce competition where both prioritise soccer, hoping to force the rival to surrender. The 'down-left' and 'up-right' solutions in Table 6.2 are both *Nash-equilibria*, where neither of them will regret their decisions once the solution is settled. Let us imagine an initial situation where Channel A broadcasts soccer and Channel B rugby. If Channel B alters its decision and instead prioritises soccer, its pay-off will be reduced from 30 to 20. If Channel A prioritises rugby instead of soccer, its pay-off will be reduced from 50 to 10. Hence, once the 'down-left' or the 'up-right' solutions have been established, neither of the channels will have any motive to move from this position, as long as the other channel maintains its initial strategy.

This case is known as the 'battle of the sexes' in *game theory* literature. It refers originally to a situation where a husband and a wife are trying to decide where to go for an evening out. The husband prefers boxing, while his wife prefers ballet. In addition, they also want to go together instead of separating. There is, however, no obvious solution to the problem since neither of them is willing to give up their first priority.

Similar situations can also be identified in sports broadcasting markets. As mentioned above, there is a tendency that a few sports attract the main interest among the general audience. Sports such as soccer, American football, Australian Rules football, rugby, basketball, baseball and Formula One motor racing are able to attract large audiences. In contrast to this, sports such as swimming, fencing, karate and orienteering are in a position where it is normally not possible to obtain any significant TV rights fees. A consequence of this pattern is that many commercial channels have spent substantial efforts on just a few sports, which also are reflected in the distribution of TV right revenues. Despite the fact that some of the most attractive events are able to generate enormous revenues; recent history contains a large number of unprofitable deals, which was illustrated in the first section of this chapter. Indeed, one major reason for these problems is that too many channels have concentrated on the same sports and hence driven up the costs. At the same time, the small sports (which are the overwhelming majority) have received moderate revenues from TV rights, if anything at all.

As seen from Table 6.1, soccer received 65 per cent of the entire Italian TV rights in 1998, while the equivalent in the Netherlands was 55 per cent. On the other hand, tennis only received 2 per cent of the total UK rights, while cycling received the same proportion of the Italian rights, despite the fact that these sports both enjoy considerable popularity in the respective nations.

Sequential decision making

A situation where rival TV channels enter the market at the same time is quite unusual. Instead, it has been more common for one to enter first, with others following in its footsteps if the original involvement turned out to be successful. The channel that enters first will obtain so-called *first-mover advantage* from cultivating relationships to sellers as well as to viewers and advertisers. There is often a tendency to duplicate such programmes. This pattern is often seen in sports broadcasting, but also in other genres of programmes, such as reality TV programmes and soap operas.

123

To illustrate the circumstances that can influence the outcome from such situations, let us alter the procedure and imagine the channels to make their decisions sequentially instead of simultaneously. This is illustrated in Figure 6.1. We assume both channels to have complete information about the rival's income and costs. Let us imagine that Channel A decides first, while Channel B makes its decision after learning what sport Channel A prioritised. To deduce the optimal solution we use *backward induction*. The upper branch illustrates that Channel B will be best off by choosing rugby (30>20) if channel A chooses soccer. This alternative gives Channel A a profit of 50. The lower branch shows that if Channel A chooses rugby, then Channel B will be best off by choosing soccer (50>10), a solution that gives Channel A a profit of 30. Hence, if Channel A chooses first, then its optimal solution is to choose soccer and earn a profit of 50. This example illustrates the first mover advantage in sequential games. If the order of the decision making is turned around so that Channel B chooses first, then we will have the opposite solution where Channel B broadcasts soccer while Channel A broadcasts rugby.

Let us for a moment change the example and imagine that Channel A has the highest income potential of the two, a situation that is illustrated in Table 6.3. Channel A's pay-off has increased by 20 in each of the alternatives compared with the

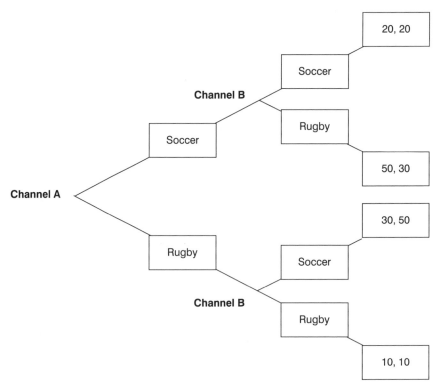

Figure 6.1 *Sequential decisions*

■ **Table 6.3** *One dominating channel (Battle of the sexes)*

		Channel B	
		Soccer	Rugby
Channel A	Soccer	40, 20	70, 30
	Rugby	50, 50	30, 10

former example. One reason for this can be differences in penetration. Advertising revenues will in general be correlated with the number of viewers. In addition, sport governing bodies and other sellers of sports rights tend to prefer channels with the highest possible penetration in order to maximise promotion effects, which in turn can stimulate recruitment to the sport as well as sponsorship revenues. Hence, channels that have the highest penetration might have to pay less than channels that reach only a fraction of the TV households, other things being equal.

Now the natural equilibrium will be that Channel A broadcast soccer while Channel B concentrates on rugby. This is known as the *focal point*, which is an outcome in which players have a common understanding that, of all the possible equilibria of the game, this one is the obvious one to choose. Focal points require a convergence of expectations on the part of the players in the game (Dixit and Skeath, 1999). Channel A has the highest income potential of the two and is unlikely to accept continuing with the least valuable sport (rugby) and let Channel B have soccer. This of course, assumes that Channel A cannot broadcast alternative programmes that create higher revenues than soccer. However, it is important to bear in mind that the down-left solution and the up-right solution both are *Nash-equilibria*. Neither of the two regret any of these solutions once they have been established. This also applies to the 'down-left' solution where Channel A has rugby. Its income will be reduced from 50 to 40 if it takes on soccer, assuming that Channel B continues to broadcast soccer.

Let us now analyse this example in the case of sequential decisions. This is illustrated in Figure 6.2 where we assume Channel B decides first. Therefore the numbers to the left in the boxes now represents channel B's pay-off, while Channel A's pay-off are the figures to the right. On the upper branch where channel B has chosen soccer, channel A's optimal solution will be to choose rugby since 50 > 40. On the other hand, if Channel B chooses rugby, then channel A will gain from choosing soccer, since 70 > 30. Hence, Channel B's optimal strategy will be to broadcast soccer. This illustrates that the order of movement can be more influential than the financial strength of the channels. However, on a long term basis, the stability of such a solution can be questioned. Even if Channel B has the first mover advantages, channel A has the highest income potential of the two. Thus Channel A is unlikely to accept playing second violin in the market on a long-term basis. This exception can be if it is subject to regulations that reduce its ability to make a profit from sports broadcasting, as is the case for PS broadcasters.

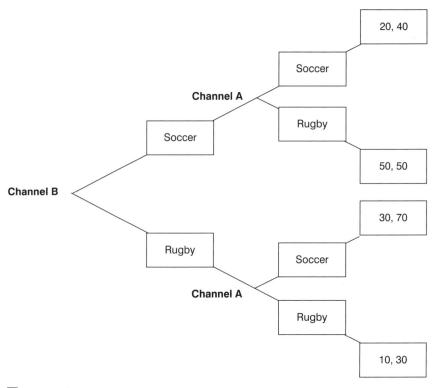

Figure 6.2 *Sequential decision making*

Recent sports broadcasting history contains a number of incidents similar to what has been illustrated above. One example is the development on the UK pay-TV market. BSkyB established a position as the sole provider of sports programmes early in the 1990s. Step by step its market position was strengthened as the number of subscribers increased. Some years later, ITV Digital also entered the market in an attempt to challenge BSkyB's position. However, this establishment did not turn out successfully and ITV Digital was taken off the air in 2002. Their bankruptcy had severe negative financial consequences for English soccer clubs outside the Premier League. One reason for ITV Digital's lack of success was that BSkyB already had the rights for the most attractive product, namely the English Premier League. Thus ITV Digital was left with the lower divisions and UEFA's Champions League matches. The value of the latter was reduced, however, since some of the matches were broadcast on the free-to-air ITV channel. It also had considerably fewer matches with English teams than the English Premier League. In contrast to the alternative that exists for Channel B in the figure above, the branches on ITV Digital's decision tree were all negative. Even if the rights ITV Digital acquired were considerably cheaper than BSkyB's English Premier League rights, they did not attract enough viewers to be profitable.

BROADCASTING IDENTICAL PROGRAMMES SIMULTANEOUSLY

Sports broadcasting history also contains other paradoxes. One such example has been several channels broadcasting identical programmes in the same market simultaneously. The two UK broadcasters, BBC and ITV, have both broadcast England's matches from World Cup soccer finals and European soccer championships for national teams on some occasions. Furthermore, ITV and BSkyB both broadcast the 2005 UEFA Champions League final between Liverpool and AC Milan. Another, and more dramatic, example was when the two Norwegian public service broadcasters, NRK and TV2, broadcast the entire 1999 World Skiing Championship simultaneously. One reason for this was their common membership in the European Broadcasting Union (EBU). Sports rights acquired by the EBU are in general offered to all members, assuming they are willing to pay the fee EBU ask for them. The two Norwegian public service broadcasters have also broadcast identical sports programmes on other occasions, such as programmes that keep viewers updated on the Norwegian premier soccer league (the Tippeliga).

Since live sports programmes are perishable goods that cannot be stored, production and consumption has to take place simultaneously. Thus, viewers are unable to watch more than one programme at a time. Such examples of simultaneous broadcasting are not efficient for the channels involved. Their programming costs are independent of the number of channels that cover the event, but not the revenues, which will decline the more channels that compete for viewers' attention. Hence, multi-channel coverage of identical events reduces income per channel while costs remain the same.

Table 6.4 illustrates the mechanism that brings about such inefficient solutions. Let us imagine that both channels have the rights to broadcast some programmes that are extremely attractive, for example, the World Cup soccer finals. We also assume that the costs of acquiring the broadcasting rights are extremely expensive. Furthermore, the competition between the two will also force them spend additional resources on programming in order to avoid losing viewers to the rival. Therefore, if both channels use their opportunity to broadcast the World Cup soccer finals, then each of them will suffer a deficit of 10.

■ **Table 6.4** *The struggle for extremely attractive programmes (Chicken)*

		Channel B	
		World Cup soccer finals	Alternative programmes X
Channel A	World Cup soccer finals	−10, −10	20, −5
	Alternative programmes Y	−5, 20	5, 5

On the other hand, if they agree to let Channel A broadcast the World Cup soccer finals, and Channel B some other programmes that attract lower audiences, say alternative programmes X, then Channel A will make a profit of 20 and Channel B a deficit of 5. Channel B can risk losing subscribers to Channel A in the case where both of them are pay-TV channels, a solution that will strengthen Channel A's market position relative to Channel B. Similar effects can occur for advertising channels. Channel A can build up a reputation as the 'sports channel' among sport governing bodies, advertisers and others involved in such activities, and benefit from it in the long run. Since the figures are symmetrical, the results will be identical if the situation is turned around and Channel B broadcast the World Cup soccer finals and Channel B some alternative programmes Y.

In the 'down-right' alternative, Channel A broadcasts alternative programmes Y and Channel B alternative programmes X, which gives both channels a profit of 5. These programmes do not attract as many viewers as the World Cup soccer finals so that revenues will be lower. On the other hand, the costs will also be lower. Since the channels broadcast different programmes, the competition will be less fierce compared to the situation when both broadcast from the World Cup soccer finals. When neither of them broadcast the World Cup matches, there is no risk of losing market position relative to its rival. It is worth noting that this solution is better for the channel that would have broadcast the alternative programmes in case the channels agreed to adopt different strategies, the 'down-left' and 'up-right' solutions.

At first sight, the case seems identical to the 'battle of the sexes' example. There is, however, one main difference between the two cases. Let us imagine that both of them have broadcast World Cups simultaneously on earlier occasions and that this lack of coordination has caused each of them a loss of 10, the 'up-left' window. We now assume that they agree a new solution where only Channel A continues to broadcast World Cup soccer finals, while Channel B concentrates on alternative programmes Y. This gives Channel A a profit of 20 while Channel B suffers a deficit of 5. Both channels would gain from moving away from the 'up-left' solution. Although Channel B will be running a deficit in the 'up-right' window, this is less than in the original solution. The problem, however, will be agreeing who should take what since both want to be the only broadcaster of soccer. While Channel A would prefer moving to the 'up-right' solution, Channel B would prefer the 'down-left' solution. So far, the logic is identical with the 'battle of the sexes' case.

The difference, however, applies to the case when both channels historically have been broadcasting alternative programmes, i.e. the down-right solution. If so, the one that continues (alone) with broadcasting alternative programmes will be worse off than if both of them continued. This illustrates the differences between the 'battle of sexes' and 'chicken' situations. In the 'battle of sexes' situation, either of the channels would benefit from moving away from the 'up-left' cell as well as the 'down-right' cell. In the 'chicken' situation, however, only one of them will benefit from moving away from the 'down-right' solution. Thus, the coordination problem, which indeed is what both cases illustrate, is bigger in the 'chicken' than in 'battle of the sexes'. Although the consequences of the worst case scenario often tend to be more negative in 'chicken' than in the 'battle of the sexes', this is not a general difference between the two cases.

The *chicken game* is well known in game theory literature. It originally refers to a game that was played by American teenagers in the 1950. Two teenagers take their cars to opposite ends of a street and then start to drive towards each other. The one who swerved and avoided a collision saved his (and the rival's) life. On the other hand, he lost his honour and was hence called the 'chicken'. The one who kept going straight won honour, and also saved his life if the rival swerved so that a collision is avoided. As one can imagine, the outcome was catastrophic for both drivers when neither of them swerved. Chapter 8 presents another 'chicken' situation between a seller of and bidder for sports rights.

In the case of repetitive matches the channels can agree to share the rights, for instance by broadcasting every other match. Agreeing such a solution can be easy if there are only two channels, but more complicated to achieve if there are other rival channels. Furthermore, since any collusion between channels can be regarded as cartel behaviour, this may well be prohibited by competition authorities.

EXCESS SUPPLY OF TV SPORT

It is often being claimed that there is too much sport on TV nowadays. As mentioned in the earlier chapters, there has been an enormous increase in the numbers of sports programmes during the last two decades. This development is likely to continue due to the introduction of digital technology which has increased the transmission capacity considerably. The only way of making these investments profitable is by offering attractive content. So far, sports programmes have been on top of the popularity lists all over the world and there are few indications of a change in this pattern in the near future.

However, it is important to bear in mind that even the most enthusiastic sports viewers have limitations with regards to how much time and money to spend on TV sport. As more viewers approach this limit, the competition for the viewers' attention approaches a *zero-sum game*. It is difficult to increase revenues unless it is possible to attract more viewers or motivate the existing ones to watch more. Then the only way of making new programmes profitable is by enticing viewers from rival channels. This, however, will reduce the average income per programme. If the competition were to become very fierce, the channels are likely to spend more resources on improving the quality of the programmes in order to prevent losing viewers to its rivals. Such retaliation will in turn increase the aggregate variable costs. If one channel implements such a strategy, then the others may not have any choice but also to adopt the same. However, the final result may be a situation where all channels adjust the production to a level where the marginal costs exceed the marginal revenues. In other words the income could have been the same, while the costs would have been lower, if the actions had been coordinated.

A similar process may also influence the values on sports rights fees. The fiercer the competition, the higher prices will be. It can also force channels to accept fixed rights fees so that they have to bear the entire risk in case revenues turn out to be lower than expected. Such investments in sports rights can be risky, particularly the long-term deals. Hence, a too fierce competition can bring about a situation where the costs increase while the revenues on each and every programme are lowered.

Table 6.5 illustrates why TV channels often end up broadcasting more sports programmes than the level that maximises profit. In this simplified example, the channels can adopt two alternative strategies; *aggressive market policy* or *moderate market policy*. The first alternative means bidding aggressively in auctions and also broadcasting many sports programmes. The second alternative is characterised by more moderate behaviour in auctions and also fewer programmes being broadcast. Let us imagine that Channel B initially follows the moderate policy. If so, Channel A will make a profit of 100 from adopting an aggressive policy, while only 70 from adopting a moderate policy. In contrast, if Channel B follows an aggressive policy, then Channel A will make a profit of 40 from also following the same strategy, while only 20 from a moderate policy. Hence, Channel A will be best off by adopting an aggressive policy whatever strategy Channel B follows, and vice versa. This implies that both channels have a *dominant strategy*, which means that their optimal decision will be the same whatever decision the rival makes.

The situation in Table 6.5 represents another illustration of a conflict between individual and collective rationality. The two channels would earn more from coordinating their efforts and agree a moderate policy, the 'down–right' solution. Nevertheless, they end up following the aggressive policy in the 'up–left' solution. This reduces profit for both, compared to if they followed a moderate policy. In this example, the outcome will be the same if the channels make their decisions sequentially.

This case is known as the *prisoners' dilemma*, which refers to a game theory example in which two prisoners must decide separately whether to confess to a crime. If one prisoner confesses, he will receive a lighter sentence and his accomplice will receive

Table 6.5 Too much sport on TV (Prisoners' dilemma)

		Channel B	
		Aggressive market policy	Moderate market policy
Channel A	Aggressive market policy	40, 40	100, 20
	Moderate market policy	20, 100	70, 70

a heavier one. If neither of them confesses, then the sentences will be lighter than if both confess. Nevertheless, the outcome will be that both confess and hence receive longer sentences than if none of them confessed. This is the best-known example of simple games, and was first analysed by Merrill Flood and Melvin Dresher and later formalised by a Princeton mathematician, Albert W. Tucker (Kuhn and Tucker, 1953).

■ **Case study 6.2** *Struggling RTL says it must bring in major sports rights*

TV Sports Markets, vol. 9, no. 4, by Miriam Sherlock

German commercial broadcaster RTL said this week that it needs to acquire major sports rights in a bid to improve its position in the country's television market. It will be an aggressive bidder for several top soccer rights in the coming months. The company, as other commercial broadcasters, has been hit by sluggish advertising. It also lost its dominant ratings position last year, with its viewing share falling heavily from 14.9 per cent to 13.8 per cent. A senior executive said that 'we are struggling as other commercial broadcasters are. The market conditions are very difficult for us all at the moment.' RTL group said that it would seek to lower its dependency on advertising by launching pay-TV channels across Europe. This month Marc Conrad quit as chief executive of RTL Television, after only three months in the job. Observers say that group chairman Gerhard Zeiler's cost-cutting strategy has been too aggressive and that the channel badly needs to strengthen its programming. One clear way to do this would be to acquire top sports content. According to the senior source, 'everything opens up in football in the next 12 months. It is clear that we must and will have some major football going forward'. RTL would be in the market for the Champions League, for German Bundesliga highlights rights and for German Cup rights. He pointed out that the Sportfive agency will start talks with broadcasters for Euro 2008 rights within the next year. RTL wasn't helped last year by the strong sports properties held by public service broadcasters ARD and ZDF: Euro 2004, the Athens Olympics and cycling's Tour de France – all big ratings winners. The Champions League, formerly held by RTL, has been shown since 2003–4 by Sat.1, after a particularly low bid by RTL. RTL certainly needs to acquire a big sports property soon. It has only two main top sports contracts: motor racing's Formula One, for which it holds the rights until the end of 2007, and a ski-jumping contract for three World Cup events held in Germany and the Four Hills competition. It is seeking to sell on the World Cup rights and, according to some in the industry, the Four Hills also. RTL denied that the Four Hills were being sold. The competition has been a crown-jewel event for RTL, but year after year has been losing viewers. It still does well, but the falls arguably mean the broadcaster is

Table 6.6 *Audience share*

	2002	2003	2004
RTL	14.6	14.9	13.8
ARD	14.2	14.0	13.9
ZDF	13.1	13.2	13.6
Sat.1	13.8	10.2	10.3
Pro7	0.9	7.1	7.0

now over-paying. Part of the reasoning for a ski-jumping sale is to save money for a Champions League bid. The Team agency is expected to start talks later this year for a deal starting in the 2006/7 season.

RTL's other rights include a package of eight Sunday matches in the 2006 World Cup in Germany, but these will not include the national side. It also holds rights for World Rally motorcycling, in a deal expiring this year, and for beach volleyball (the 2005 world championship in Berlin and the German championship).

Too experimental?

RTL's audience share fell by 1.1 percentage points last year, allowing it to be overtaken by ARD – despite the fact that the public service broadcaster suffered a small fall itself. ZDF was the main winner among the top channels. Perhaps more important, RTL's share of the 14–49 age group, the broadcaster's target audience and the group that is critical for attracting advertising income, fell heavily from 18.2 per cent to 16.8 per cent. One analyst said that the channel needs to return to a tried and tested formula. 'It has tried cutting costs and that hasn't worked. It has experimented too much in its programming and that hasn't worked. It tried too many niche programmes – which cost little money and brought in little advertising. It needs to concentrate on what it has always done well – a mixture of top general entertainment programming and sports.' A more aggressive approach towards acquiring top sports rights will be costly – but not necessarily as costly as it might have been. Commentators had expected Haim Saban's ProSiebenSat.1 to bid strongly for rights in the coming months, but that is no longer clear with Saban negotiating to sell his stake to Axel Springer (*TV Sports Markets*, vol. 9 no. 3).

Selling ski jumping

RTL bought the rights for ski jumping's Four Hills and the three German World Cup events as part of a wider €75 million (£51.7 million), five-year deal from 2002–3 to 2006–7. It has sold on the other events and is now talking to broadcasters about the World Cup events. RTL says that it is not, as some sources claim, selling the Four Hills. The ratings are good, but have fallen heavily over the years. The Four

Hills, for instance, attracted 9.4 million viewers in 2001–2, followed by 9.2 million, 6.5 million and, this winter, 5.6 million. Ski jumping still does well in the ratings, according to one senior executive. 'It is still a desirable sports property. It brings in the same sort of figures as Bundesliga highlights and some soccer matches. It just no longer does as extraordinarily well as when RTL acquired the rights. The problem for RTL is it is now vastly overpaying for the ratings that it gets.' The RTL deal, with the German Ski Federation, Deutsche Skiverband, was for all German World Cup skiing and ski jumping. But the broadcaster sold back the skiing rights to the federation in 2002 (they were then sold to ARD and ZDF, which also hold the rights for World Cup ski jumping in Switzerland). RTL remains the host broadcaster and the worldwide television rights distributor for the three World Cup ski-jumping events (at Oberstdorf, Willingen and Titsee-Neustadt) and it also gets the two Four Hills events in Austria, through an exchange deal between the German and Austrian ski federations.

Solutions to 'prisoners' dilemma' situations

If the example presented in Table 6.5 is repeated, the channels will understand that mutual gains can be achieved from a coordination of strategies, that is agreeing to follow a moderate policy. Such an agreement will spread the viewers on fewer programmes and hence increase the average income per programme. Furthermore, rights fees are likely to be reduced if they agree which sports rights to bid for, rather than competing on each and every item being sold.

There are indications that tacit agreements existed between Australian broadcasters until the start of this century, although it cannot be proved. For many years, Australia has had three commercial free-to-air networks, Channel 7, 9 and 10. These have all been involved in sports broadcasting. However, instead of competing for all the specific products, the channels concentrated on separate sports. Channel 7 was the broadcaster of AFL, which has been the most expensive Australian TV product. In addition, it also broadcast other sports such as tennis. Channel 9 concentrated on cricket and also on rugby league after acquiring these rights from Channel 10. As Table 6.7 shows, the AFL rights also increased in the 1980s and 1990s, but this was not due to any fierce competition between the channels. However, this peaceful climate came to an end when Channel 9, Channel 10 and Foxtel (the pay-TV platform) also got interested in the AFL rights and challenged Channel 7's position. Indeed, in 2002 these channels succeeded in bidding away the rights from Channel 7. As a consequence of this, the deal from 2002 to 2006 was worth 100 per cent more annually than the former deal with Channel 7. Although the rights fees increased also during the 1990s, this growth was considerably lower than the leap in 2002 where a real competition took place. Channel 7 and Channel 10 have agreed to cooperate for the selling of the AFL rights starting in 2007.

Table 6.7 Australian Football League TV rights

Period	Total fee (Aus $)	Annual fee (Aus $)
1976–1981	3 million	0.5 million
1987–1992	30 million	6 million
1993–1995	47 million	15.7 million
1996–1998	90 million	30 million
1999–2001	120–150 million	40–50 million
2002–2006	490 million	98 million

Sources: Shilbury and Turner (1995); Howorth Communications (2002); Macdonald and Borland (2004)
Note: Equivalent to US$250 million on 1 January 2002.

For the Australian TV networks, the solutions during the 1980s and 1990s have similarities with the 'down-right' solution in Table 6.5. By not competing for the same rights, bidding wars were avoided, and rights fees kept on a low level. The period starting in 2002, however, is probably closer to the 'up-left' solution.

Such incidents can be found across several European markets, for instance in the UK. The BBC and ITV operated a buyer duopoly in soccer without any competition for many years. This kept sports rights considerably cheaper than if they had been competing, even if some of the programmes achieved very high rating figures. This was illustrated in 1985 when both channels refused to broadcast Premier League matches as a reaction to the FA's demand for more money. The alliance between BBC and ITV gave them the advantages illustrated in the 'up-left' solution. However, in 1988, this collaboration came to an end when ITV broke out from the collaboration and acquired the rights solely for an annual fee of £11 million, which more than tripled the value of the existing deal. In recent years, other companies with more aggressive market behaviour have entered the market, in particular BSkyB. Similar examples, from 'down-right' to 'up left' and the opposite way, have been seen in many European markets since the early 1990s.

Similar incidents took place in Norwegian broadcasting, where the NRK and TV2, the two public service broadcasters, competed very fiercely for sports rights throughout the 1990s. This included the double broadcasting from the 1999 World Skiing Championships, as mentioned earlier, in addition to other incidents where the rivalry between them pushed rights fees far beyond the levels that were common some years earlier. This competition came to an end after some years, when they realised that it was possible to keep sports rights cheaper by colluding instead of competing. One illustration of this is their sharing of Norwegian soccer rights. However, in 2006, this alliance came to an end when NRK started collaborating with Modern Times Group (MTG).

TV channels can increase their joint market power by forming alliances, for example by sharing rights or agreeing tacit agreements of not competing with each other. However, the duration on such alliances can be short lived. This was illustrated in December 2004 when Canal Plus paid a record €1.8 billion to broadcast France's Ligue 1 matches over three years. This ended the collaboration between Canal Plus and TPS, another pay-TV platform that had shared French soccer rights. To achieve the rights exclusively, Canal Plus had to pay €130 million (a 60 per cent increase) more per year than in the former joint deal. Canal Plus acquired four packages: two sets of live games, a highlights package and a group pay-per-view match. As a consequence of this, the French Ligue 1 deal will become the most expensive broadcast contract in Europe, overshadowing the current £1.1 billion deal between BSkyB/BBC and the English Premier League.

■ *Case study 6.3* *Did winner Canal Plus lose or loser TPS win? And Sky?*

TV Sports Markets, vol. 8, no. 23, by Miriam Sherlock

Commentators are virtually certain that Canal Plus's exclusive €1.8 billion (£1.24 billion) three-year deal for the French football league rights is not commercially viable. They say that the company vastly overpaid and misjudged the market. It would not be able to justify spending €600 million a year on rights which are worth €375 million under the present deal. At the same time, competition lawyers are extremely surprised that the European Commission will not investigate the exclusive deal, given its strong objection to BSkyB's capture of the exclusive rights for the English Premier League. Canal Plus, which has long stated its intention to win exclusive rights for its channels and digital platform, Canal Satellite, hugely outbid rival platform Télévision par Satellite for each of the rights packages on offer (see table). Its overall €600 million a year bid for live rights and a highlights package for three years, from next season, contrasted with TPS's €327 million a year. The two companies share rights under the present deal. The Canal Plus fee is well above the expectations of nearly all analysts – and dwarfs the reserve price set by the French league of €425 million. Observers argue that, in paying so much, the company may have compromised its position as the leader in the French pay-TV market. One or two, however, suggest that the move could serve to force TPS to the merger table. Would TPS be able to survive without a share of French football rights? But the more common question is whether it is Canal Plus which has put itself in the weaker position and will most need a merger. And will Canal Plus have any cash left to compete against TPS for other top rights? On the regulatory side, competition lawyers argue that the European Commission is acting inconsistently in deciding to leave the Canal Plus deal alone. Some argue that the lack of action may have repercussions for the commission if it seeks to challenge future tender processes in other countries, particularly any exclusive purchase of the English Premier League rights by BSkyB.

Justified gamble?

Critics argue that the new deal will lead to Canal Plus paying double for much the same rights that it has now. Under the present deal Canal Plus holds most of the league's rights (the first-choice and third-choice live matches and seven pay-per-view matches, with TPS showing only one live match exclusively). Canal Plus pays €305 million a year and TPS €70 million. So Canal Plus has paid a high premium for exclusivity. Whatever the company's reasons, critics believe that it is unlikely to attract enough new subscribers to cover the additional cost. The market for the premium channel has more or less peaked over the last few years, so will the company, which already holds the bulk of football rights, be able to offer potential subscribers a significantly improved product? Analysts at UBS Warburg estimate that the Canal Plus premium channel, which has 4.88 million subscribers, will have to add more than one million to recoup the additional cost of the new contract. Analysts at Merrill Lynch forecast that it will add only an extra 150,000 or so, because most soccer fans already take its service. UBS forecasts that the deal will push the premium channel, which is expected to report a €100 million profit for 2004, into loss by 2006. One informed source thought that it was 'very strange' that Canal Plus bid so much. The company obviously did its sums to see what it could afford and what money would take the rights out of TPS's hands. But it still overbid heavily. How can you rationalise a deal in which you are paying €600 million for rights which your rival values at only €327.5 million?' He questioned whether the company would have been better off paying much less for a non-exclusive deal (*TVSports Markets,* vol. 8, no. 19). Some commentators regard the Canal Plus bid as largely strategic. The company simply could not afford to lose either of the first two packages to TPS, so it had to put TPS out of the running with a high bid. It had to pay a high price in order to secure its own future. It may not have wanted to pay so much but, if it had to, the fee would be part of a longer-term plan to force TPS into a merger. Holding the exclusive rights would put Canal Plus into a strong negotiating position, and the value of a merger would compensate for overpaying for the rights. As one industry expert put it: 'The league's rights were so important that Canal Plus could not afford to fail to win them. It didn't necessarily need exclusivity but it needed to be sure it had the main rights. The way the rights were packaged meant that the company had to go exclusive and pay a high price to make sure.' The problem with that argument, according to several commentators, is that Canal Plus may have so overstretched itself financially that it has limited its ability (1) to market the league matches effectively and (2) to make further rights purchases. Canal Plus is likely to share the cost of the deal between its premium channel (the bulk) and Canal Satellite. Under the present deal Canal Satellite, which has 2.83 million subscribers, pays for the pay-per-view rights and the Canal Plus channel the rest.

EC stance

The decision by the European Commission not to launch an investigation into the Canal Plus deal has taken lawyers and many other commentators by surprise. They ask how the commission can pay no attention to this exclusive deal when it tried to break up the exclusive deal between the English Premier League and BSkyB: it said the league must next time award its rights to more than one broadcaster. The French competition regulator, the Conseil de la concurrence, does not object to the legislation that allows exclusive deals in France. Canal Plus may be the dominant French pay operator, but it put in the highest bid for each of the four individual packages of rights on offer. The regulator said earlier this year that the exclusive acquisition of rights by a dominant pay-operator could have a negative effect on the market, but the three-year limit for any deal would ensure that rival operators do not go out of business. Even so, several lawyers argue that it is illogical for the European Commission not even to look at the French deal, even if it were subsequently to find no fault. 'There is always the element of a precedent being set and for this reason the Commission should at least have investigated the deal,' according to one lawyer. Commentators suggest that, despite appearing to be discriminated against by the Commission's acceptance of the Canal Plus deal, BSkyB could be a major beneficiary. They argue that the Commission will not be able to forbid exclusivity in England now that it has accepted the Canal Plus deal – so long as the Premier League auctions its rights in a similar way to the French league. According to a European pay broadcaster, the Commission's acceptance of the French deal was 'a very good sign for future negotiations across Europe, a clear signal that exclusive deals are permitted'. So, as a senior competition lawyer put it, it will be hard for the Commission to argue that 'what is OK for Canal Plus today is not OK for BSkyB tomorrow'. The Canal Plus deal showed that one broadcaster's estimate of the rights value was higher than anyone else's and it is difficult to see where there is an abuse in that. But, as others point out, the two cases are different. There was competition in France, there was not in England. In the English case, the Commission queried the composition of the Premier League's rights packages and said that they were too heavily weighted in favour of BSkyB, precluding competition. In the French case, 'it seems that the league structured its rights in such a way that a broader range of bidders could bid and competition was achieved'. The Commission could still forbid an exclusive deal in England or elsewhere. According to one lawyer, 'it could argue that an exclusive deal in England is more damaging to competition and to the development of the market than in France, where real competition was generated'. Some lawyers believe that the Commission's attitude over the French league follows on naturally from the precedent which the Commission allowed to be set with the Premier League. According to one lawyer, the BSkyB case 'established that a dominant operator could win exclusive rights for the league. The commission tried to force a different outcome but failed, with the end result that it lost credibility. The best it could do was to say that it will prevent an exclusive deal next time.' Having backed down in the Premier League case, it would be difficult for the Commission to intervene elsewhere, particularly where a national regulator and all the parties concerned appear happy with the deal. 'The French case is thus entirely consistent with Commission policy and with what the Commission allowed in England. Why should the Commission have been led to a different conclusion in the French case?' Lawyers agree in the main that the French deal presents no competition issues. The league issued a transparent tender and split the rights into small enough packages to allow competition. The outcome – that a dominant pay-operator won an exclusive deal – is the result of the workings of the market. As a general principle, the Commission is there to regulate the conditions of the sale and competition, not the outcome. The Commission has also, since May this year, been seeking to devolve competition rulings to the national level.

The French league was last year forced to scrap a controversial three-year exclusive television deal with Canal Plus, due to start this season, worth an overall €1.44 billion. After a complaint by TPS about the way the rights had been awarded, the Conseil de la concurrence blocked the deal on the grounds that the award had a serious anti-competitive effect on TPS, the sector and consumers. The league was eventually forced to extend its then existing rights contract, held jointly by Canal Plus and TPS, for a further year to cover the present 2004/5 season, at the same price as for the previous year.

Merger power

Several observers believe that Canal Plus would have put itself in a strong position to push TPS out of the market – had it won an exclusive deal at a reasonable price. But it is Canal Plus and not TPS that is now calling for a merger. Canal Plus said this week that there was not room in the French market for two viable pay-operators, particularly because new technologies such as digital-terrestrial television and ADSL are emerging. The company was open to talks about a merger or an acquisition. The potential threat from ADSL was evident in the exploratory €15 million per season bid by France Telecom for the pay-per-view rights. Next time around, France Telecom is likely to put in a more significant bid. Analysts at Merrill Lynch, as analysts elsewhere, believe that Canal Plus overpaid for the rights. They suggest that the deal makes sense only in the event of a merger, which would serve to strengthen pay-TV's share of the market. But TPS, owned by commercial broadcasters TF1 and M6, may be in no hurry to negotiate. It has followed a careful growth strategy, according to one commentator. Its deals have always had to make sense from the perspective of the shareholders, which have chosen to develop profitability slowly. Merrill Lynch argues that TF1 and M6 need contemplate a merger only in the event that TPS starts losing money. But the broadcaster should be able to survive without a merger.

Even if collaboration can keep rights values down, it is important to bear in mind that any negotiated solution in the 'up-left' corner can be difficult to uphold, as the recent development in the French market illustrates. Indeed, the 'up-left' solution in Table 6.5 is an unstable solution where both channels will benefit from breaking the agreement, given the right circumstances. The reason for this is that both channels will increase their profit by breaking away from a 'down-right' solution, assuming the other channel does not do the same thing. Channel A will increase its profit by moving to the 'up-right' solution and the same applies to Channel B, which increases profit by moving from 'down-left' to 'down-right'. This illustrates the core of the phenomenon: the potential to benefit from breaking any negotiated deal, given that the other actor follows it.

Some instruments can help the channels to uphold negotiated solutions. Profit maximising TV channels will balance the gains and costs when deciding whether to comply with the agreement or to break it. Let us imagine that one of them keeps its promise while the other does not. The one that cheats might expect the other channel to retaliate, for example by also conducting an aggressive market policy. Factors such as: the risk of being discovered; the threat of any retaliation from the other channels; and the potential strength of this retaliation will influence whether any of the channels can be tempted to break the agreement.

In repeated games the sequential nature allows the players to adopt strategies that depend on behaviour in previous plays of the games. Such strategies are known as *contingent strategies*, where most are *trigger strategies*. Channels using a trigger strategy play cooperatively as long as rivals do so, but any defection on their part 'triggers' a period of punishment of specified length. Two of the best-known trigger strategies are the *grim strategy* and *tit-for-tat*. The *grim strategy* entails cooperating until your rival defects from cooperation. Once a defection is discovered you punish your rival be choosing the cheat strategy yourself, and in every play for the rest of the game (Dixit and Skeath, 1999).

Tit for tat is not as harshly unforgiving as the grim strategy. One of its advantages is the ability to solve the prisoners' dilemma without requiring permanent punishment. Playing *tit-for-tat* means cooperation as long as your rival cooperates during the most recent play of the game and cheating if your rival cheated during the most recent play of the game. Thus the retaliation phase lasts only as long as your rival continues to cheat.

Several factors will influence whether it is profitable to cheat, as well as how to react when rivals are cheating. If the gains from cooperation are large, this also means that the future costs of cheating are large if the cooperation breaks down. Another factor will be how quick cheating is detected. The quicker and surer the response is, the higher is the cost of cheating. Furthermore, if a channel decides to cheat it will have to decide whether to cheat once or forever. The fact that the *tit-for-tat strategy* entails *forgiving* can make it more tempting to cheat than if the rival follows the *grim strategy*.

To exemplify these considerations, let us assume that the channels in Table 6.4 agree that both should broadcast few programmes, a strategy that gives each of them a pay-off of 70. If one of them decides to break this agreement, then its income in the next round will increase to 100 while the rival's income is reduced to 20. However, in the following round the cheater's income is reduced to 40 since the rival also will start cheating, by broadcasting many programmes. The pattern of the outcomes in the following rounds depends on how the channels react on each other's moves.

$$NPV_1 = 100 + 40*(1/1+r) + 40*(1/1+r)^2 + \ldots + 40*(1/1+r)^n \quad (6.1)$$

Equation 6.1 illustrates Channel A's revenue if it cheats in the first period and Channel B's response is the *grim strategy*. As seen, Channel A will earn 100 in the first period and then 40 in each of the following periods.

$$NPV_2 = 100 + 40(1/1+r) + 20(1/1+r)^2 + 100(1/1+r)^3 + 40(1/1+r)^4 + 20(1/1+r)^5 + \ldots \quad (6.2)$$

Equation 6.2 presents Channel A's outcome if Channel B chooses the *tit-for-tat* strategy as a reaction. Here we assume that Channel A cheats in the first period and receives a payoff of 100. Channel B adopts the same strategy in the second period, which lowers Channel A's outcome to 40. In the third period Channel A reinforces the original deal and broadcasts few programmes, while Channel B continues cheating. This reduces Channel A's outcome to 20. In the fourth period, however, Channel A is back to cheating while Channel B adopts Channel A's strategy from the former period and broadcasts few programmes. This gives Channel A a payoff of 100. As an alternative, in the third period, Channel A may convince Channel B that it will not cheat again and persuade Channel B to implement the same strategy immediately. This would have given each of the channels a pay-off of 70 in this round.

$$NPV_3 = 70 + 70(1/1+r) + 70(1/1+r) + \ldots + 70(1/1+r)^n \quad (6.3)$$

Equation 6.3 presents Channel A's income if both channels stand by the agreement and broadcast few programmes forever.

Profit maximising channels will maximise the net present value (NPV). Hence, which strategy the channels adopt will depend on the differences in the nominal pay-offs between the alternatives as well as on the discount factor, r. The higher the discount factor, the lower is the net present value of future revenues. This can make cheating more profitable than keeping the agreement, assuming the channels follow the grim strategy. The conditions can be different if other channels enter the market. This can lead to fiercer competition and hence lower pay-offs in the future.

It is important to remember the special cost structure of broadcasting when analysing the behaviour of the channels. The very high degree of sunk costs reduces cost-saving abilities, for example by broadcasting fewer programmes or spending less effort per programme. Hence, those channels that already have entered the market may find themselves in a position where there are no other options than to continue spending a considerable amount on sports programming.

STRATEGIC MOVES

The previous sections have analysed the possibility of influencing rivals (and collaborators) by means of threats. In this section we will discuss another instrument, namely strategic moves. Figure 6.2 showed how the order of the moves can influence the outcome. Indeed, what it illustrates are the potential gains from manipulating the order. In other words, the *first mover advantages*.

The main purpose with strategic moves is to alter the behaviour of the rival. There are two categories of strategic moves, namely *conditional* and *unconditional*. If Channel A declares that it will follow a specific strategy, irrespective of what its rival does, this is an example of an unconditional move, which can also be called a *commitment*. The purpose of such a statement is to change the order of the game at the following stage, achieving *first-mover advantage*. In the example presented in Table 6.2, Channel A can make a statement that it will use all its resources on acquiring soccer rights, irrespective of the strategy of Channel B. Its objective is to remove the lowest row in Table 6.2, Channel A's rugby row, so that Channel B's alternative outcomes are presented in Table 6.8. If Channel B believes the threat, then its optimal decision is to choose rugby. The result would be a pay-off of 30, while the soccer alternative only gives 20.

Several alternatives exist for how to conduct such strategies. The simplest one is to declare one's intentions in public, for example that it will only concentrate on soccer in the future. To convince the market that this strategy is serious, it might be necessary to submit bids on a number of attractive soccer rights, and not spend any resources on other sports, for example on rugby. Another way of making the strategy known to everybody is acquiring stakes in soccer clubs.

If decision making is sequential, such a strategy is identical with eliminating the rugby branch from Channel A's nodes. This is presented in Figure 6.3, which is developed from Figure 6.2. Figures to the left show Channel B's profit, while figures to the right show Channel A's profit. Channel A's message is that it will only

■ **Table 6.8** *Removing Channel A's rugby row*

		Channel B	
		Soccer	Rugby
Channel A	Soccer	40, 20	70, 30

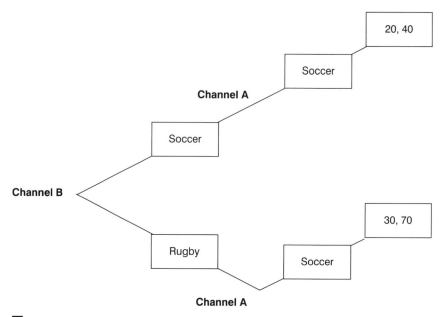

Figure 6.3 *Channel A acquiring first mover advantages*

spend resources on soccer, whatever strategy Channel B adopts. Hence, Channel B's optimal choice will be to concentrate on rugby, even in cases when Channel B is the one that formally moves first.

Conditional strategic moves

The former section illustrated the ability to take advantage from using *threats*. Threats are examples of conditional strategic moves, which mean that one tries to establish a reaction function. If Channel A adopts strategy X, then Channel B's reply to this will be strategy Y. Let us say that Channel B has the second move in a sequential game. Before it makes its move, however, Channel A announces how it will respond to Channel B's move. As already mentioned, Channel A's declaration can be a threat where the purpose is to frighten Channel B from making decisions which are unpleasant for Channel A.

An alternative to threats is to offer promises to the rival. In the example above, Channel A can promise Channel B that it will stay away from rugby assuming Channel B will stay away from soccer. Conditional strategic moves can take different forms depending on what the actors try to achieve and how they set about achieving it. A company that wants to block its rivals from doing something try to *achieve deterrence*, while a company that want to induce the rival to do something try to *achieve compellence*. In the example, Channel A can threaten Channel B with means that will lower Channel B's pay-off unless it concedes to Channel A's wishes. Alternatively,

Channel A can promise that it will respond in a way that leads to a higher pay-off for Channel B, assuming it follows the suggested strategy, in other words, staying away from soccer.

Conditional strategic moves are reducing one's own choices in the second round. At first sight such behaviour might sound irrational. The potential gain, however, appears if it influences the rival to make decisions which outweigh the disadvantage from giving up some alternatives. In the case of a threat, the reduction in freedom in the second stage of the game has a strategic value. The example illustrated how Channel A can take advantage from altering Channel B's expectations about Channel A's future responses.

In order to be effective, both threats and promises need to be credible. This means that the actor who is threatened believes that the rival really will take the steps it threatens to do. In the example, Channel A will have to do something that convincingly makes Channel B believe that Channel A will not give in to the temptation to deviate from the stipulated action when the time comes. As a rule of thumb, threats of punishment are not credible if the channel that threatens it will be worse-off than it would be following another strategy that does not involve any punishment. Any threats from actors that are unable to pursue the strategy they declare are not credible, and thus unlikely to achieve deterrence. Channel A has two ways of making such a strategy move credible in the example. First, it can remove the other moves from its own set of future choices. Second, it can reduce the pay-offs from those moves so that the stipulated move becomes the actual best one.

Let us imagine that Channel A declares that it will submit bids on all attractive soccer rights that are going to be auctioned in the near future. However, if it is known to be in serious financial problems, for example due to losses on former sports broadcasting deals, then Channel B may have no reason to worry. The same applies if the most attractive soccer rights have just been sold to other channels, in deals that have durations of several years. Likewise, there is no reason for Channel B to alter its behaviour if Channel A would have done what it threatens to do anyway.

Companies that have been successfully involved in some specific activities for some time are likely to continue along this path. One relevant example is BSkyB's success with involvement in soccer and particularly the English Premier League. There are no doubts that it is the acquisition of these rights that has been the major income and subscription generator. Surveys have indicated that it could risk losing more than 50 per cent of its subscribers without these programmes. Hence, there is no reason to believe that BSkyB would have any plans of giving up these rights in the future. This was illustrated when the European Commission demanded the English Premier League to split up the rights in four packages as an attempt to remove BSkyB's monopoly. The result of this, however, was that BSkyB submitted bids, and won all four packages. Although the company agreed to offer one package to other channels, no one was able to meet their asking price. It remains to be seen whether the European Commission will succeed in having other TV companies acquiring a piece of the English Premier League next time the rights are being auctioned.

Similar responses should be expected from the American-based ESPN, the French-owned Canal Plus, as well at Foxtel, the leading pay-TV platform in Australia. These companies have all been successful in sports broadcasting. It is unlikely that any of them will be willing to share the products that have brought them success without a fight.

Chapter 7

The pricing and selling of TV sports rights

This chapter will focus on different aspects related to the selling of sports rights. It begins with a discussion about the production process, including a description of the *input-output relationship*. It then focuses on the ownership issue, including a discussion of *individual* versus *collective sale* procedures. This section also gives attention to the *competitive balance* and *uncertainty of outcome*, which is an important element of sports contests as commodities. Some empirical data showing the distribution of TV rights in European soccer leagues are also presented. The final section of the chapter analyses the export of sports programmes beyond the domestic market.

The broadcasting of live sports programmes must be done on what is called the *lowest meaningful level*. This would be the individual match in team sports, while in individual sports it can be a race, match or other forms of contests, depending of the nature of the sports. Below this level, it will be technically impossible to film in a meaningful way. This does not mean that it is totally meaningless to film from an individual car in a race or only focusing on one player in a club match. However, the majority of viewers would demand to have an overview of the whole game or the whole race (Cowie and Williams, 1997).

Table 7.1 provides some illustrations of relationships between inputs and outputs in the production of sport competitions, with competitors/clubs representing the inputs, and competitions/races/matches the outputs.

Live sports programmes are extremely perishable goods and cannot be stored without losing most of their commercial value. The interest for a sport contest is very *time sensitive* and the interest for watching (and listening) drops substantially once the contest is over and the results known. This particularly applies to sports where the entertainment dimension is highly correlated with the uncertainty of outcome. The drop in value will be smaller in sports where the aesthetic performance is of importance, for example in figure skating and gymnastics. The high degree of time sensitivity represents a major difference from other entertainment products, such

Table 7.1 Input and output in the production of sporting events

Sport	Competitor/Player	Match/ Competition	League/Tournament
Soccer	Ronaldinho	Brazil–Germany	World Cup soccer finals
Motor racing	Fernando Alonso	Australian Grand Prix	Formula One World Championship
Basketball	Yao Ming	Houston Rockets v. Chicago Bulls	National Basketball Association (NBA)
Tennis	Serena Williams	Williams v. Hingis	Wimbledon

as literature, films and music since all these products can be stored without loosing most of their commercial value (Gaustad, 2000).

THE OWNERSHIP ISSUE

Sports rights serve to some extent the same purposes as copyrights do for books, films and music. In contrast to these areas, however, there has not been any clear understanding of copyrights in sporting events. Hence, various practices have been followed. For many years ownership was not a controversial issue in sports broadcasting, a picture that particularly characterised the situation in Europe. In its negotiations with outside bodies the BBC, as an example, claimed that its right to cover events was analogous to that of the press. Consequently, fees were regarded as 'facility fees', payment offered by way of compensation for inconvenience, and did not constitute a payment for broadcast rights (Gratton and Solberg, 2004). This is definitely not the case any more, which is mainly a consequence of the enormous increase in value of the most attractive products.

In team sports there will usually be two potential owners: the home team or a sport governing body. Recent history contains several disagreements, and some disputes have even ended up in court. In 1996, the Dutch club Feyenoord won a Supreme Court judgment that challenged the Dutch soccer association to act on behalf of the teams.[1] Another example took place in Germany in 1998 where the German Federal Court of Justice undermined the German Football Association's sales of UEFA Cup matches and the Cup Winner's Cup matches and awarded the rights to the German clubs.[2]

Some factors can make the *ownership issue* complicated. In team sports, the *home team* is the sole bearer of the economic risk to a match unless it is played on neutral ground. This represents an argument for regarding the home team as the sole owner. It has to provide the stadium, security, advertise the game and sell tickets. In many cases the visiting team hold the right to hold a rematch and hence has a chance to market this game and sell rights of an equal value. On the other hand, *the league* contributes to the product by its organisational and administrative inputs. Furthermore, the fact that a match is a part of a tournament or a league often makes it more valuable than if it was just a match between two clubs. One such example was the 2004 UEFA Champions League final between AC Monaco and FC Porto. Neither of them belongs to the ultra class of attractive clubs, except in their respective nations, at least not compared to clubs such as Manchester United, Liverpool and Real Madrid. Thus, an ordinary match between these two teams would only receive moderate attention apart from in France and Portugal. However, the fact that this was the final match in UEFA's Champions League, probably the most prestigious soccer tournament for clubs worldwide, made a substantial difference. Therefore the match received enormous attention, which in turn also influenced its commercial value.

The duration of sports rights deals can vary considerably, from a single event at a specific point of time, up to periods running over several years. Furthermore, such products can cover several alternatives, for instance live programmes and delayed highlights.

The ownership issue can itself influence the value as well as the quality of the products. Private ownership is one of the most important motivations that society has to make people interested in investing, creating and maintenance. It is this connection between the owner's control over a product and the owner's right to make a profit from it that creates the motivation effect from the ownership. According to Merges (1995), the motivation behind the idea of copyrights and the juridical protection of immaterial goods is to combine the initial owners' motivation to produce immaterial goods with society's interest that these goods actually are being produced. This is based on the philosophy that property rights motivates the owner to spend efforts on upholding the quality of the commodity. In other words, there could be an incitement problem without some sort of property rights. The purpose of 'property rights' is to protect the ownership for those who produce products and similar items where there is no natural 'physical protection' (Gaustad 2000). A consequence of this, however, is that some sports rights have become extremely expensive and hence transferred enormous profits from TV channels to the initial owners of the rights.

Furubotn and Pejovich (1974) highlight three factors that tend to influence the economic benefits from property rights. The first is the right to use the commodity and to restrict others from using it. For a commercial channel the value of acquiring such rights is very much influenced by the degree of exclusivity. Not many viewers would be willing to pay any pay-per-view fees if the programmes can also be seen on free-to-air channels.

The second factor is the ability to make a profit from the commodity. The income of advertising channels comes from screening commercials in connection to the programmes, and any restrictions on this ability will reduce the value of the acquisition. In Europe, TV advertising was prohibited in all but the UK, Italy and Luxembourg until the mid-1980s. Indeed, TV broadcasting was dominated by non-commercial broadcasters that received their entire income from licence fee or public grants. Hence they were also unable to make any profit from broadcasting. Thus, sports rights were considerably cheaper than in North America where there was a fierce competition between the networks and where the market was considerably less regulated than in Europe. Although the regulations were dramatically liberalised in the late 1980s, European broadcasting is still considerably more regulated than in North America. This also reduces the abilities of advertising channels to make profits from sports broadcasting (Solberg, 2002). Indirectly, the commercial value of sports broadcasting can also be reduced by other regulations, for example a prohibition of advertising on the arena.

The income of pay-TV channels comes from charging the viewers. Hence, they must also be able to prevent those who are unwilling to pay the subscription fee or the pay-per-view fee from watching. Reception of TV signals belong to the category of an (impure) public good, which satisfies the non-rival criterion, but not the non-excludability criterion. The latter means that it is possible to exclude viewers that are unwilling to pay the fees being charged. Indeed, having this ability represents the basis for the existence of pay-TV channels. Unfortunately for them, however, it is possible to watch illegally by means of pirate cards. In Italy, the number of pirate cards has been estimated to be 2 and 4 million.[3]

The third factor is the right to alter the commodity and its form. Having such a possibility can be extremely important when the competition becomes fierce, both between channels and sports. The number of TV channels has increased considerably across the whole world since the early 1990s. Many of the new entrants have spent substantial amounts of money on sports programming. This development has also triggered the competition for the viewers' attention. As a consequence of this, many sport governing bodies have taken substantial steps in order to uphold the popularity of their sport and its events, sometimes in collaboration with the TV channels. Sports such as skiing, biathlon and skating have even altered the way the competitions are performed or introduced new competitions.

Some TV rights deals guarantee interviews with players and coaches before and after the matches, or even during the breaks between the periods. The contracts can also include clauses that require the interviews to take place so that names of sponsors and advertisers are present in the background. However, these instruments do not guarantee any income increase to the competitor. There is a limit for how many viewers that are interested in watching sports programmes. As the maximum potential is coming closer, the struggle for attention approaches a 'zero-sum game'. Hence the competition can have the character of a 'prisoner's dilemma' (see Chapter 6). The channels that invest cannot expect any increase in income, but only the prevention of a decline. Under such conditions, the result may well be that all the TV channels and sports spend too many resources on upholding the popularity of competitions. In other words, beyond the level where the marginal costs of using additional inputs equal the marginal gains from the additional output. Hence, the benefit from using more resources is in avoiding losing market position, not in making any additional profit or income. Nevertheless, those that are unwilling to be part of the commercialising process will be running the risk of being left behind by those that are willing to take the steps which involve more commercialising.

Another factor is the ability to sell a product in a way that maximises the seller's interest. A sports competition, as well as any other good and service needs to be promoted to uphold its commmercial value. The responsibility for such efforts are usually in the hands of sport associations or other sport governing bodies, local event organisers, but also by commercial players such as TV companies. However, any vagueness regarding the juridical ownership issue reduces the motive to spend resources on commercialising the product. Thus, it is important that the ownership is clearly defined. Very few (if any) would be willing to invest in any item where the juridical ownership issue is vague.

■ **Case study 7.1** *IAAF revamps series in search of golden TV deals*

TV Sports Markets, vol. 9, no. 6, by Ben Speight

The International Association of Athletics Federations is considering an overhaul of the Golden League series of grand prix meetings as it prepares to sign a new television deal for the series' international rights. The federation wants to make the series more attractive to television, having failed to get free-to-air coverage in the major European markets. The league has undergone changes before and has been a continual subject of debate within the sport. Despite the television problems, it is thought likely that Dentsu, the Japanese agency which handles the television rights, will be appointed for the next rights period when its contract runs out after this season. The agency has the right of first negotiation and a matching rights option. Istvan Gyulai, federation general secretary, said that the federation 'had got to be happy' with getting coverage in 180 territories and Dentsu had done a good job. 'But it is disappointing that we haven't got free-to-air television in the top markets.' A number of format changes are being examined. These may include expanding or cutting the number of events from the present six; rescheduling the meetings to make a better fit with other athletics events; and trying to ensure that the top quality performers take part. Critics believe that although Dentsu is likely to retain the rights, it will offer a lower rights fee than last time. The lack of big-market interest, it is said, made it difficult for Dentsu to get a return on the estimated $15 million (£7.8 million/€11.3 million) it paid for the television rights for three years, from 2003 to 2005. But, according to one Golden League event organiser, the IAAF cannot agree a deal for less money because that will lead to a cut in the fees which the IAAF pays the event organisers for their international rights. Zurich, the top event, gets $1.2 million a year, the smaller events between $300,000 and $400,000. Gyulai believes that getting a decent fee will not be a problem. He said that 'Dentsu and several other agencies have bid and all the offers could finance the Golden League as it is'. Two agencies understood to be interested in the rights are Sportfive and IMG. The deal under which the event organisers centralise their international television rights expires after this season. So, if they cannot get the IAAF to offer enough for the next contract period, they have the option to quit the league or sell the rights themselves – both arguably unattractive. The organisers already handle their own domestic rights. Dentsu has the international television for the Golden League as part of a wider three-year deal for marketing, worth an overall $20 million. It sells the television rights via a servicing company, Athletics Management and Services. It also holds the non-European television and marketing rights for the IAAF's World Athletics Series, which includes the world championships and the World Athletics Final, the final of the season's grand prix. The eight-year deal runs from 2002 to 2009. The Golden League was set up in 1998, built around the earlier Golden Four grand prix of Zurich, Brussels, Oslo and Berlin. There are now six events, the others being Rome and Paris.

Format changes

The Golden league is generally regarded as a good product. It makes athletics understandable because it brings events together in what seems an irregular calendar. But observers say several changes could be made:

- Number of events: Some think that the series should be expanded, others that it should be cut to the original Golden Four events which broadcasters found easier to schedule.
- Scheduling of events: The series should lead up to the annual major athletics event, such as the Olympics or European or World Championships, rather than continue afterwards, sometimes as an unwanted anticlimax. There would be more 'editorial sense' for a broadcaster to acquire the series. But event organisers would have to change their traditional slots in the calendar.
- Improving quality: The series attracts a top field with the incentive of a $1 million jackpot for each meeting. But few top athletes want to commit to all six events.
- Finally: The Golden League has no direct relationship with the World Athletics Final, the climax of all the grand prix rather than the Golden Six. A more direct link would strengthen the league.

TV coverage

AMS says that it is difficult to sell the Golden League to terrestrial broadcasters in the top European markets because they already show a lot of athletics. The European Broadcasting Union buys the IAAF's World Athletics Series and the

European Athletics Association's top events, leaving little space for the Golden League. Pay-TV broadcasters have bought Golden League rights in Europe's top markets: Sky Italia in Italy, Canal Plus in France and BSkyB in the UK. In Germany, the series is shown on the German window of Eurosport. But Spain, the fifth market, is expected to agree a terrestrial deal soon. Terrestrial already does well in Europe's second tier markets. The whole series is shown live by NOS in the Netherlands, RTBF and VRT in Belgium, Nelonen in Finland, TV4 in Sweden, NRK in Norway and DR2 in Denmark. The IAAF has agreed 'in principle' to renew a deal with the European Broadcasting Union, the umbrella organisation of public service broadcasters, for the World Athletics Series until 2009. The present deal expires after this season.

SPORT CONTESTS AS JOINT PRODUCTS

Sports competitions fall into the category of *joint product*. It takes two clubs to produce a match and several clubs to produce a league or a knock-out tournament. A match cannot be hosted if one club achieves the status as a monopolist. Similarly, it takes at least two competitors to produce an individual contest. This also creates interdependency between the competitors. Neither an individual competitor, nor a single club can produce a contest without having at least one rival. Gerrard (2000) describes this relationship as:

> co-operative competition, where clubs co-operate in economic terms to produce sporting contests and tournaments.

Furthermore, spectators that attend a sporting event or watch it on TV want there to be some degree of uncertainty regarding the outcome of the contest. Therefore, the clubs must remain independent and competitive in sporting terms in order for contests to be legitimate.

INDIVIDUAL AND COLLECTIVE SALE OF BROADCASTING RIGHTS

A part of what attracts people to sporting events is the *uncertainty of outcome*. This is based on the philosophy that spectators in general prefer contests between clubs or individuals that are even. In team sports, uncertainty of outcome reflects the *competitive balance* of teams participating in a tournament. Where many teams have a similar probability of winning, the league has a high degree of competitive balance. In contrast, there is a low degree of competitive balance when only a small number of teams have a high probability of winning. Competitive balance depends primarily on the distribution of playing talent across teams, which in turn depends on the relative economic revenues of the teams (Gerrard, 2000).

151

According to Cairns *et al.* (1986), the uncertainty of outcome can refer to *match outcome, seasonal outcome* (uncertainty related to which team will win the championship or are in the contention for places where they qualify for other tournaments), and *long run outcome* (whether a team is dominating over a period of several years).

The uncertainty of outcome dimension represents a two-edged sword for teams and their supporters. Although both of them prefer to win, many find it boring if one or a few teams become too dominant. Thus, too much superiority could reduce the interest for matches and thus also the club's income. In European soccer, as an example, premier league clubs attract considerably lower audiences in cup matches against clubs from lower divisions than when they play against other clubs from the premier league. Hence, clubs (and leagues) are facing a permanent challenge to find a balance between the desire to win and at the same time upholding a sufficient degree of *competitive balance* to make the league attractive for the general audience.

The *uncertainty of outcome/competitive balance phenomenon* is well known in the sport economics literature. In his famous article, Rottenberg (1956) argues that the interest in the sport, and hence the total attendance and revenue, will be greater the closer the competition between the competitors is. This basic principle applies to individual contests as well as to team sports.

According to Fort and Quirk (1995), professional club sports leagues are classic examples of business cartels. However, sports leagues differ from other cartels in one important and paradoxical respect, since they are in the business of selling competition, leading to what Neale (1964) termed 'the peculiar economics of professional sports'. Unlike any conventional industry, clubs must combine together to produce a product. Thus, they also have an interest in upholding the economic health of their rivals. It is in all teams' own interest to ensure that none of them become too dominant.

Therefore, leagues use a variety of mechanisms to protect the collective interest in upholding uncertainty of outcome/competitive balance. This includes various forms of cross-subsidisation of the smaller clubs by the larger clubs. Such a philosophy does not correspond with basic principles in other industries where companies at each level along the value chain would prefer to be the sole supplier or buyer. In other words, being a monopolist or monopsonist, which would provide them with more market power than if they had to compete with rivalling companies. This is different in sport because of the joint product element. The importance of upholding the competitive balance has allowed sports clubs to establish co-operations that would be in violation to *anti-trust policy* in other industries.

The income potential of a club is influenced by its drawing power, which reflects the ability to attract the interest from spectators, TV viewers and sponsors. A club's drawing power can be influenced by:

- demographical factors;
- socioeconomic conditions in the market of its supporters;

- the history of the club;
- the popularity of the sport;
- the availability of substitutes.

Demographic factors can influence ticket revenues, and also influence TV revenues. Nowadays the fan base of clubs does not necessarily follow the old geographical boundaries. Indeed, clubs such as Manchester United, Liverpool and Real Madrid seem to have more supporters in foreign markets than in their geographical home markets.

Figures 7.1, 7.2 and 7.3 present the basis for a simplified model that illustrates the relationship between the distribution of input (talent) between clubs and competitive balance. The curves reflect the relationship between talent and income for two clubs with different drawing power. We will analyse the market equilibriums under two different regimes, namely *profit maximising* and *win maximising*. The former alternative is the traditional objective of many companies operating in competitive markets, and the behaviour of the firms is analysed thoroughly in many microeconomic textbooks. In principle, a club operating in such a regime will hire more talent as long as the marginal revenue exceeds the marginal costs. A club operating in a win-maximising regime will be hiring talent as long as the costs are covered.

In the sport economics literature, there has been a consensus that North American clubs behave like profit maximisers, whereas in Europe, Australia and other continents some kind of utility maximisation seems to be the objective (Fort, 2003; Vrooman, 1997; Kesénne, 1996; Sloane, 1971; Rottenberg, 1956). Sloane (1971) considers European soccer clubs as utility maximisers where the utility function of club owners also includes sporting performance. According to Vrooman (1997), European club owners are willing to sacrifice some financial return in order to achieve better sporting performance. It would probably be more correct, however, to regard these two regimes as polar cases where the behaviour of North American teams is closer to profit maximising while the behaviour of European teams is closer to win maximising, but that teams on both continents emphasise both objectives. In recent years some signs indicate that the gap in objectives has narrowed. Several European teams have entered the stock exchange, which in turn require them to have a reasonable profit rate to be attractive.

Figure 7.1 measures the total revenues (TR) along the vertical axis, while Figure 7.2 measures the marginal revenues (MR) and average revenues (AR). The two horizontal axes measure *talent* (L). It is important to bear in mind that talent is not identical to players in this context. Indeed, talent is unequally distributed among the players so that a player of extremely good quality will have many talents, while a player of ordinary quality will have fewer talents. In our model, a player with many talents has higher productivity than a player with fewer talents. The MR curves represent the additional revenues of hiring more talent (winning more) for the two

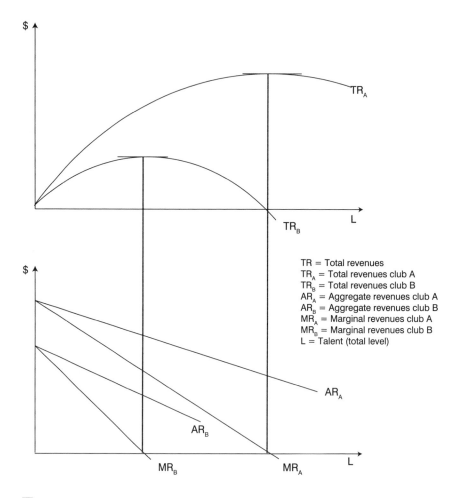

Figure 7.1 *Total revenues from hiring (top)*
Figure 7.2 *Average and marginal revenues from hiring talent (bottom)*

clubs. The AR curves represents the total revenues divided by the amount of talent. Club A has the highest drawing power of the two clubs and thus also the highest income potential. Hence, its MR curve and AR curve lie above club B's curves for any given winning per cent. We also assume that the winning per cent (P) of a team is affected by its amount of talent. Hence, the horizontal curve can alternatively be measured in winning per cent. The winning per cent can vary from 0 to 1, where P = 1 means that a club is 100 per cent likely to win, while P = 0 means that it is 100 per cent likely to loose.

In Figure 7.3 we have taken one step further and now imagine the two clubs to have established a *two-club tournament*. The figure shows the equilibrium distributions

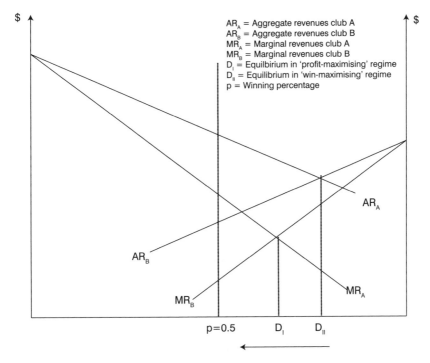

Figure 7.3 *Competitive balance in a two league tournament*

of talent in the two regimes. The curves are identical to those presented in Figure 7.2, with the exception that club B's demand for talent is read from right to left. Hence its winning per cent is at its lowest at the right end of the x-axis, contrary to club A, which winning per cent still is at its lowest at the left end. Talent (L) is assumed to be 100 per cent mobile between the two clubs. Hence, any player can be sold from one club to another at any time. The total supply of talent is constant, and we also assume the minimum wage level any player is willing to accept is lower than the MR curves and AR curves over the entire interval. This guarantees that the clubs will hire all the talent that is available so that $L_A + L_B = L$. The winning per cent is influenced by a team's ratio of talent where $P_A = L_A / (L_A + L_B)$. In a two-club world, the sum of the winning per cents must be equal to one. This means that $P_A + P_B = 1$ everywhere along the axis, or that $P_A = 1 - P_B$.

By hiring more talent the club wins more matches, which in turns bring in more income from spectators, TV channels and sponsors. However, the figures also reveal that the growth in income decreases. In mathematical terms, this means that the first derivate of the income with respect to talent is positive, while the second derivate is negative. Also note that the total revenues of the clubs, $TR_A + TR_B$, are maximised where the respective marginal revenues, MR_A and MR_B respectively, are zero.

155

The *marginal revenue curve* (MR) represents the demand for talent from a club operating in a *profit maximising regime*. The *average revenue curve* (AR) is the demand curve for a club operating in a *win maximising regime*. The fact that the AR curve is situated above the respective MR curve at any point along the x-axis, illustrates that a club operating in a win-maximising regime will spend more on talent than if it alternatively operates in a profit-maximising regime. Clubs operating in win maximising regimes will spend their entire income on talent.

The total income of the two clubs ($TR_A + TR_B$) is maximised where the marginal revenues of the two clubs are equal, i.e. at D_I. Outside this point of distribution, TR can be increased simply by redistributing talent. To the left of D_I club A's marginal revenue is higher than club B's marginal revenue. Hence any transfer of talent from club B to club A will increase TR. Contrary, to the right of D_I a transfer in the opposite direction would increase TR. D_I is the equilibrium in a profit maximising regime.

Similarly, D_{II} will be the equilibrium in the win-maximising regime. Outside this point, we have a situation where one team would be willing to over-compensate the other club for hiring talent. Hence, market forces will drive the equilibrium towards D_{II}.

Figure 7.3 illustrates that both of the two equilibriums will be characterised by imperfect competitive balance. Club A has more talent than club B and thus will win more matches, which applies to both regimes. It is also worth noting that it will be more dominating (winning more matches) in a win-maximum regime than in a profit-maximising regime. Hence, the competitive balance will be worse in the win-maximising regime. This will always be the case when large-market clubs dominate the small-market clubs, according to Kesénne (2004). The reason for this is that clubs operating in win-maximising regimes will spend any additional income on talent. Clubs in a profit-maximising regime, however, will spend more as long as the marginal revenue increase is greater than the increase in marginal cost.

The D_I and D_{II} equilibriums should both be regarded as results of individual sale producers.

Maintaining sufficient uncertainty of outcome is often seen as a necessary requirement for the long-term sporting and financial viability of tournaments and requires that tournament organisers foster a relatively high degree of competitive balance (Gerrard 2000). The fact that TV audiences tend to be larger when big city teams participate in playoffs and championship series provides profit incentives for a league to adopt policies that promote less competitive balance (Fort and Quirk, 1995). Although this might be correct on a short-term basis, sport governing bodies fear that a long-run imperfection in competitive balance can reduce the interest relatively to other sports and sporting events. Therefore, many of them have established various forms of cross-subsidising, which transfers revenues from teams with high drawing power to teams with low drawing power.

In Figure 7.3, any movement towards p = 0.5, either from D_I or from D_{II} will improve the competitive balance. Indeed, redistribution of TV right revenues represents one of the most common instruments that sport governing bodies use to uphold competitive balance. Such redistribution does not require the TV rights to be sold collectively. Clubs that sell their rights individually can also agree to share income. However, since the main purpose with agreeing collective sale procedures often is to redistribute income, the clubs involved in such deals are probably more willing to share income than clubs that sell their rights individually. Another difference between the two alternatives is that the transaction costs will be lower in the case of collective sale. While individual sale will require as many sale operations as there are teams, collective sale will only require one.

The effectiveness on the competitive balance from redistributing income will be different in the two regimes. In a profit-maximising regime, deals where the distribution formula is independent of the team's performance will not have any influence on the competitive balance. There can be two distribution formulas, relating to how income is collected and how income is redistributed. What matters for the competitive balance is the net effect. To improve it in a profit maximising regime the *net-formula* must motivate team A to spend less on talent and give team B the opposite motive. This can apply to deals where the income is collective independently of playing success (e.g. collective deals), and then redistributed on the basis of performance. According to Szymanski (2001):

> What matters for competitive balance is the investment decision of the teams, which in turn depends on the access of teams to the income pool ex ante, rather than ex post share out. Income that is collected as lump sum tax will not distort incentives, while redistribution on the basis of performance will give equal incentives to all. Hence, teams with a small drawing power are no longer deterred from investing in talent because of the limits imposed by their local market ...
>
> In theory, collective selling and the distribution of TV income purely on merit (e.g. league ranking) will enhance competitive balance by giving small market teams equal access to the TV market. A club with a small local market can finance a successful team if TV income is the dominant source of finance.

However, in a profit-maximising regime it is important to bear in mind the importance of the distribution formula with regards to the ability to influence competitive balance. To alter it the deal must be constructed so that it *influences the club's decision* to hire talent. It is not enough to transfer money from large clubs to small clubs. The redistribution arrangement must shift the two clubs' demand curves for talent differently. To improve the collective balance, the intersection between the new curves must be to the left of the original intersection.

In a win-maximising regime, however, any redistribution income will alter the competitive balance. The reason for this is that win-maximising clubs reinvest all additional income (above their costs) in talent. Hence, an increase in TR_B and reduction in TR_A will improve the competitive balance. In Figure 7.3, such redistribution will shift AR_A to the left and AR_B to the right. Theoretically, however, it is also possible that the competitive balance can be worsened, that is a move to the right of D_{II}. The can happen if the distribution formula is constructed so that the large clubs receive more than if there was no redistribution of income. However, we find it unlikely that clubs that agree on collective sale procedures will agree such distribution formulas.

It is also worth noting that the total income of the two clubs ($TR_A + TR_B$) will increase as long as the new solution is moved closer to D_I. Total income is maximised where $MR_A = MR_B$. It can also be shown that the players' wages will increase as long as the new solution is moving closer to D_I, than the original solution, D_{II}.

In real life, the relationship between income and talent is a bit more complicated than in simplified models in textbooks. With some exceptions, clubs make their decisions about hiring talent before the season starts. The income in accordance with performance will be distributed after the season is over. Hence, the clubs will have to calculate how much value additional talent can generate when they decide how much talent they will hire. Such calculations will also involve uncertainty. Players can be injured or lose their form for other reasons. In addition, sport competitions involve various forms of coincidences. There are numerous examples where dubious (and even wrong) decisions by referees have had enormous financial effects on club's revenues. The ability to handle risk varies among clubs. Large clubs with a strong financial base might be willing to take more risks than small clubs. Such circumstances also need to be taken into account when the ability to improve the competitive balance by redistributing TV rights is analysed.

The practice of collective sale has not been 100 per cent accepted by all competitive authorities across the world. One major problem with such a procedure is the concentration of rights in the hands of one seller (or few sellers), which reduces the number of rights available. This reduces the level of competition, which in turn increases the market power of the channel(s) that acquire the rights. Such undesirable elements are strengthened even further when contracts are agreed for a long duration, and/or covering a large number of events. There is no doubt that a league can be regarded as a cartel, given the special circumstances of the industry. As a rule of thumb, any cartel behaviour is regarded as a violation of anti-trust regulations. However, an alternative approach is to regard a league as a *multi-plant firm* that competes for consumer expenditures with other sporting leagues (Neale 1964). In addition to redistributing income from large clubs to smaller clubs, a league will also handle other jobs, for example schedule matches so that televised games do not clash with other matches in the league, thereby causing any negative effect on attendances.

In North America, the collective selling of broadcasting rights has been accepted by the competition authorities, despite the fact that it has also been declared as a horizontal collusion of competing clubs. The Sports Broadcasting Act of 1961 provided an antitrust exemption from the anti-trust laws in reaction to broadcasting activity for the NFL, NBA, NHL and MLB, but not for other professional sports. This was perceived to be in the best interests of competitive balance, and hence also for spectators and TV viewers. Collective sale has been the procedure for national broadcasting rights, with the income being equally shared between the clubs. In addition, other regulations such as 'black-out' rules that regulate the ability to broadcast matches in the area where the match takes place also exist. The NFL clubs currently practise a 'black-out' rule which prohibits the broadcast of matches in the home area of the clubs unless all tickets offered for sale are sold out 72 hours before the game.

The reason for allowing these exemptions from general anti-trust regulations was the special circumstances of sports leagues and their distinctive needs for a governance structure including horizontal arrangements, in particular the aim to enhance competitive balance. In addition, clubs have sold rights to local TV stations individually with the home team receiving the entire income. In some leagues, particularly the MLB and NHL, this has generated enormous differences in revenues between clubs from large metropolitan areas and clubs from smaller cities. In 2003, the team at the bottom of the income ladder in MLB (Montreal Expos) only earned 30 per cent of the club at the top (New York Yankees). Contrary to this, the distribution of the NFL rights has been more even. In 2003, the lowest income earner (Arizona Cardinals) earned 53 per cent of the income of the top earner (Washington Redskins).[4] The NFL sells the entire broadcasting rights in national deals, with the income being equally distributed between the teams.

In Europe, the issue of collective selling of broadcasting rights of league games has been decided differently by the various jurisdictions. In the UK, the Restrictive Practice Court (RPC) accepted in 1999 the collective agreement between the FA Premier League (FAPL) and BBC/BSkyB. Although the deal was regarded as cartel behaviour, the RPC regarded the benefits that occurred from the agreement (redistribution of wealth to smaller clubs) to outweigh any potential detriment through a reduction in competition. The European Commission has required the FAPL to divide up its packages of media rights to bring in other broadcasters to prevent BSkyB from monopolising the broadcasting of FAPL matches. However, since no broadcaster was able to meet a designated reserve price, BSkyB kept all the rights when the current deal (from 2004–7) was agreed. This monopolistic situation comes to an end, however, with the start of the 2007/08 season, where PL rights will be shared between BSkyB and Setanta Sports, the Irish broadcasting company.

In France, the national football federation was been assigned the right to sell the games collectively by law. It has the sole authority to exploit the broadcasting rights of all the games it organises. The law came into force in 1992 and was confirmed by the French Supreme Court in 1994 (Heubeck, 2004).

■ **Case study 7.2** EC is being far 'more radical' over Premier League

TV Sports Markets, vol. 9, no. 9, by James Pickles

A European Commission plan to break UK pay-operator BSkyB's exclusive hold on live English Premier League soccer appears remarkably heavy-handed in comparison to the Commission's approach in other European markets. The plan – to force the league to split its next television rights tender into technology-specific packages – would be far more radical, for example, than the structure of packages approved by the Commission for this summer's sale of Bundesliga rights. It also appears inconsistent with the exclusive deal agreed by the French league last December with Canal Plus, which passed without any Commission opposition. The plan has a precedent in Italy, where the Commission imposed conditions on another Murdoch-owned platform, Sky Italia, restricting it to acquiring only satellite rights and enabling competitors to exploit the rights via other mediums, which Mediaset duly did by buying digital terrestrial rights. But that condition was a corrective measure designed to counterbalance the anti-competitive effects resulting from the commission's approval of the merger of pay-operators Telepiù and Stream to create Sky Italia. Brussels will face a fierce battle if it tries to impose similar conditions on BSkyB, which has received no favours. One reason for the inconsistency is the change of policy adopted by the Commission last May, when it decided to devolve competition decisions to national regulators for all but the most severe cases. The Canal Plus deal was a new case and was approved by the French regulator, the Conseil de la concurrence. But the Commission's investigation into the Premier League began in 2000 and, so the argument goes, has yet to be closed and will remain with the Commission. The Premier League would almost certainly resist any attempt to impose technology-related packages. Aside from potentially having a crippling effect on the Premier League's revenues, the uncertain pace of technological convergence is making major rights-holders reluctant to break down their rights too specifically. Neither UEFA nor FIFA did so in their recent tenders for Euro 2008 and the 2010 World Cup and they also opted to bundle broadband internet rights with the main television rights packages. The IOC bundled all its media rights together in its recent deal for the 2010 and 2012 Olympics. The commission refused to comment on the proposed strategy, saying merely that it was continuing talks with the Premier League about the best way of structuring the next television rights deal based on the provisional agreement made in 2003. The league, said the commission, then agreed that from 2006–7 there would be 'at least two television broadcasters of live matches, that it will create balanced packages of matches showcasing the

Premier League as a whole, and that no one broadcaster will be allowed to buy all of the packages'. Some lawyers query the appetite of the Commission for another fierce battle with the Premier League and BSkyB. It received a bloody nose last time and the league can expect strong political support against any measures that might significantly reduce its television income.

Bundesliga packages

The agreement earlier this year between the Commission and the German league stipulates that rights for the top two Bundesliga divisions be split into nine packages. There is no restriction on who acquires the packages. The packages include: two live rights packages, available to free-to-air and pay broadcasters; three highlights packages, two of which must be on free-to-air, including one that contains the rights for a minimum of two live matches a season; one live internet rights package; and one live or near live package of mobile phone rights.

In 1999, the Italian Competition Authority decided that the collective selling of broadcasting rights were in violation of anti-trust law. Since then the broadcasting rights have been sold individually by the home clubs. As a consequence of this, the distribution of Serie A TV rights is considerably more unequal than in any other league across Europe, which is well illustrated by comparing the figures in Tables 7.3 to 7.9. In the 2004/05 season, Juventus, which heads the revenue list, earned more than the bottom nine clubs in total. Moreover, the four top clubs earned 52 per cent of the total income, leaving 48 per cent to be shared by the remaining 16 clubs. Indeed, this practice caused such big problems that the start of 2002/03 season was delayed by two weeks. The smallest clubs were disappointed by the low amount they were offered by the TV channels and threatened to boycott the games. To solve the conflict, the large clubs had to pay the difference between the amount offered by the TV channels and what the small clubs asked for.

In Germany, the German Competition Act has included an anti-trust exemption that has allowed the Bundesliga clubs to continue to market their broadcasting rights collectively. This practice has also been accepted by the European Commission. In January 2005, the German football league and the European Commission agreed to legally binding commitments in the sale of packages of media rights. These are split into nine different packages, four for TV broadcasting, two for the internet and two for mobile phone streaming. Some of the rights are available only for leagues/governing bodies, others only for clubs, and others subject to negotiation between clubs and associations.[5] The European Commission has allowed UEFA to sell the Champions League rights collectively, in an agreement that has a pattern similar to the German deal. Hence, UEFA has been asked to split up the rights into several small packages on a market-by-market basis. The reason for this is to avoid the situation that only one channel gets control of all the matches.

Table 7.2 shows formulas for how TV rights are distributed in some European soccer leagues. Except for Sweden, all the deals distribute a portion of the income in accordance with the team's position in the league. Some of them also reward the number of TV appearances. Hence, the deals try to combine motives of stimulating performance with the desire to uphold the competitive balance.

Contrary to this pattern, Italian and Greek clubs have sold their TV rights individually. Spanish clubs have used a mixture of collective and individual sale procedures, with the larger clubs selling the rights individually while the other clubs have conducted a collective sale. As seen from Tables 7.3 to 7.9, the income in the Italian and Spanish leagues is considerably more unequally distributed than in any other leagues. In Spain, Real Madrid earned more than the bottom seven clubs in total. The two most valuable clubs, Real Madrid and Barcelona, earned 37 per cent of the total, leaving 63 per cent to be shared among the remaining 18 clubs.

Table 7.2 *European TV rights deals, soccer leagues distribution formulas by 2005*

Collective agreements	
Austria	50% equally shared and while 50% variably distributed by Austrian Top football so that he clubs are being honoured for using Austrian players.
Belgium	Some shared equally – while the remaining distributed in accordance with position last six seasons and appearances on pay-TV.
England	50% equally shared, 25% in accordance with league position and 25% in accordance with the number of TV appearances.
France	50% equally shared, 30% in accordance with league position and 20% in accordance with the number of TV appearances.
Germany	50% equally shared while the remaining is distributed in accordance with the club's positions the three previous seasons as well as the current season.
Island	70% equally shared – 30% in accordance to league position and number of TV appearances
Norway	40% equally shared, 30% in accordance with league position and 30% in accordance with the number of TV appearances.
Russia	Some is equally distributed, while the remaining is distributed in accordance with league position. The exact proportions are unknown
Scotland	52% equally shared and 48% in accordance with league position
Sweden	100% equally shared
Switzerland	The league is split in two stages – 50% is distributed in accordance with the position in the first stage and 50% in accordance with the position in the second stage.
Turkey	According to league position. Top 3 receive 40% while the remaining 15 clubs share 60%.

Source: Deloitte, *Annual Review of Football Finance*, 2004; Peter Elman, *TV Sports Markets*; Greg Mailer, Scottish Premier League; Tommy Theorin, Swedish Soccer Association; Boye Skistad, Norsk Toppfotball

Table 7.3 *TV rights English Premier League, 2005/06 season*

Club	Income (€ million)	Share of total (%)	League position
Manchester United	39.4	7.0	2
Chelsea	39.0	6.9	1
Liverpool	36.7	6.5	3
Arsenal	36.5	6.5	4
Tottenham Hotspur	34.6	6.1	5
Blackburn Rovers	30.6	5.4	6
Newcastle United	29.7	5.3	7
West Ham	28.9	5.1	9
Wigan	28.9	5.1	10
Bolton Wanderers	28.6	5.1	8
Everton	28.1	5.0	11
Charlton Athletic	25.5	4.5	13
Fulham	25.1	4.4	12
Manchester City	24.5	4.3	15
Middlesbrough	24.1	4.3	14
Aston Villa	22.3	3.9	16
Birmingham City	22.2	3.9	18
Portsmouth	21.7	3.8	17
West Bromwich	20.0	3.5	19
Sunderland	19.0	3.3	20
Total	565.4		
Parachute payment for relegated clubs			
Crystal Palace	6.6		
Leeds United	6.6		
Leicester City	6.6		
Norwich City	6.6		
Southampton	6.6		
Wolverhampton	6.6		

Source: Deloitte *Annual Review of Football Finance,* 2006

Contrary to this, the two top earning clubs in the English Premier League, Arsenal and Manchester United, earned only 15 per cent of the total TV revenues.

The fact that sports clubs agree various forms of cross-subsidisation does not automatically solve the problem of imperfect competitive balance permanently. The stability of such agreements is often influenced by whether teams will benefit from breaking the agreement or not, which can be illustrated by means of Figure 7.3.

Table 7.4 *TV rights Italian Serie A, 2006/07 season*

Club	Income (€ million)	Share of total (%)
AC Milan	66	14.3
Inter Milan	55	11.9
Roma	37	8.0
Fiorentina	37	8.0
Palermo	34	7.4
Lazio	28	6.1
Cagliari	20	4.4
Torino	20	4.4
Sampdoria	18	3.9
Udinese	18	3.9
Catania	16	3.5
Parma	15	3.3
Atalanta	14	3.0
Messina	13	2.8
Chievo	13	2.8
Reggina	13	2.8
Empoli	12	2.6
Livorno	12	2.6
Ascoli	10	2.2
Siena	10	2.2
Total	461	

Source: 'Final deals for Serie A lead to row with government', *TV Sports Markets*, vol. 10, no. 17

To the left of D_1, club A would make more money than club B from the last unit of talent being hired. At the level were $P = 0.5$, club A will be willing to pay W_A for hiring more talent in a profit-maximising regime, while club B only would require W_B to be willing to sell. Both clubs will gain from a trade of talent, even if it violates the intention of the agreement. Hence, any income-generating agreements between the two clubs resulting in this distribution of talent contain an element of instability. A similar form of instability applies to any solution in win-maximising regimes. If $AR_A > AR_B$, then club A is willing to compensate club B with more than what is necessary to make club B willing to sell.

The 'cheating element' does not make sense in a two-club tournament. Why should two teams agree a deal with each other, and then break it? However, the circumstances become considerably more complicated when a league consists of 14–20 clubs. In European soccer the wage levels have increased enormously during the

■ *Table 7.5* TV rights Spanish Primera Liga, 2005/06 season

Club	Income (€ million)	Share of total (%)	League position
Barcelona	65.0	19.3	1
Real Madrid	65.0	19.3	2
Valencia	24.0	7.1	3
Atlético Madrid	20.0	6.0	10
Deportivo La Coruña	18.0	5.4	8
Villareal	14.0	4.2	7
Espanyol	12.0	3.6	15
Athletic Bilbao	11.0	3.3	13
Real Sociedad	10.0	3.0	16
Real Betis	10.0	3.0	14
Real Zaragoza	10.0	3.0	11
Sevilla	9.0	2.7	5
Osasuna	8.6	2.6	4
Cadiz	8.6	2.6	19
Alaves	8.6	2.6	18
Real Mallorca	8.6	2.6	12
Málaga	8.6	2.6	20
Getafe	8.6	2.6	9
Celta de Vigo	8.6	2.6	6
Racing Santander	8.0	2.4	17
Total	336.05		

Source: 'World Football League and TV Rights' *TV Sports Markets*

1990s and early 2000s. In contrast to North America, Australia and other markets, European team sports do not normally have any salary cap regulations. Therefore many clubs have suffered from enormous financial deficits. Indeed, some of them would have gone bankrupt if it was not for support and patience from creditors. Under such circumstances it can be difficult to reject selling talent to larger clubs, even if this will worsen the competitive balance. Hence, agreements to the collective sale of TV rights do not guarantee that the problem of poor competitive balance will be solved permanently.

Conflicts between the need for upholding *uncertainty of outcome* and the income distribution that market forces generate also exist in individual sports. According to newspaper articles, star athletes are often offered substantial revenues just to participate in a competition. In addition, many organisers also offer extra revenues for setting world records. The distribution formulae tend to reflect the market value

■ **Table 7.6** *Scottish Premier League , 2003/04 season*

Club	Income (€ million)	Share of total (%)
Celtic	7.9	12.5
Rangers	7.3	11.5
Hearts	5.7	8.9
Dunfermline	5.3	8.4
Dundee United	5.2	8.2
Motherwell	5.0	7.9
Dundee FC	4.9	7.7
Hibernian	4.7	7.5
Livingston	4.6	7.2
Kilmarnock	4.4	7.0
Aberdeen	4.3	6.7
Partick Thistle	4.1	6.5
Total	63.5	

Source: Greg Mailer, Scottish Premier League

■ **Table 7.7** *Swedish Premier league – Allsvenskan, 2004 season*

Club	Income (€)	Share of total (%)
Malmø	664,300	7.1
Halmstad	664,300	7.1
Gøteborg	664,300	7.1
Djurgården	664,300	7.1
Kalmar	664,300	7.1
Hammarby	664,300	7.1
Sundsvall	664,300	7.1
Ørebro	664,300	7.1
Elfsborg	664,300	7.1
Helsingborg	664,300	7.1
Landskrona	664,300	7.1
Ørgryte	664,300	7.1
AIK	664,300	7.1
Trelleborg	664,300	7.1
Total	9,300,000	

Source: Tommy Theorin, Swedish Soccer Association and Peter Elman, *TV Sports Markets*

Table 7.8 Norwegian Tippeliga, 2006 season

Club	Income (€ million)	Share of total (%)	League position
Rosenborg	1.85	15.9	1
Brann	1.61	11.1	2
Vålerenga	1.23	8.5	3
Lillestrøm	1.12	7.7	4
Lyn	1.10	7.7	7
Start	1.02	7.0	6
Viking	0.94	6.5	11
Stabæk	0.90	6.2	5
Tromsø	0.89	6.1	10
Fredrikstad	0.83	5.7	8
Molde	0.78	5.4	14
Sandefjord	0.78	5.4	9
Ham-kam	0.77	5.3	13
Odd Grenland	0.72	5.0	12
Total	14.54		

Source: 'Slik fordeles TV-pengene', *Dagbladet*, 13 December 2006

Table 7.9 Top three clubs' share (percentage)

Spain	46
Italy	43
Norway	36
Scotland	33
England	22
Sweden	21

Source: Peter Elman, *TV Sports Markets*

of an event, both with respect to gate receipts, TV right values and sponsorship income.

The list of products in Table 7.1 contains individual events as well as of events that are part of larger tournaments. As an example, sports such as skiing, skating and biathlon all have established world cup tournaments that consist of a number of individual events. Tennis has the Grand Slam tournaments (Australian Open, French Open, Wimbledon and US Open). Athletics (on some continents known as Track and Field) has the Golden League events. The Formula One World Championship consists of 19 separate races held at different places around the world.

By tying the events together in a multi-event tournament, the *uncertainty of outcome* is also given a *seasonal element*. Furthermore, it can also make the events more prestigious and thus enable event organisers to attract more competitors of good quality. This can in turn raise the interest among spectators, sponsors and the media.

EXPORTING TV SPORT PROGRAMMES

In recent years, there has been a growth in the values for domestic leagues in overseas markets. Table 7.10 shows the right fees for the 'big five' leagues within their own domestic markets as well as the international rights. The French Ligue 1 was the most expensive in the domestic European football broadcast rights market by 2006, while their international fees were moderate. The English Premier League (EPL) was the second highest revenue generator in the domestic market during the 2006/07 season, but will take over the number one position from the start of the 2007/08 season when the new deal with BSkyB and Sentana is initiated. The EPL was the most valuable league on the international market during the 2006/07 season, followed by the Spanish and Italian Leagues. For the EPL , the revenue from overseas sales are expected to reach €980 million (over three years), i.e. about one-third of the domestic TV revenues when all deals are completed (*TV Sports Markets*, vol. 11, no. 1). The Spanish and German international deals are for the period 2008/07–2008/09 while the other three deals are for the period 2003/04–2006/07. The international fees cover all nations outside the leagues own domestic market.

Table 7.11 presents the TV right fees for the three most valuable European football leagues on overseas markets (the English Premier League, the Italian Serie A and the Spanish Primera Liga) in the Japanese, Dutch and French markets. In addition it also includes the fees for the domestic leagues in these three markets. The table uncovers both similarities and differences between the three different nations. The French Ligue 1, which is a member of the 'big five', was by far the most expensive of the three in their respective domestic markets. Its gross value was

■ **Table 7.10** *TV rights of premier leagues in the 'big five' football nations: domestic and international markets, 2006/07 season*

	Domestic market (€ million)	International market (€ million)	International fees as percentage of domestic fees
French Ligue 1	647	7.5	1.2
English Premier League	609	160.0	26.2
Italian Serie A	568	80.0	14.1
Spanish Primera Liga	450	106.6	23.7
German Bundesliga	413	25.0	6.1

Source: *TV Sports Markets* (2006), vol. 10, no. 19; *TV Sports Markets* (2006), vol. 10, no. 16; *TV Sports Markets* (2006), vol. 10, no. 4; *TV Sports Markets* (2005), vol. 9, no. 1

Table 7.11 *TV right deals in Japan, Netherlands and France, 2006/07 season*

League	Annual TV rights		International leagues as percentage of domestic league (%)
	Total (€ million)	Per capita (€)	
Japan			
J-League	33.0	0.26	
English Premier League (EPL)	13.1	0.10	39.7
Italian Serie A (SA)	23.1	0.18	70.0
Spanish Primera Liga (SPL)	15.0	0.12	45.4
EPL+SA+SPL	51.2	0.40	155.0
The Netherlands			
Dutch Eredivisie	71.0	4.31	
English Premier League	2.5	0.15	3.5
Italian Serie A	2.0	0.12	2.8
Spanish Primera Liga	4.0	0.24	5.6
EPL+SA+SPL	8.5	0.52	12.0
France			
French Ligue 1	647.0	10.63	
English Premier League	9.0	0.15	1.4
Italian Serie A	10.0	0.16	1.5
Spanish Primera Liga	5 .0	0.08	0.8
EPL+SA+SPL	24.0	0.39	3.9

Source: Constructed on basis of information from *TV Sports Markets* vol. 10, no. 10 and vol. 10, no. 16

almost nine times the value of the Dutch league and more than 18 times the value of the Japanese J-league.

Table 7.11 also illustrates some major differences in values on overseas leagues compared to the domestic leagues. The Japanese market assessed the overseas leagues highest. The fees for the English, Italian and Spanish premier leagues combined accounted for 213 per cent of the fees in France and more than 600 per cent of the fees in the Netherlands. These differences were also reflected when comparing the overseas leagues with the domestic leagues. In Japan, the three overseas leagues accounted for 155 per cent of the Japanese J-league, with the Italian Serie A alone accounting for 70 per cent of the J-league. This was different in France where the overseas leagues combined only accounted for 4 per cent of the French Ligue 1. The situation in the Netherlands was somewhere between the other two markets, although considerably closer to France than to Japan. Here the overseas leagues combined accounted for 12 per cent of the Dutch Eredivisie.

Due to differences in the size of the population, comparisons in per capita terms represent a supplement for those who aim for a thorough picture of the interest for football and football leagues in the respective nations.[6] The French league was the most valuable asset also in per capita terms, worth 2.35 times the Dutch league and 38 times the Japanese league in their respective domestic markets. The pattern described above, however, did not occur for the overseas leagues. In per capita terms, the English Premier League, Italian Serie A and the Spanish Primera Liga combined were (only) 3 per cent more expensive in Japan and 33 per cent in the Netherlands than in France.

These figures illustrate that there exists a major difference between these three nations in their assessment of their own domestic premier league, and their capacity or desire to import a quality overseas league. The French Premier League turned out to be many times more expensive than the others, both in terms of gross values and per capita values. The interest for overseas leagues was quite moderate in comparison to their own domestic premier leagues. This pattern also reflects the situation in the other 'big five' markets; England, Spain, Italy and Germany. These nations have traditionally been very successful in international tournaments, for both national teams and club football. Hence, sports fans in these nations do not have to watch matches in overseas leagues to find top quality.

European club football has also attracted considerable attention across other Asian nations. By 2004, the English Premier League football was the most watched sport in Malaysia, Thailand and Singapore.[7] In 2005, it was the most popular televised football league in China, rising from third position two years ago. According to an Internet survey, 83 per cent of Chinese football fans preferred watching the English Premier League to matches in the China Super League (CSL).[8]

Currently the rights to broadcast UEFA's Champions League are sold to 233 nations, including 53 in Africa, 58 in North and South America, 55 in Europe, 32 in Asia, 13 in the Middle East and 22 in Oceania. As many as 1.5 billion people had the possibility to watch the 2005 final between Liverpool and AC Milan.

The professional team tournaments in North America are also being broadcast outside the primary market in the USA and Canada. In 2003, NHL matches were broadcast in more than 160 countries around the world. NBA matches were seen in 214 countries around the world during the 2004/05 season. A total of 157 different television channels broadcast NBA programming in 43 different languages, of which 18 are in China.[9]

The Japanese TV company, SKY PerfecTV broadcasts the following international soccer competitions:

- UEFA Champions League;
- Italy/Serie A;
- English Premier League;
- Holland/Eredivisie;

- Germany/Bundesliga;
- France/Ligue 1;
- Portuguese/Futebol SuperLiga;
- Scotland/Premier League;
- USA/Major League Soccer;
- Brazil/National Championship;
- Argentina League.

Of these, most attention is given to the English Premier League and the Italian Serie A. Viewers can choose between pay-per-view, pay-per-day, and pay-per-series.

MODELLING THE EXPORT OF TV SPORT PROGRAMMES

Figure 7.4 illustrates the profit maximising solutions for a sports programme that is broadcast by one single channel in two separate markets, which we call *domestic* and *foreign*. We assume the programme is broacast on a pay-per-view basis. The vertical axis measures the viewer's monetary assessment of the programme (willingness to pay), while the horizontal axis measures the number of (potential) viewers. D_D represents the demand-curve in the domestic market, while D_F is the demand curve in the foreign market. We assume the two demand curves to be independent of each other. Furthermore, the channel can only charge one price within each of the markets. In other words, internal price discrimination is precluded. On the other hand, third degree price discrimination, which allows the two equilibrium prices to be different, is acceptable. This, however, assumes viewers in one market are unable to take in signals from the other market.

AC_d and AC_f reflect the average broadcasting costs for the *domestic* and *foreign* markets respectively. The fact that both AC curves are declining illustrates economies of scale advantages. AC_d refers to the entire programming and broadcasting costs that accrue to the domestic market. Due to the high degree of 'first-copy costs', a large proportion of the programming costs will not be altered if it also is broadcast in nation B. Therefore, the AC_d curve is situated above the AC_f curve. The AC_f curve refers to costs that only relate to the foreign market, such as transmission cost and costs associated with local commentators.

The channel will first set the price on the market that yields the highest revenues, which in this case is the domestic market. The profit maximising solution is at the level where the marginal revenue is zero, i.e. $MR_d = 0$. Similarly, the optimal solution in the foreign market is where the marginal revenue is zero, i.e. were $MR_d = 0$.

Note that the profit-maximising *price–quantity* solution does not take into account the marginal costs as would be the case for private goods. The reason for this is that production costs not are influenced by the quantity being consumed.

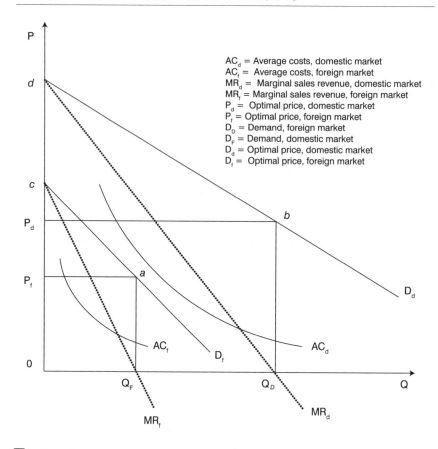

Figure 7.4 *Broadcasting TV sports programmes in two markets*

This means that neither the numbers of viewers nor how many each of them are watching will influence the costs. Indeed, this follows logically from the public good characteristics mentioned above. As a consequence of these characteristics, the *profit maximising* solution and *revenue maximising* solutions are identical. The average costs influences the solution, but only requires an interval where demand exceeds the costs, i.e. where $D_d > AC_d$ and $D_f > AC_f$.

The decision whether to export the programme to the foreign nation should only be based on revenues and costs that accrue to this market. Since the main programming costs have already been covered in the primary market, it takes less to make export profitable.

The following equation expresses the total profit from the two markets:

$$TR = (P_d - AC_d)*Q_d + (P_f - AC_f)*Q \qquad (7.1)$$

Theoretically, it is possible to increase sale revenues by conducting price discrimination, which means that each individual pays his or her maximum *willingness to pay*. Such a policy would increase the profit from the domestic market with an area equivalent to $P_f ac$, and $P_d bd$ from the foreign market. However, in the real world, it usually turns out to be impossible to implement such a pricing policy. Therefore, producers are often restricted to second or third degree price discrimination.

■ *Case study 7.3* 'We'll catch up' Premier League

TV Sports Markets, vol. 9, no. 5

Italy's Serie A will soon close much of the gap in international television sales between itself and England's Premier League, according to the Sportfive agency this week. Sportfive and Rai Trade, the commercial arm of Italian state broadcaster Rai, have sold the international rights for Italy's Serie A in a joint venture for the last six years. Serie A and Spain's Liga are the strongest in Europe in soccer terms but the estimated annual €80 million a season which the agency makes on Serie A is only a little over half the annual €150 million which the Premier League earns from its highly successful international sales strategy. Oliver Ciesla, Sportfive vice president of television rights, said that it was misleading to compare the present value of Serie A, based on deals with broadcasters mostly done three years ago, with the value of Premier League deals done last year. In the deals which the agency had already concluded for the coming seasons – albeit for an incomplete championship – the value of Serie A had increased sharply. 'We probably won't be able to match the Premier League's €150 million a season but we will close the gap considerably.' He expected strong competition for the Serie A rights in any market where there is a strongly developed pay-TV industry. Independent experts expect the strongest competition to be in Japan and the Far East generally and, within Europe, in France and Scandinavia. The Premier League's sales strategy was highly influential on industry thinking but Ciesla claimed that Sportfive's long-term approach might prove to be smarter. 'We will not follow the route that the Premier League went down of forcing licensees with which we have had a long-term relationship into an auction. 'The Premier League's tender process was well planned and well executed and took people by surprise and it was able to benefit from that. But it left a lot of scorched earth behind it and many of the people who lost out were unhappy with the way it was handled. The league will not get away with the same approach next time.'

CULTURAL DISCOUNT

The ability to earn extra revenues from exporting sports programmes also has to do with factors as the demand side, such as the *cultural discount*. The cultural discount reflects the reduction in value on media products when they are shown beyond the home market. In general, the cultural discount is lower for sports programmes than for many other media products. Sports in general have the same rules world wide, which is a characteristic that is favourable for export. Hence, it is not necessary to understand the language to enjoy watching a sporting contest in another country.

However, there can be large variations on a sport-by-sport basis. Nations that have close historical and cultural relationships often share similar interests in sports. One such example is the close bonds between the UK and their former colonies. As an example, cricket and rugby are major sports in many of these nations, but only attract moderate interest elsewhere in the world (with some few exceptions).

In addition, people in neighbouring countries often share similar sporting interests, a phenomenon which partly has to do with similarities in climate conditions. Cross-country skiing, as an example, are major sports in all the Scandinavian countries, while alpine skiing traditionally has been popular in southern European countries where the climate and landscape offer good conditions to cultivate the sports.

As mentioned above, viewers of TV sports programmes in general have preferences for watching competitors and clubs from their own nations. The fact that many clubs have recruited players from other nations has stimulated the interest for sports programmes in external markets. Many European soccer clubs have a large number of foreign players, also from non-European countries, as seen from Tables 7.12 and 7.13, which are based on surveys conducted by the Sir Norman Chester Centre for Football Research at University of Leicester, UK. The English Premier League has recruited a large number of foreign players, as Table 7.13 reveals. Indeed, there have even been matches where one of the clubs only had foreign players.

Table 7.14 illustrates the situation of non-domestic players in the dominant European soccer leagues during the 2004/05 season. Only 44 per cent of the players in the EPL were English, and this was even less in the top four clubs where only 32 per cent of the players were of domestic origins. The figures for the EPL are quite significant when compared to other leagues across Europe. In most other leagues, the figures of non-domestic players were quite a bit lower. Having said that, the non-domestic players represented nearly half of the contingent in the German Bundesliga (48 per cent), 38 per cent in the French leagues and just under a third of players in the Italian and Spanish leagues (31 and 29 per cent respectively). The most interesting aspect of Table 7.14 lies in the column in which the percentage of foreign players representing the leagues top 4 clubs is identified. The top four clubs in the EPL are represented by 68 per cent of foreign players, while the Italian top four clubs have over half their playing staff from non-domestic representatives.

Table 7.12 *Foreign players in European Premier Divisions (1999)*

Spain	200
Germany	185
Italy	163
Netherlands	161
England*	116
France	80

Source: http://www.le.ac.uk/fo/resources/factsheets/fs16.html
Note: *Only players from outside Britain

Table 7.13 *Foreign players in FA Premier League starting line-ups (percentage)*

1992/93	22
1993/94	26
1994/95	27
1995/96	29
1996/97	32
1997/98	43
1998/99	44
1999/2000*	54

Source: http://www.le.ac.uk/fo/resources/factsheets/fs16.html
Note: *Forecast

Table 7.14 *Percentage of foreign players (2004/05 season)*

	All clubs	Top 4 clubs
English Premier League	56	68
Italian Serie A	31	58
German Bundesliga	48	45
French Ligue 1	38	36
Spanish Primera Liga	29	36

Source: Football-europe.com. http://football-europe.com/Data/Players/ForeignPlayers.html

The top four clubs of the particular leagues represent in many cases the 'power-clubs' of their domestic competition. These clubs tend to dominate their particular league. The capacity of the top clubs to include non-domestic players on their roster is highlighted in Table 7.15. As can be clearly seen, in the case of Arsenal, less than 20 per cent of their players were English. Of the other nine clubs identified, over two-thirds of their playing list comes from outside their country of origin.

■ **Table 7.15** *Clubs with highest percentage of foreign players (2004/05 season)*

Arsenal (England)	81
Roda (Netherlands)	75
Chelsea (England)	73
Inter Milan (Italy)	73
Portsmouth (England)	72
Liverpool (England)	71
Ajax (Netherlands)	70
Blackburn (England)	69
Bolton (England)	67
Feyenoord (Netherlands)	64

Source: Football-europe.com. http://football-europe.com/Data/Players/ForeignPlayers.html

While a club such as Portsmouth cannot be said to be a powerful top-ranked team in the EPL, they have identified the need to import many of their players in order to merely remain competitive in their domestic league.

While this freedom of movement of labour across Europe has had a pronounced impact on the recruitment of players by leading clubs, a further attribution can be made for the wealth that has been generated in leagues such as the EPL through broadcast rights fees. Much of this wealth has been transferred to the players through salary increases. This circumstance creates a unfulfillable prophecy in its own right. While increased revenues are being generated through the sale of broadcast rights, the more talented athletes are attracted to the clubs and leagues that have generated this increased revenue. The clubs in turn pay more for the services of the more talented athletes, who in turn demand increased salaries when the league renegotiates its new broadcast rights deal. The end result is that international football has been characterised by enormous differences in revenues between rich clubs and less richer clubs – as well as between rich leagues and less rich leagues.

THE INFLUX OF ASIAN PLAYERS

Despite the fact that Europe has been regarded as the dominating football continent since the 1990s, the majority of TV viewers following the World Cup football finals has come from Asia, as illustrated in Table 7.16. One reason for this is that Asia is the most populated continent on earth. However, it also has to do with a growing interest for football in Asia and in particular for European club football.

This development coincides with a growth in import of Asian players into European football. This may in part be a result of the impact of the success associated with the Japanese and Korean national teams following the 2002 FIFA World Cup, but there is also a strong link to the move by some of the larger European clubs towards developing a presence in the larger Asian markets. Table 7.17 identifies some of the Asian players who have pioneered the move into European football clubs.

Table 7.16 *Aggregate TV audience, World Cup football finals*

	Asia	Europe	Latin America	Africa
1994: USA	15.8 billion	6.8 billion	4.3 billion	3.4 billion
1998: France	14.0 billion	6.4 billion	4.5 billion	5.4 billion
2002: Japan/Korea	11.1 billion	4.1 billion	4.4 billion	5.2 billion

Constructed on basis of information from various numbers of TV Sports Markets 2005.

Table 7.17 *Some Asian players in European football*

Player Home nation	History
Hidetoshi Nakata Japan	The most famous Japanese player in European football. Along with David Beckham, Nakata can take the credit for making football a serious challenger to baseball in Japan (http://ballz.ababa.net/uninvited/nakata.htm, 2005). Played for five Italian Serie A clubs (Perugia, Roma, Parma, Bologna and Fiorentina). On loan to Bolton (EPL) 2005/06 season
Shinji Ono Japan	Signed by Feyenoord (Netherlands) in 2001 season, where he has played since than. Ono did not come alone to Holland, but his arrival marked the beginning of an journalist invasion, who followed every step Ono took, for half a year and had to write a page a day about him. Holland was stunned by all the attention the he got, but as soon as he had played his first match they understood Feyenoord had signed a new superstar (http://www.absoluteastronomy.com/encyclopedia/s/sh/shinji_ono.htm, 2005).
Junichi Inamoto Japan	Signed for Arsenal on a loan deal in 2001. Signed later on for Fulham, West Bromwich and Cardiff (on loan from West Bromwich). Has a contract with West Bromwich for the 2005/06 season
Li Tie China	Signed for Everton on a one year's loan deal in 2002 as a part of the club's sponsorship deal with the electronic giant Keijan. Signed a three year deal in 2003 (http://www.evertonfc.com/index.php, 2005).
Jihai Sun China	Joined Manchester City in March 2002 from Dalian Wanda, the Chinese club he joined in his native land after returning from a loan spell with Crystal Palace in London. Became the first Chinese player to score in the English Premier League. Having scored the best performances in the Premiership among Chinese overseas players, Sun has been China's hottest football icon, according to the newspaper, China Daily. He was also elected as the most valuable City player by English fans, in the first month following his transfer.
Don Fangzhuo China	Signed by Manchester United in 2004 – currently (2005/06 season) on loan to Antewerp FC, Belgium.
Ji-Sung Park Korea	Signed by Manchester United from PSV Eindhoven (Netherlands) for a fee of £4 million. Originally signed by PSV in December 2002

Such import of overseas football players to Europe is not a new phenomenon. During the 1980s, several Latin American players were recruited by European football clubs, and in recent years the import has also involved players from Africa and Australia, in addition to Asia. While there never been raised any doubts that Latin-American players were recruited because of their skills as football players, this has not necessarily been the case for Asian players. Indeed, in some cases, clubs have been accused of more taking into account commercial concerns, than emphasising the player's skills. The following story how Everton Football Club became the biggest football team in China in a few short months in 2002/03 is an interesting case study of sport in the global marketplace (Gratton, 2003):

> In July 2002, Everton became the first European football club to sign sponsorship deal with a Chinese company. The deal with Keijan, China's top mobile phone manufacturer, was for two years and was reported to be worth £1 million per season. As part of the deal two Chinese internationals, Li Tie and Li Weifeng were to come to Everton on 12-month loans. Everton also planned to tour China, set up a Chinese based club, and create a Mandarin page on its official website through which it could sell merchandise.
>
> Keijan, in reverse, saw the deal as a way of extending its brand into Europe. Also by televising Everton's games live in China it gave the company an opportunity to raise its profile in China, where it faced stiff competition from European and Japanese brands. By the time the 2002/03 season began in August 2002 Everton had overtaken Liverpool and Manchester United as China's favourite team. During the early part of the season one of the Chinese players Li Tie established a regular place in Everton's first team line up, something many did not expect at the beginning of the season, and Everton enjoyed their best ever start to a Premiership season. On January 1st 2003, 365 million Chinese viewers watched Everton play Manchester City live on Chinese television. As well as Li Tie in the Everton line-up, Manchester City also had their Chinese star Sun Jihai playing. The result was a television audience in the Far East 200 times larger than the same game would have attracted in England. By February 2003, the Chinese version of Everton's website had received more than three million hits since it was set up in August 2002.

The use of multinational squads to promote sports tournaments on overseas markets has not been unique for football, as similarities to this pattern are also found in North American professional team sport. Teams in the National Hockey League (NHL) have imported several European players over the years. In 2003, the number of foreign players amounted to 273 – that was an average of 9.1 per team. This made approximately 40 per cent of the total, and Table 7.18 shows the players' native nations. Such a high proportion of foreigners stimulated the interest for NHL matches outside North America, and particularly in Europe which has been the main overseas provider of players. During the 2003 season, NHL matches were broadcast in more than 160 countries around the world.

Table 7.18 *International players in the National Hockey League (2003/04 season)*

Nations	Number of players
Czech Republic	71
Russia	64
Sweden	50
Finland	38
Slovakia	25
Germany, Latvia, Ukraine, United Kingdom	6, 5, 4, 3
Other	7

Source: nhl.com (2005)

The National Basketball Association (NBA) has also received substantial attention on overseas markets, and particularly in Asia. NBA matches were broadcast in 214 countries, in 43 different languages around the world during the 2004/05 season. This involved a total of 157 different television channels – of which 18 are in China (nba.com, 2005). One major reason for this has been the import of players from Korea and China, among others. The best example of how effective such a strategy can be is Yao Ming, the Chinese basketball player, who has been very successful in the NBA. Yao, who currently (2006) plays for Houston Rockets, was the first player from outside the United States to be selected with the first pick in the NBA draft. He was also elected on the All-Star game starter each of his first three seasons in the league. His success has increased the interest for NBA substantially in China. Houston Rocket's matches have been watched by 30 million Chinese viewers, reflecting a figure of 30 times more than the number of American viewers (foreignpolicy.com, 2005).

One interesting aspect associated with this broadcasting identity is that the commercial values do not necessarily correspond with the values on the domestic market. The National Football League (NFL) has been the most popular TV sport in the US market, but has not achieved the same position on the international market, simply because the sport is hardly played outside North America. As an illustration, the 2005 Super Bowl was the most popular sport programme world wide this year and attracted a global average TV audience of 93 million viewers. Of this, the US accounted for more than 90% - equivalent to an average of 86 million.

The UEFA Champions League final between Liverpool (UK) and AC Milan (Italy) came second on the popularity list, with an average audience on 73 million. Different from the pattern for the Super Bowl, however, the interest for the Champions League final was distributed across many nations. The match achieved its highest ratings in Italy, Turkey and the UK. These three were the top-rating markets due to Italy and the UK providing the two finalists, and Istanbul hosting the match. In total, these three nations accounted for 40% of the total global audience (exchange4media.com, 2005).[11]

Note that these figures are based on live broadcasts only, and also that they refer to the average ratings across the entire length of the broadcast. This is in contrast to peak and/or cumulative figures quoted by some companies in the sports industry, i.e. totalling all the viewers who watched the event at all, regardless of how long. This is a very important distinction to draw since minute-by-minute data is the standard approach used in establishing industry standard trading currencies worldwide (exchange4media.com, 2005).[12]

One reason for this is that the NFL has not had any international sport governing bodies working on promoting their sports on a global market. Therefore, American football does not have any prestigious international championship, either for national teams nor for clubs. This represents a major difference from (European) football, where FIFA, UEFA and sport governing bodies on other continents regularly stage international tournaments, both for clubs and national teams.

This difference is also reflected by the distribution of power between teams/clubs and the sport governing bodies. Compared to European football, the teams in the North American professional leagues have considerably more power vs. their respective sport governing bodies. One illustration of this is the annual collision between the NHL-play off and the International Ice Hockey Federation's (IIHF's) World Championship. The players in the NHL are not allowed to participate in the World Championship before their team is eliminated from the NHL play off. That many of the best players not are allowed to participate of course reduces the prestige and popularity of the World Championship. This is different in football, where FIFA has the power to declare specific periods only for international matches, i.e. the qualifying matches for national teams. The clubs are obliged to let their players go to these matches. These international matches, including both the qualifying matches as well as the final tournaments, are excellent promotion efforts for football towards a global audience.

HETEROGENEOUS GOODS

The number of TV sport programmes has increased enormously in recent years across the whole world. This includes programmes from domestic as well as international competitions and tournaments. As mentioned above, matches from the most attractive European soccer tournaments are broadcast internationally in Europe, as well as on other continents such as Asia, Oceania and the American continent.

Although sports fans often have preferences for one particular sport, most of them are interested in several sports. Hence, viewers can choose between a considerable number of substitutes. North American TV viewers can watch American football, basketball, baseball, ice hockey, car racing, wrestling and many other sports. Australian TV viewers can choose between Australian Rules Football, two rugby tournaments, cricket and soccer. Europeans can choose to watch soccer, skiing, skating, rugby, basketball, and car racing. Some of these sports will have several tournaments going on simultaneously, which makes it impossible for one person to watch all of it live.

Such situations are known as a *monopolistic competition*, which means that consumers (viewers) can choose between goods that are quite similar, but not identical. The sellers will be the sole supplier of their specific good or service, but will meet competition from other suppliers of similar products. A car dealer, as an example, can be the sole supplier of Mercedes cars within its geographical region, but not the only seller of cars. As illustrated above, TV viewers are offered a wide range of sports programmes.

People in general are interested in several sports, although many have preferences for one specific sport. This was illustrated by a fans survey conducted by the English FA Premier League in 1997 among more than 28,000 fans of top clubs. Table 7.19 shows that English soccer fans preferred their own domestic premier league, but also that they were interested in watching soccer from foreign leagues.

TV sports markets can also be regarded as *oligopolies*, which refer to markets where there are few producers/suppliers. This provides them with more market power compared to a situation of perfect competition, but not as much as in a monopoly. Figure 7.5 illustrates the seller's dilemma with conducting the optimal price policy. Take as an example a pay-TV channel broadcasting sports programmes where it charges a fee of P*. If the fee is increased, the demand will be reduced along the D(p) curve. Since the viewers can watch similar programmes on other channels, the reduction in demand is likely to be stronger than if it was a pure monopoly. This assumes that the prices on other programmes are unchanged. On the other hand, if the channel reduces the fees, then the rival channels that also broadcast sports programmes might retaliate by reducing their fees. This is in order to prevent losing viewers to the other channel. This pattern of reaction refers to the *kinked demand curve*, which is a well-known phenomenon from oligopoly theory. It was introduced by Paul M. Sweezy, in his article in the *Journal of Political Economy*, where

Table 7.19 English football fans preferences (percentage)

Match of the Day (highlights from the English Premier League)	89
Live Premiership, Sunday	58
Live Premiership, Monday	53
Live Italian Football	28
Live Football League	25
Live Scottish League	14
Live Spanish League	7

Source: Sir Norman Chester Centre for Football Research, University of Leicester, Chapter: Fact Sheet 8: British football on Television http://www.le.ac.uk/footballresearch/resources/factsheets/fs8.html

181

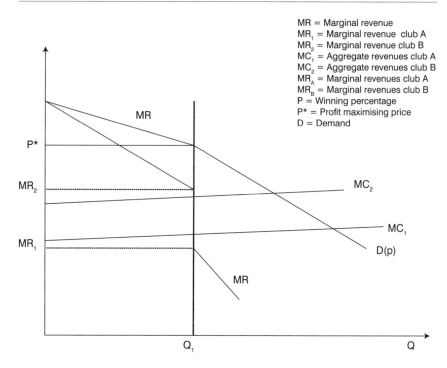

MR = Marginal revenue
MR₁ = Marginal revenue club A
MR₂ = Marginal revenue club B
MC₁ = Aggregate revenues club A
MC₂ = Aggregate revenues club B
MRₐ = Marginal revenues club A
MR_B = Marginal revenues club B
P = Winning percentage
P* = Profit maximising price
D = Demand

Figure 7.5 *Kinked demand curve*

he argued against the assumption that everything else would remain unchanged if the oligopolist changed his price (Sweezy, 1939).

The *kinked demand curve* has an associated marginal revenue curve (MR) that breaks at the point of the kink in demand. A profit maximising TV channel will offer its programmes up to the point where marginal revenue equals the marginal cost. However, the gap in the MR curve means that the marginal cost curve can fluctuate between MR_1 and MR_2 without effecting the optimal price and quantity.

The core of this theory is that the demand curve contains two distinct segments, one for prices higher than P* that is more elastic, and one for prices lower than P* that is less elastic. In other words, the marginal costs can increase or decrease without inducing a profit-maximising oligopolistic firm to change price or quantity on programmes.

The rationale behind this pattern is that any price reductions will be retaliated by price reductions from the rivals. Price increases, on the other hand, are not likely to be followed. If firms face such demand curves, then P* is the optimal price for any marginal cost curve that cuts the vertical section of the marginal revenue curve between MR_1 and MR2. Hence, P* is the profit-maximising price for both MC_1 and MC_2 in Figure 7.5.

Many viewers of sports programmes will have preferences for one specific product, as was illustrated in Table 7.14. However, there is a limit on how much money they are willing to spend on it. This particularly applies to viewers that are interested in more than one team or one tournament. The same applies to viewers who are more interested in sport of good quality than on following specific teams. As an example, if the fees on English Premier League matches increase relatively to the fees on Italian Serie A matches, some of the international TV viewers may decide to cancel their subscription on TV channels that offer EPL matches and instead watch Italian matches. Hence, a price increase on EPL matches may not cause any corresponding increase on Italian Serie A matches, while a reduction might do. Such effects were seen in some European countries during the 1990s when pay-TV channels bid attractive soccer rights away from free-to-air channels. As retaliation to this, some of the free-to-air channels that were outbid started to broadcast other attractive sports programmes at the same time as soccer matches were screened on pay-TV channels. This made it more difficult for pay-TV channels to reach a sufficient number of subscribers to be profitable, particularly in countries where there were many free-to-air channels. Some preferred to watch skiing on a free-to-air channel rather than soccer on a pay-TV channel.

Germany has traditionally been the European country with the highest number of free-to-air channels. Hence, German viewers have been able to watch a large number of sports programmes free of charge. This has made it more difficult to motivate them to pay for watching sports programmes, compared to other countries with fewer free-to-air channels. Therefore, the main German pay-TV company, Premiere, has not been as successful with recruiting subscribers by means of soccer as other pay-TV platforms across Europe, in particular the UK-based BSkyB.

Chapter 8

The auctioning of sports rights

Auction seems to have become the common sale procedure for the most attractive sports rights. It has been a standard procedure in North America since the 1970s, and has gradually become more common in Europe, Australia as well as other continents.

This chapter will analyse the effectiveness of auctions as sale procedures of sports rights, from the perspectives of sellers as well as buyers. Various auction procedures exist, and several factors can influence the outcome: the final price as well as other contract terms that influence the distribution of the income that the broadcasting of the programmes generates. This includes factors such as the number of bidders, their monetary valuation of the product and attitudes towards risk.

An auction does not automatically guarantee the seller higher revenues than any other sale procedure. In other words, an auction is in itself not sufficient to maximise revenue to the seller, it has to be staged effectively. The effectiveness will be influenced by a wide range of factors. Some of these are within the realm of the seller, but not all of them.

The Oxford English Dictionary defines an auction as a 'public sale in which articles are sold to the maker of the highest bid'. The essence of any bidding situation is that the bidders value the item for sale differently, but no one knows exactly how highly anyone else values it. The seller is unsure about how much each buyer is willing to pay. Even if such information were available, it would not guarantee that the seller would exploit the amount the highest bidder is willing to pay. This will be discussed more thoroughly in this chapter.

The profitability of sports broadcasting depends on the gap between the revenues and costs. High rating figures, combined with relatively low programming costs, can generate substantial profit. The distribution of this profit, however, can be greatly affected by the sale procedures. In principle, auctions do not influence the economics of sports broadcasting itself, only the distribution of the profit. Effective auctions can increase rights fees significantly given the right circumstances. The higher the fees are, the larger the proportion of the profit falls to the seller. In general, the purpose of staging an auction is to maximise the seller's proportion of this profit.

The most important factor with regards to the distribution of the profit will be the level of competition, on the demand side as well as on the supply side. A seller of sports rights will benefit from being the sole provider of such products, while there is at the same time fierce competition at the demand side. In contrast, the buyer of sports rights would prefer to be the sole purchaser while at the same time there are a large number of sellers.

CONTEXT

This becomes evident if we compare the values of Olympic rights in the USA and Europe, which is illustrated in Table 1.3. As the table illustrates, the US rights have been considerably more expensive, particularly until the 1990s. The main reason for this was differences in competition level between the two continents. Several networks have submitted bids for the US rights since the 1970s. One episode that illustrated the effectiveness of auction was the sale of the 1980 Moscow Summer Olympics rights for the US market as described in detail by McMillan (1991). At that time, the rights were sold by the local organising committee (LOC), and not by the IOC as is the current procedure. The Moscow organising committee was very effective in orchestrating a bidding war between the three main networks ABC, CBS and NBC. The LOC first asked for US$210 million, which they later admitted was 300 per cent of what they expected. Then the networks were urged to compete in an unending series of bids. At some stage new sealed bids were submitted every 24 hours. The networks made every effort to keep their bids secret, but without success since the LOC leaked details to their rivals. At some stage the networks threatened to boycott the process completely in protest against the broken promises. This, however, did not have any effect, since the LOC succeeded on playing one off against another. As a result of this, the real value increased by 140 per cent from the 1976 Olympics in Montreal, Canada. For North American networks, the commercial value of the Olympics are much higher when staged on the American continent than in Russia because of differences in the time zones. Hence the real increase in value exceeded the 140 per cent growth.

Such a pattern did not occur in Europe at that time since public service broadcasters operated as monopolists in most markets. Hence, the demand side was characterised by a total lack of competition despite the fact that some sports programmes attracted very high rating figures. Domestic products were in general sold to the national public service broadcaster that did not have any rivals. Major international events such as the Olympics or the World Cup finals were acquired by the European Broadcasting Union (EBU)[1] and subsequently distributed to their member channels at prices based on full cost coverage (Solberg, 2002a).

This came to an end in 1996 when EBU was challenged when bidding for the Olympic rights for the first time ever. Rupert Murdoch's News Corporation submitted a bid of $2 billion for the entire games from 1996–2008. Thus, EBU was forced to increase their bid dramatically compared to what they paid in the past. EBU submitted a bid of $1.44 billion, which was 0.6 billion less than News Corporation (Solberg, 2002a). The IOC accepted the lower bid from the EBU since it wanted the Olympics broadcast on free-to-air television.

The importance of competition also becomes evident by studying the European rights as a proportion of the US rights. For the Olympic Games in 1980, 1984 and 1988, the European rights accounted for respectively 8, 8 and 10 per cent of the US fees. For the period from 1996 to 2008, however, the European fees accounted for 50 per cent of the US fees. If the IOC had accepted Murdoch's bid, the European rights would have cost 93 per cent of the US rights.

The potential effectiveness of auctions has also been illustrated by developments in the UK. Here, TV sport was a buyer's market until the 1990s. Throughout the 1970s, soccer coverage was handled by negotiation between the BBC and ITV, and the Football League and the Football Association in what Whannel (1992) describes as 'the old cosy BBC/ITV sharing of soccer'. It was not until late in the 1980s that ITV became a serious threat to the BBC in soccer coverage when it pushed up the price of broadcasting rights for the 1988–92 period by 250 per cent and outbid the BBC to obtain exclusive rights.

In 1992, the pattern was totally revolutionised when Rupert Murdoch's BSkyB entered the scene. BSkyB acquired the rights for the first time ever for a fee of £304 million, but not before it was given an opportunity to submit a final bid after learning of ITV's final bid of £262 million.[2] The £304 million deal, which also included highlights fees from the BBC, constituted a massive rise in the fees that was almost five times the value of the deal ITV acquired in 1988. When new deals were agreed in 1997 and 2001, BSkyB was faced with challengers. Therefore the rights fees also increased significantly, as seen in Table 8.1. This was different in 2004, however, when BSkyB did not face any serious competition. The annual price was reduced by 9 per cent, from the previous deal, and the fee per match by as much as 57 per cent. In 2007, however, BSkyB faced competition from Setanta (who won two packages), NTL and Disney's ESPN. Informal rumours indicated that Channel 4, Five, ITV and the BBC also submitted bids (TV Sports Markets, 2006). Therefore, the right fees increased with 70 per cent.

Effective auctions have also driven up rights fees on North American team sports. Due to limitations in capacity, most of the packages have been sliced up and shared by more than one network. Nevertheless, the sellers have succeeded in playing the networks against each other when auctioning the different pieces. The NFL rights have been the flagship and the most expensive product. As seen in Table 8.2, the rights fees have become extremely expensive, and on some occasions even unprofitable for the networks. Nevertheless, some networks seem to have calculated

Table 8.1 *Deals between English Premier League and TV Companies, 1983–2007*

	1983	1985	1986	1988	1992	1997	2001	2004	2007
Length of contract (years)	2	0.5	2	4	5	4	3	3	3
Broadcaster	BBC/ITV	BBC	BBC/ITV	ITV	BSkyB	BSkyB	BSkyB	BSkyB	BSkyB/Setanta
Rights fee (£m)	5.2	1.3	6.3	44	191.5	670	1100	1000	1700
Annual rights fee (£m)	2.6	2.6	3.1	11	38.3	167.5	367	333	567
Live matches per season	10	6	14	18	60	60	66	138	138
Fees per live match (£m)	0.26	0.43	0.22	0.61	0.64	2.79	5.56	2.41	4.1

Source: Williams (2002: 3); 'The Labour Market in the Football Industry', *TV Sports Markets*, vol. 9, no. 1

Table 8.2 *TV rights, National Football League (NFL)*

Period	Network	Annual fee($ million)
1987–89	CBS, NBC ABC, ESPN	497
1990–93	ABC, CBS, NBC, ESPN, TNT	901
1994	NBC (Superbowl)	40
1994–97	ABC, FOX, NBC, ESPN, TNT	1,097
1998–2005	ABC, FOX, CBS, ESPN	2,200
2006–10*	CBS, NBC, Fox, ESPN, DirecTV	3,735

Source: Gratton and Solberg, 2004; Rodney Forts web site: http://users.pullman.com/rodfort/SportsBusiness/BizFrame.htm

Note: *The end of these deals varies from 2010 to 2013. When this chapter was written NFL had still to award rights for another package of eight late-season games.

the costs of being without NFL matches to be higher, mainly due to the risk of losing indirect impacts. In 1994, Fox became a major competitor to the 'big three' broadcast networks at that time, ABC, CBS and NBC after acquiring NFL rights for the first time ever when they outbid the longtime rights owner CBS to broadcast. The rights gave Fox many new viewers (and affiliates) and a platform for advertising its other shows. In order to bump out CBS, Fox triggered a 91 per cent surge in NFL rights fees. Four years later, it was NBC that walked away as CBS returned with the result that the NFL rights fee doubled.

Another example that illustrated the effectiveness of auction took place in 1996 when FIFA auctioned the rights for the World Cups in 2002 and 2006 to the German Kirch corporation and the Swiss ISL marketing agency. This contradicted the pattern of former sale procedure where they had been sold to a consortium of public service broadcasters (including EBU), which hardly faced any competition. This change in pattern was also reflected in the prices. FIFA made 2.8 billion Swiss Francs (about US$2.24 billion) for the 2002 and 2006 tournaments. Of this, 1.3 billion Swiss Francs was for the 2002 tournament, which was an increase of 500 per cent compared to the 1998 World Cup in France.

AUCTION PROCEDURES

There are two categories of auctions, *private-value* auctions and *common-value* auctions. In *private-value auctions* each player's valuation is independent of those of the other players. An example is the sale of antiques or paintings to people who will not resell them. In such auctions, the bidder cannot extract any information about his own value from the valuations of the other players. Knowing all the other bids in advance would not change his valuation, although it might well change his bidding strategy. At the time of the bidding, each bidder knows exactly what winning would be worth to him or her, but does not know what it would be worth to others.

This is different in *common-value auction*, where the item being auctioned has approximately the same value to all bidders. However, the bidders do not have precise information of the about the value of the item, and thus have to estimate it on basis of the information that is available. Each bidder is guessing the item's true value at the time of bidding, and does not know the other's guesses. In such auctions, the purpose of the buyers will often be to use the item in some kind of commercial activity, for instance to resell it or to use it as an input in some kind of production.

The two theoretical models can be regarded as extreme cases. Real world auctions will have elements from both categories, which also applies to auctions of sports rights. The values of sports rights will be closely related for commercial channels, but not necessarily 100 per cent identical. Pay-TV channels and advertising channels earn their revenues from different sources. Furthermore, pay-TV channels belonging to different broadcasting platforms may not have the same numbers of subscribers. Thus, income generating potential also varies. Neither do all advertising channels have the same penetration. Hence, the channels will not have identical revenue from broadcasting sports programmes.

The most common auction procedures are:

- English auction (open – first cry);
- Dutch (descending);
- sealed – first bid;
- sealed – second bid.

Of these alternatives, *English auction* and *sealed – first bid*, or combinations of them, have been the most common procedures when sports rights have been

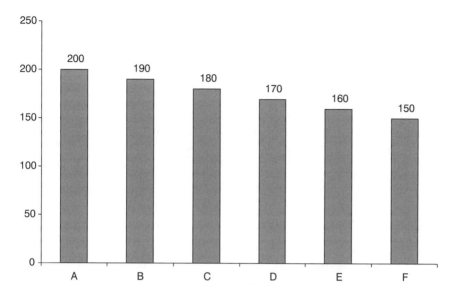

Figure 8.1 *TV channels' evaluation of sports rights*

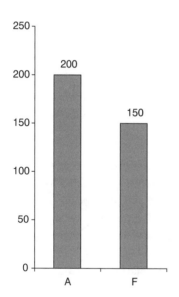

Figure 8.2 *TV channels' evaluation of sports rights*

auctioned. Therefore, the remainder of the chapter will concentrate mainly on these two procedures. Before going into details on the characteristics of them, let us first look at two hypothetical situations that are illustrated in Figures 8.1 and 8.2. Figure 8.1 presents a situation where six different channels (A–F) are bidding. The graphs show the reservation prices for each channel: their maximum willingness to pay (WTP). In Figure 8.2, the number of bidders has been reduced to two, channel A and channel F.

Hypothetically, the two situations can also refer to the same market, but to different points of time. For instance, it could be the case that six channels competed against each other the first time the rights were auctioned, while channels B–E had disappeared the next time, some years later. One reason for this could be that channels B–E had gone bankrupt, while another reason could be that they had merged (into channel F). The following sections will use these two figures as illustrations when discussing the effectiveness of two alternative auction procedures.

English auction

In an *English auction*, the process starts with a (low) bid, which is then raised successively until one bid remains. The winner is the one with the highest bid, and who then pays the price he or she has bid. A player's strategy in the series of bids will be a function of the following factors (Rasmusen, 2001):

- their own evaluation of the item;
- their prior estimate of other bidders' valuations;
- the past bids of all the players.

The dominant strategy in this procedure will be to keep bidding just small amounts more than the previous bid until it reaches one's own valuation, and then to stop. The bidding process ends when the price reaches just above the valuation of the player with the second-highest valuation.

Sellers that are profit- or income-maximisers will try to exploit as much as possible of the highest bidders real evaluation: its reservation price. What is important in an English auction is the gap between the two bidders that have the highest reservation prices. The narrower the gap, the higher the price will be. In an English auction, the dominant strategy will always be to bid slightly above the rival's bid. Hence, this procedure gives a market price of 191 in the former example and 151 in the latter example. It is worth noting that the outcomes from the two auctions are different despite the fact that company A's valuation is identical. This illustrates how important the level of competition is for the auction price.

Revealing information

It is impossible to estimate the income from broadcasting the programmes 100 per cent accurately when the item being auctioned covers a bundle of events that take place some time in the future. The income will be influenced by a number of factors, of which many will be uncertain at the point of time when the bids are submitted. First, there can be unforeseen positive and negative shifts in demand due to fluctuations in the business cycle and the popularity of the sport. In international competitions, the participation (and performance) of competitors and teams from the respective countries will be of importance. There are several examples of where the elimination of certain teams has reduced the commercial value of a tournament in the respective countries severely (Solberg and Hammervold, 2004). The Italian channel, Rai, considered suing FIFA since TV pictures revealed that Italy was eliminated from the 2002 World Cup soccer finals due to a mistake by the assistant referee.[3] Second, there is also the risk of excess supply if too many TV companies broadcast too many similar sport programmes simultaneously. The consequence can be lower rating figures than what was predicted when decisions were made over the value of the rights. Such uncoordinated actions can create severe financial problems due to the high proportion of sunk costs that characterises this industry. These two factors are the major reasons why so many TV companies have been hit by the winner's curse, which is a situation where the winner of an auction is worse off as a consequence of overestimating the value of an item and thereby bidding too much (see Chapter 6). The winner's problem is that he or she realises this too late. Income turns out to be lower than expected, while it is impossible (or at least extremely difficult) to reduce costs.

Since all bidders try to estimate their own valuation of the rights for a specific event, open auction procedures can work to the advantage of the seller, given the right circumstances. Some bidders may have limited information on the revenues that the deal can generate. For them, it can be useful to learn how much the rivals are bidding, which in turn can help them to adjust their initial assessment of the valuation of the rights. Hence, the unveiling (and sharing) of information that is integrated in an English auction can improve abilities to estimate the income potential correctly. This can in itself motivate risk-averse buyers to bid more aggressively.

■ *Case study 8.1* Biathlon wins huge fee increase from TV rivalry

TV Sports Markets, vol. 9, no. 10, by Miriam Sherlock

The International Biathlon Union will receive almost a 500 per cent increase in television rights fees in a four-year deal with the European Broadcasting Union (EBU), the umbrella organisation of public service broadcasters. The deal, covering all international biathlon events from 2006–7 to 2009–10, is worth an overall €40 million (£27.1 million). It renews an existing four-year EBU deal worth €7 million. Under the new deal, like the present one, the EBU will handle the sale and worldwide distribution of the rights. The huge increase in the fee is largely because of a rival bid from the IMG agency for the global rights. There was also strong interest from German commercial broadcaster RTL for the German rights. There might well have been a good increase anyway because, according to one source, the rights were 'massively undervalued in the present deal'. German public service broadcasters ARD and ZDF are the guarantors of the new deal and will shoulder the bulk of the cost, paying at least 50 per cent of the rights fee. The other main EBU biathlon broadcasters are YLE in Finland, NRK in Norway, RTR in Russia, TVR in Belarus and RTV in Slovenia. The sport is particularly popular in Germany because of the success of German stars Sven Fischer, Uschi Disl and Kati Wilhelm. It is a 'very good television property,' according to a senior executive. This is partly because of its range: there are team and individual competitions, and men's, women's and mixed events. There is also strong competition within each event and over the course of a season. Thus, of the 27 events in the 2004–5 World Cup, events were won by 10 different men and 14 different women. Biathlon, according to the executive, also 'gives broadcasters several hours of programming per event and is far less weather dependent than other winter sports such as alpine skiing and ski jumping. The new deal covers the Biathlon World Championships in 2007, 2008 and 2009 and the World Cup, European Championships and European Cup competitions.

Sealed – first bid auction

In this procedure each bidder submits one bid and without having any information on the rivals' bids. The highest bidder acquires the rights. A company's bid will be a function of (Rasmusen, 2001):

- their own valuation;
- their prior beliefs about the rivals' valuations.

Since the bids are kept secret, risk-averse bidders are not provided with the same support to predict the value as in an English auction. This can be a major disadvantage if many sellers are risk averse. Nevertheless, the fact that information about the rivals' bids is kept secret can also work to the seller's advantage, given the right circumstances. This particularly applies to cases when there is a wide gap between the highest and the second highest bids.

Channel A will not be willing to bid more than 151 if it is public knowledge that channel F's reservation price is 150 in Figure 8.2. However, since the bids are kept secret, channel A does not have this information. The seller's challenge is to take advantage of this situation and encourage channel A to bid more than 151. In sealed auctions, the bidder with the highest valuation will face two potential traps. First, the danger is to bid more than necessary. Second, by being too greedy, and bidding too low a price, the bidder will be running the risk of missing out on a deal that could have been profitable. The bidders will have to balance these two contradictory threats when deciding the strategy.

Although the main purpose with bidding in auctions is to win the competition, some bidders might be led by strategic motives. History tells us that the bidders on sports rights over time tend to be the same companies. Until digital technology, no single company had the resources necessary to broadcast all sports programmes, mainly due to limitations on frequencies. Nowadays, this bottleneck is effectively removed due to a manifold extension in transmission capacity in recent years. Nevertheless, it is still unlikely, or at least very rare, that one single broadcaster can afford to acquire the entire range of attractive sports rights, the reason being that this would simply be too expensive.

Under such circumstances, some companies may enter the auction mainly to push up the prices. The reason for this is to weaken the ability of the winner to submit bids on the next occasion a package of sports rights is being auctioned. In the case of sealed bid auctions, it may not even be necessary to submit a bid to achieve this aim. Leaking information that it considers doing so may well be sufficient.

As mentioned earlier, the two Norwegian public service broadcasters, the Norwegian Broadcasting Corporation (NRK) and TV2, competed quite fiercely for sports rights in the late 1990s. One of these incidents was in 1998, when TV2 submitted a very high bid for skiing rights that they knew NRK also was extremely eager to acquire. TV2's main purpose, however, was not to win the contract, but to force their rival to pay the highest possible price in order to weaken NRK's ability to submit an expensive bid on the next occasion sports rights were up for sale. As TV2 rightfully calculated, NRK outbid TV2, but to do so, they were forced to pay a price which was 400 per cent higher than the value of the former deal.[4]

COLLABORATION

Channels that participate regularly in repetitive auctions will learn that bidding wars can be avoided by collaborating. This can avoid a permanent state of a *prisoner's dilemma*, and prevent profit from being transferred to the supply side, or at least reduce the transfer. Indeed, the channels can also establish some sort of tacit agreement where they desist from bidding on specific rights. Although such collaboration is regarded as illegal cartel behaviour, sellers of sports rights as well as competition authorities may find it difficult to prove that potential bidders have collaborated. No one can force anyone to submit bids on all the sports rights that are being auctioned, and it can be very difficult to prove that this is due to illegal collaboration. In addition, many competition authorities across the world have made exceptions where TV companies have been allowed to agree such collusion. As mentioned elsewhere in the book, there are indications that such tacit agreements existed on the Australian market during the 1980s and 1990s.

Collusion between buyers will strengthen their market power as a group at the cost of the seller, assuming it is effective. On the other hand, any reduction in the number of buyers will strengthen the market power of the remaining companies. Even if the cartel member's income increases, this does not guarantee that the collaboration will last forever. Indeed, it is sometimes claimed that the success of a cartel will in itself represent the biggest threat with respect to its duration. The cartel members will balance out the potential advantages and disadvantages against each other when they decide whether to uphold the collusion or not. The benefit from breaking the agreement can come from two sources. First, acquiring the deal solely can increase one's profit, assuming the income from broadcasting exceeds the costs. Second, if one of the rivals goes bankrupt, this will reduce the future competition and hence strengthen the market power of those that survive.

Sellers will do anything to prevent collusion as it reduces their income. Whether they will succeed is also influenced by the auction procedure they choose. In an English auction, all information about the bids will be immediately released. Hence, if one cartel member breaks out from the agreement, the others will discover it immediately. This also creates a disciplinary effect on the members. Thus, sellers who have any fears about buyer collusion should not stage English auctions. This is different in sealed auctions where a surprise bid will not be revealed until the auction is finished (Cowie and Williams, 1997).

On the other hand, breaking out from the collusion can also have long-term negative consequences. The future competition can grow fiercer if the companies who were cheated on survive, and there is also the risk of retaliation. The consequence of this can be a permanent state of bidding wars, and hence a permanent state of the *prisoner's dilemma* (see Chapter 6). Furthermore, by breaking the deal, the confidence between the companies will be reduced, which in turn worsens the climate for colluding on later occasions. The benefits of collusive deals depend on factors such as the prices of inputs and outputs, as well as the level of competition on the supply side. These factors can vary over time and so also will the gains from collusion.

TV channels that offer a narrow menu of programmes will be more vulnerable to losing attractive content. Such conditions can tempt the cartel members (which also are rivals) to break any agreement, as a way of getting rid of troublesome rivals. So far, pay-TV channels have concentrated their activity on acquiring popular sport programmes and films. Relying on such a small menu of programmes can be risky. According to BSkyB's own market surveys, more than 50 per cent of their subscribers would consider cancelling the subscription if it was not for the English Premier League rights (Solberg, 2002a). On the other hand, several pay-TV channels are bundled together with other channels by transmission companies. To some degree, such forms of bundling can outweigh the disadvantages of narrow programme menus on the separate channel. Advertising channels involved in sports broadcasting tend to have a broader menu of programmes. Hence, their entire existence will not be threatened from losing out on a package of sports rights, as can be the case for a pay-TV channel that cannot rely on any other programme genres.

■ *Case study 8.2* UEFA will gain from end of Italian collusion

TV Sports Markets, vol. 9, no. 10, by Frank Dunne

UEFA expects to enjoy a significant increase in the value of the next round of Champions League rights in Italy because the television market is in a period of unusually healthy competition. European soccer's governing body hopes to make up much of the 38 per cent fall in the rights value last time around. The main reasons for the competition are the ending of the strategic alliance – or collusion – between Silvio Berlusconi's Mediaset and Rupert Murdoch's Sky Italia; pressure on state broadcaster Rai to acquire some top soccer after having lost its exclusive World Cup coverage; the emergence of Telecom Italia as a rights player; and the likelihood that two agencies will make a speculative bid for the rights. UEFA's negotiating position for the next deal, from 2006–7 to 2008–9, has also been boosted by the re-emergence of Italian clubs as a force in Europe after a period of several years in the wilderness. AC Milan has contested two of the last three finals. The last deal, from 2003–4 to 2005–6, was negotiated at a time when commercial broadcaster Mediaset and pay-TV platform Sky Italia were in the honeymoon period of their alliance. It was also the first deal after UEFA had reduced the number of matches in the competition by scrapping the second group phase. The two broadcasters made a de facto joint bid – against the rules of the tender – of €59 million a season. With no other broadcaster bidding for the rights, UEFA's marketing agency Team had little option but to accept. In the previous four-year deal, Mediaset paid €95 million a season. The Berlusconi-Murdoch alliance ended abruptly with Mediaset's surprise move on the digital-terrestrial rights for Serie A last year (*TV Sports Markets*, vol. 8, no. 12). Any lingering doubts there may have been that the two companies are now genuine, even bitter, rivals evaporated two weeks ago when Sky's parent company News Corporation lodged a complaint with the European Commission. It complained that the Italian government, led by Berlusconi, has provided illegal state aid to boost the take-up of digital-terrestrial television.

Bidders

Mediaset is thought almost certain to bid for the exclusive rights for all live games, with a view to spreading coverage across its free-to-air channels and its digital-terrestrial service. Sky, too, is thought to be considering a bid for exclusive live rights for all games, even though it does not have a free-to-air outlet of its own (whereas Mediaset, Telecom Italia and Rai have pay and free outlets). Both can expect competition from Rai which, according to director general Flavio Cattaneo, would bid for all rights and would also look to split games between its free-to-air channels and its digital-terrestrial service. Cattaneo came under intense pressure for losing the live rights for 39 games of the 2006 World Cup finals to Sky (*TV Sports Markets*, vol. 9, no. 9). The Champions League rights award last time led to questions being asked in parliament about the lack of a bid from Rai. Rai's critics on the Left suspected that a Rai board answerable to the Berlusconi government had not wanted to compete against Mediaset. So it remains to be seen whether Rai's bid is a genuine, aggressive bid or simply a gesture to appease the critics. Telecom Italia is also considering a bid for its commercial channel La 7 and its digital-terrestrial service. Last time, the company was still a shareholder in Sky and had no strategic interest in bidding separately. Bids are also expected from two Italian agencies which, it is said, want to acquire the rights in a gatekeeper role. One agency is Telecalcio, a joint venture set up by Rodolfo Hecht, founder of Media Partners, and Mario Rasini, former chief executive of Telepiù, the Canal Plus company that merged with Stream to form Sky Italia. The second agency is the Rome-based agency Bianchi and Group. Neither would appear to have much chance of success but their interest could be exploited by Team to force up the price.

Exclusive deal?

Some bidders will bid for all the available packages, but that would go against the spirit of a UEFA agreement with the European Commission in 2003 about the collective selling of the rights. The agreement was designed to open up competition from a range of operators. There are, however, precedents for Team selling all the rights to a single company. It has done so twice with Modern Times Group in Scandinavia – in 2002 and again this year – and it would be prepared to do so with another company in another market if the offer were right.

MINIMUM PRICES

Asking for a *minimum price* represents another instrument for sellers that find themselves in a situation similar to the one in Figure 8.2. If successful, this can keep profit at the supply side that would otherwise have gone to the demand side, in cases when there is a gap between the highest and the second highest willingness to pay (WTP). The minimum price will also be the final price in case there is only one buyer that is willing to submit a bid at least at this level.

However, it cannot be taken for granted that the bidder with the highest evaluation will automatically accept to pay the minimum price. Live sport programmes are perishable goods that cannot be stored (Gaustad, 2000). Once a competition is over and the result known, the commercial value of TV programmes drops considerably. This is a situation that both the seller and the buyer with the highest valuation will be aware of, which in turn can result in a *chicken* game between them. See Chapter 6 for more details about the chicken situation.

The example in Figure 8.2 contains some of these elements. To illustrate the main aspects, let us imagine that a package of sports rights is being auctioned, and that one of the bidders has a reservation price that is considerably higher than any other. For the case of simplicity, we assume that the broadcasting of the programmes will generate an profit of 200.

Moreover, we assume that the seller and the bidder can only adopt two alternative strategies. We call the first alternative the *tough strategy*. Anyone following this strategy is absolutely unwilling to admit any concession to the other party. A seller will not accept anything less than the minimum price, while a buyer will refuse to pay the minimum price. In contrast, a seller adopting the *soft* strategy can accept a bid lower than the minimum price, while a buyer who follows the *soft* strategy can be willing to pay the minimum price (or even more).

Table 8.3 shows the pay-off matrix in the four alternative solutions. The figures to the left represent the buyer's pay-off, while the seller's pay-offs are to the right. In the 'upper-left' window, both adopt the soft strategy, which gives each of them a pay-off of 100. In the 'down-left' window, the buyer follows the tough strategy while the seller has adopted a soft strategy. This solution gives the buyer a surplus of 150, and the seller a surplus of 50. In the 'up-right' window the buyer adopts a soft strategy and the seller a tough strategy. The pay-off matrix is 100 per cent symmetrical so that the seller now makes a surplus of 50, while the buyer will obtain 150.

In the fourth alternative, both follow a tough strategy. The seller sets the minimum price above the level that the buyer is willing to pay, and neither of them is willing to give any concessions. As the table shows, the result of being too stubborn can be that no deal is agreed, with the result that the seller and the buyer give away the opportunity of sharing a profit of 200.

The situation described in Table 8.3 can now turn in to a negotiation process between the two, where both try to agree a deal that is as favourable for themselves as possible. The fact that the production and the consumption of live sports programmes have to take place simultaneously puts a pressure on them to agree a deal before the competition takes place. No deal is identical with the 'down-

■ **Table 8.3** Seller and highest bidder playing (Chicken)

		Seller	
		Soft	Tough
Buyer	Soft	100, 100	50, 150
	Tough	150, 50	0, 0

right' window, which gives no profit. However, if one of the actors is more capable of doing without the profit than the other, it might be tempting to adopt a 'wait and see' strategy, hoping it will persuade the other actor to adopt a soft strategy. In general, the one that has the strongest financial base will be more capable of surviving without the profit. This, of course, would represent an advantage if the actors enter into any negotiation.

Furthermore, whether or not the actors have other alternatives will also influence their willingness to compromise. A channel that alternatively can broadcast other profitable programmes might be unwilling to alter its strategy. On the other hand, some sports programmes are difficult (or impossible) to replace with other programmes. The World Cup soccer finals cannot be replaced by just some other soccer matches. A title match in heavy weight boxing cannot be replaced by just another boxing match.

Table 8.3 contains two *Nash solutions*, namely the 'down-left' and the 'up-right' windows. This means that none of the actors will regret their decisions once either of these two solutions has been established. Ideally, the buyer will prefer the 'down-left' solution, while the seller will prefer the 'up-right' solution. However, both of them will accept the opposite solution, once it is established. In the 'up-right' solution, the buyer's pay-off will be reduced from 50 to 0 if he alters his strategy. Hence, the optimal choice is to follow the soft strategy, assuming the seller continues following the tough strategy. The same picture characterises the behaviour of the buyer in the 'down-left' solution.

The pay-off matrix in Table 8.3 presents a coordination problem scenario that can be quite realistic on some occasions. The total profit can be substantial if the seller and the buyer manage to agree a deal. At the same time, the result can be disastrous if they are too greedy and unable to admit the concessions necessary to find a solution.

Sellers of sports rights also receive other revenues, of which some might be influenced by TV promotion. Sponsorship deals are worth more the more attention the event receives in the media. This can put pressure on the event organiser to sell the rights a long time before the event, and also to prefer channels with the highest penetration.

The effects on gate receipts, however, can be both positive and negative. Some (potential) spectators may stay at home instead of going to the game if the event is on TV, particularly when on a free-to-air channel. This can represent a double edged sword for the TV channel since the quality of live programmes are best with sold-out stadiums and a lively audience. On the other hand, the promotion effect created by TV broadcasting can increase attendances, particularly events of long duration. The net effect will depend on the strength of these two effects.

At the start of the twenty-first century, TV channels and transmission companies have recently invested heavily in the digital technology, or in the process of doing so. Such investments are extremely expensive and can be regarded as sunk costs.

The only way of making them profitable is by offering content that the viewers and advertisers are willing to pay for. Since sports programmes attract high rating figures, TV companies often find themselves compelled to continue bidding for sports rights. This can, at least to some degree, help sports that otherwise would have been lagging behind in the competition for financial resources.

REVENUE SHARING

As mentioned above, the list of factors that influence the profitability of sports rights is long. Some of them can vary substantially over time and hence cause severe fluctuations in the rating figures (and income). Thus, it is no surprise that a number of companies have been hit by the *winner's curse* and suffered substantial financial losses on unprofitable deals. Many deals endure over several years, and some of them are even sold before the participants have qualified. Some are also sold before it is decided where the event will take place. Such procedures add further to the risk, since differences in time zones can influence the value of advertising slots substantially.

If the competition is fierce, the buyers may also have to accept bundles where the popularity of the specific products varies considerably. As an example, many European TV companies acquired the 2006 World Cup soccer rights, together with the 2002 tournament, before Germany was elected as the host nation. Since year 2000, the Olympic rights have been sold in bundles. The 2000–8 Games were sold before the host of the 2006 and 2008 Games were selected, a pattern that also partly applied to the sale of the 2010 and 2012 Games.

In addition, unforeseen negative shifts in the demand from viewers and advertisers may also occur. The so-called *September eleven effect*, as an example, severely reduced advertising in connection with sports broadcasting, particularly in North America. Hence, the channels acquiring expensive long-term deals would be running a high risk if the fees were fixed. Such conditions can reduce the number of bidders, particularly those that are risk averse.

For the buyers, the risk will come from two sources. First, there is the risk of losing out on deals that could have been profitable, which will motivate risk-averse bidders to bid more aggressively. Secondly, there is the risk related to the income, which is due to factors that have been discussed throughout this book. This latter element will have the opposite effect and can reduce the bids considerably in case there is a very high degree of risk, or if a high degree of risk aversion exists among the bidders. If so, the seller might benefit from accepting deals where it shares the risk with the winning bidder. One alternative could be to agree a *royalty fee* that ties the price (partly or totally) to the income from broadcasting the programmes. Indeed, such clauses were agreed for some of the US Olympic deals late in the 1980s and the 1990s (McMillan, 1991), which also applies to more recent deals. When NBC sold more than $615 million in advertising for the 1996 Atlanta Games, a 50:50 revenue sharing arrangement automatically kicked in, netting the IOC an additional $36 million (Slater, 1998).

An alternative to fixed fees is *revenue sharing* (royalty fees) that ties fees to the income from broadcasting the programmes. The principle is illustrated in the equation below, where the price is split into a fixed fee, P_0, and a royalty fee, $a(R - C - P_0)$, which is a proportion of the profit from broadcasting the programme. The equation only includes costs and income directly connected to the programme. Such an agreement will share the risk between the seller and the buyer, contrary to fixed fees where the buyer bears the entire risk alone.

$$P = P_0 + a(R - C - P_0) \tag{8.1}$$

where
P_0 = fixed fee
R = gross income from broadcasting the programmes
C = realised production- and broadcasting costs
a = sharing parameter, i.e. the proportion of the broadcasting channel's net surplus $(R - C - P_0)$ that the seller receives

The equation illustrates that the seller can choose from the following three alternatives when asking for bids (McAfee and McMillan, 1987):

1   Set the royalty rate, a, and call for bids on P_0, the fixed fee.
2   Set the fixed payment P_0, and call for bids on the royalty rate, a.
3   Call for bids on both the fixed payment P_0 and the royalty rate a simultaneously.

The effectiveness of the three alternatives depends much on the attitudes towards risk. If buyers are risk averse, this is an argument for increasing the proportion from the royalty fees, in other words increasing a. Risk-averse bidders will be willing to pay more in return for being sheltered from risk, in effect incorporating an insurance premium in their bids. Hence, they will bid higher in the less risky case of revenue sharing than in the fixed-price case, when the winner bears all of the risk.

Furthermore, royalty fees also reduce the inherent differences among the bidders. In that way it strengthens the competitive pressure that bidders with relatively low estimates of the value of winning can put on bidders with high estimates of the value of winning. This can increase the total payments by the winning bidder. The smaller the differences in the valuations of winning between the bidders, the more aggressive the bidding will be. These two effects can work to the seller's advantage because they raise their share of the revenue. As a rule of thumb, the more risk averse the bidders are, relative to the seller, then the higher is the optimal royalty rate (McAfee and McMillan, 1987).

On the other hand, revenue sharing agreements can also cause situations of *asymmetric information*, which in these cases are *moral hazard problems* where the seller cannot control all the actions of the winning bidder afterwards. If the sharing parameter, a, increases, this reduces the buyer's motives for any ex-post sales efforts. Hence, royalty fees can diminish the total income that is to be shared between the seller and the winning channel. Indeed, if $a = 1$, the seller will receive the entire extra income, which totally eliminates the seller's motive to pursue any ex-post sales efforts.

Another example of a moral hazard effect relates to the measurement of the fee. It is the income and costs from broadcasting the programme that decides the fee. Since the TV company has more accurate information on these variables than the seller, it is in a position where it can manipulate information to its own advantage by underreporting the income and exaggerating the costs. Although some information will be available to the general public, for instance rating figures, this does not apply to all the variables. Information on discounts and special agreements with advertisers are usually treated with confidentiality.

The optimal revenue-sharing rate from the seller's point of view is determined by balancing these three factors, namely increased competition, reduced risk and weakened incentives that revenue-sharing induces.

Indirect revenues are usually left out from the basis on which royalty fees are calculated. Although the buyer might be willing to include it, the seller will nevertheless find it difficult to measure and control its actual value. As for the general royalty fees, the buyer will be able to manipulate the value when reporting to the seller.

Indeed, this is another moral hazard situation. The TV channel will gain from reducing the revenue-sharing proportion. As an example, it can offer sports programmes cheaply to viewers that are willing to subscribe on long-term deals. Such a policy might be unprofitable, judged purely on bases of the direct revenues and costs. Nevertheless, it may well pay off on a long-term basis if it attracts a sufficient number of subscribers.

A similar policy can be applied towards advertisers, for example by offering discounts on advertising slots connected to the sports programmes, assuming the advertisers are willing to agree long-term deals on other programmes. The rationale behind such agreements is to take a calculated short-term loss, hoping this can be outbalanced by a future pay-off. Sellers of sports rights often find it difficult to find out information about such strategies.

As a conclusion, neither *minimum prices* nor *royalty fees* guarantee sellers of sports rights the same rights fees as when there is a fierce competition on the demand side. Nevertheless, these two instruments can reduce the transfer of profit from the supply side to the demand side, given the right circumstances.

Finally, we turn to the other two auction procedures, *Dutch auction* and *sealed bid – second price auction*. To our knowledge, neither of these two alternatives has so far been adopted by sellers of sports rights. Nevertheless, there is still a possibility that they could become more popular in the future. In the *Dutch auction*, the auctioneer starts with announcing a bid that is expected to be higher than anyone assesses the item to be worth. Then the asking price is continuously lowered until some buyer stops the process and agrees to pay that price. When to submit a bid will be a function of:

- one's own valuation;
- prior beliefs of the rivals' valuations.

When the price called by the auctioneer is above your own valuation, let us call it X, you choose not to bid. If no one has bid by the time the price gets down to X, you may choose to do so. However, the channel has two options. It can bid now and get zero profit, or it can wait for the price to drop lower. Waiting a bit longer can increase the profit, but it also increases the risk of losing the rights to a rival. Indeed, this is the same dilemma as in *first cry – sealed bids* auctions, being greedy and risk losing profitable deals or bidding quickly and risk leaving money on the table. This procedure does not produce any information as it does not allow anybody to observe the rival bids, as is the case in an English auction.

In *second cry – sealed bids* auctions each bidder submits only one bid, the highest bidder pays the amount of the second-highest bid and wins. As in the former procedure, the player's bid will be a function of his value and prior belief about other players' valuations. The major difference, however, is that the final price is influenced by the competitors bid, not by the winner. By bidding high, the channel can win the rights, but what it will have to pay is out of its control. The dominant strategy will always be to bid one's valuation. Truthful bidding is never worse and sometimes better than bidding either above or below one's true valuation. In other words, no matter what the rivals bid, it is always in one's best interest to be truthful. Hence, bidding one's true valuation is the dominant strategy. This procedure is well known for its ability to make the bidders reveal their true valuation. However, to our knowledge, it has not been used when auctioning sports rights.

Chapter 9

Market intervention in sports broadcasting

This chapter will focus on direct regulations in sports broadcasting that regulate which channels are allowed to broadcast specific events. Examples of such regulations are the European Listed Events and the Australian Anti-Siphoning List, which prevent pay-TV channels from broadcasting events that are of special value for society. First, it discusses the welfare economic rationale behind such regulations. On the basis of this, it then provides a thorough analysis of the European and Australian regulations.

The book has given substantial attention to factors that influence the market value of sports rights. Although it has not been defined precisely, these analyses have assumed some form of private ownership of the rights. In some cases the owner has been the local event organiser, in other cases a sport association or other sport governing bodies, for example the International Olympic Committee (IOC). However, as mentioned elsewhere in this book, there have been several juridical disagreements regarding the ownership issue.

The opposite of private ownership is when a product belongs to the public domain. This means that everybody in society can use it free of charge. Public parks and street lights are examples of such goods. If a sporting event is regarded as a property in the public domain, this means that any TV channel can broadcast it and without having to pay any broadcast rights fees. If an event is not in the public domain the owner can prevent any TV channel broadcasting it unless they pay a fee. Another alternative is to allow the broadcasting of some highlights of the event free of charge in news programmes.

In Europe, the ownership of sporting events did not cause any disagreements between event organisers, sport governing bodies and the media until the mid-1980s. The climate between these actors was peaceful, and there were few controversies regarding sale procedures and ownership issues. This, however, came to an end when the broadcasting markets were deregulated and market forces took over. Gradually, more actors involved in sports broadcasting also became aware of income generating potential. It is this awareness that has paved the way for the enormous value increase on sports rights fees. A similar development has taken place in other markets across the whole world with the exception of Africa, although with some differences in the timing.

The prospect of making income from sports broadcasting, directly and indirectly, has stimulated the actors involved to pay more attention to the ownership issue than before when sports rights were not treated as commodities. This development towards more commercialisation has also created a different climate where judicial disagreements have become quite common. Nowadays, all companies that want to broadcast attractive sporting events must be prepared to pay a fee.

This development, however, has not reduced the amount of TV sport compared to some years ago. Indeed, statistics reveal that never before has there been so much sport on TV, on free-to-air channels as well as on other platforms. What has raised concerns among politicians is not the total amount of TV sport, but fears that some special popular events that traditionally have been available for everyone should migrate to pay-TV channels that only a small proportion of the population can watch. This applies to events such as the Olympic Games and World Cup soccer finals, which traditionally have been broadcast on free-to-air channels. The ability to watch such events without having to pay any extra fees has traditionally belonged to the public domain.

The development where market forces move such events away from free-to-air channels to pay-TV channels also reduce the amount of goods that belong to the public domain. In that way, it can be regarded as a cost for society, as it reduces welfare. The objective of regulations such as the Listed Events and the Anti Siphoning is to move sporting events back to the public domain sphere. On the other hand, any regulations that regulate the ability to keep sporting events out of the public domain sphere reduce the owner's ability to make a profit. As a rule of thumb, the higher degree of the public domain, the lower the commercial value of the ownership will be. A high degree of public domain reduces sellers' freedom to exploit the commercial value of the product. The negative relationship is illustrated in Figure 9.1. A regime of strict juridical protection improves the owner's ability to make profit from the product. This means that he or she can sell it to the highest bidder in the case of an auction.

The figure illustrates a static relationship. Such a relationship might be correct on a short-term perspective, but not necessarily on a long-term basis. Owning the broadcasting rights to an event also provides the owner with the motive to increase its commercial value. As discussed in Chapter 4, a profit or income maximising channel will gain from improving the quality as long as marginal revenues from these efforts exceed the marginal costs. This can stimulate the owner to improve the quality of the product. Hence, private ownership can provide the public with more products of better quality than if it belongs to the public domain.

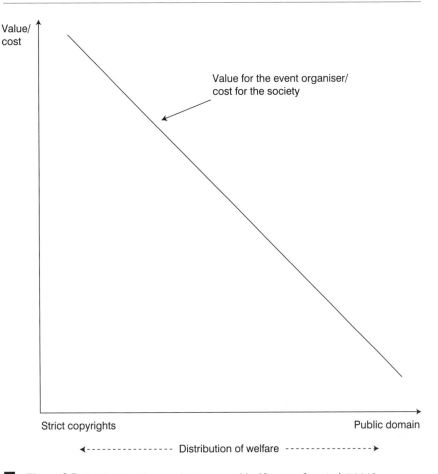

■ **Figure 9.1** *Public domain vs. private ownership (Source: Gaustad, 2006)*

Throughout the 1990s, the growth of pay-TV channels raised concerns regarding the general public's ability to watch popular sport. European politicians were alarmed in 1996 when News Corporation almost bid the Olympic Rights away from the European Broadcasting Union (EBU). Their fear received more fuel when FIFA, the same year, sold the 2002 and 2006 World Cup Soccer finals to the German Kirch corporation and the Swiss ISL marketing agency, instead of to the EBU as they had done in the past. As a consequence of this, viewers in many nations would not be able to watch the entire tournament on free-to-air broadcasters as in the past. In 2005, the EBU lost the rights for Euro 2008 to Sportfive, a media agency, for a fee of more than €600 million.[1] Whether a part of this tournament will be shown exclusively on pay-TV channels remains to be seen. As mentioned elsewhere in this book, live matches in European premier soccer leagues have mainly been broadcast exclusively on pay-TV channels since the late 1990s. In general, free-to-air channels have been restricted to showing highlight programmes. In Australia the growth of pay-TV channels in the 1990s caused a fear of a similar development, so that people in general not would be able to watch their favourite sports on free-to-air TV.

A consequence of this development is that governments on the two continents have invented regulations that define sports programmes as a part of the public domain. Late in the 1990s so-called *Listed Events regulations* were established in several European countries, while the *Australian Anti-siphoning List* was launched in the mid-1990s. Before going into details on these two regulations, we will first discuss the theoretical rationale behind such interventions in sport broadcasting.

Welfare economic theory of broadcasting regulations identifies three sources of market failures that can legitimise any governmental intervention:

- public goods;
- merit goods;
- externalities.

These aspects have already been discussed in Chapter 3 in connection to the content regulation of *public service broadcasters*. This chapter will only concentrate on direct interventions in sports broadcasting. However, some similarities can be found in these two chapters, since the rationale are based on the same principles.

PUBLIC GOODS

Pure public goods have already been defined as goods that are characterised by the *non-rival* and *non-excludability* criteria, of which the reception of TV signals satisfies the former criterion. According to welfare economics, charging for television programmes introduces inefficiency, because the fee deters people from watching even though the resource cost of their viewing would be zero. Hence any positive prices on programmes will generate *market failures* in terms of *efficiency losses*. This principle is not confined to sports programmes, however, but to any category of programme. The high degree of first-copy costs that characterises such media products is another welfare economic rationale for making the programmes available for large audiences. Programming costs are independent of the number of markets the programmes are transmitted to. The same applies to the number of viewers within these markets.

MERIT GOODS AND EXTERNALITIES

The concept of *merit goods* was first introduced by Musgrave (1958) and has since been developed and interpreted by Head (1974), who defined them as: 'goods that individuals would choose to consume too little of due to imperfect knowledge'. Merit goods could arise because some individuals have imperfect knowledge and information of the consequences of their actions on their welfare. Pozner (1972) extends Head's definition and also includes 'unaccounted-for externalities' as another feature of merit goods. According to Pozner, the main rationales of merit goods could arise because some individuals have imperfect knowledge and information of the consequences of either of the two alternatives:

- a person's actions on his or her welfare;
- actions taken by other individuals on his or her own welfare, i.e. unaccounted-for-externalities.

Since merit goods are beneficial for the entire society, there is also a welfare economic rationale for governments to intervene in the market and correct this situation so that the consumption and production of merit goods is encouraged. The welfare implication of such information is that the individual cannot be left alone to judge of what is 'good' or 'bad' for him or her. This is based on a paternalistic philosophy that governments know better than the consumer themselves what is best for them. Traditional examples of merit goods are cultural goods, for example public sculptures and opera concerts.

Such impacts are also generated by sporting activities, including sports broadcasting. For example, exercising is good for people's health. Staying more healthy and living longer improves quality of life.

Although such associations are obvious, many of us do not take them (sufficiently) into consideration when we decide how much to exercise. This can be due to lack of knowledge about the positive impacts. Another reason can be lack of opportunities. In addition, it can also be equity related. Some people may not be able to afford to exercise as much as they would like to if swimming pools and sports centres adopt a pricing policy based on profit or income maximising. These examples represent a rationale for governmental intervention, for instance by subsidising sports activities and promotion of sports.

Such objectives can also be achieved by sports broadcasting, for example if the broadcasting of sporting events can stimulate people to exercise. If so, this also represents a rationale for market intervention. First, by ensuring that the events are broadcast on TV, and second, that they are broadcast on channels with the highest possible penetration. Hence, more people will be stimulated than if the events were only broadcast on pay-TV channels that maybe only 20 per cent of the population can watch. Moreover, the fact that people have different tastes could represent a welfare economic rationale for presenting a diversity of TV sports and events.

Another example is enhanced pride and self-esteem that people enjoy when national competitors have successes in international competitions. Common enjoyment of international success in sporting events might strengthen people's feeling of having national identity. Although we are not aware of any surveys, we nevertheless believe that many Greeks became more proud of being a Greek after they won the 2004 European Championship in soccer. Such achievements can create a festival atmosphere and a state of celebration, which is a well-known phenomenon across the whole world. According to reports in the media, more than 750,000 people lined the route of the city parade when Liverpool Football Club returned after winning the final of the 2005 UEFA Champions League.[2] However, these effects are not confined to the nations that win medals in international contests. For example, when Jamaica qualified for the World Cup soccer finals in France in 1998, the government declared the following day a national day of celebration, and most employees were given a day off work.

Externalities are usually referred to as the result of an activity that causes incidental benefits or costs to others with no corresponding compensation provided or paid by those who generate the externality. The costs or benefits are not included in the supply price or the demand price and hence are not in the market price. What makes it a problem is the lack of motives to incorporate these consequences when they decide how much to do of the actions that cause externalities. The pollution caused by each and every driver of a motor car is minor. Therefore, it would not make any difference if one or only a few drivers decided to take the bus instead. However, if this is the judgement of all potential car drivers then this is the mechanism that can make pollution a problem for society.

Sports broadcasting can generate externalities in several ways, directly and indirectly. As already mentioned, it can encourage people to exercise. This will benefit the whole of society if it reduces absenteeism from work, which in turn will increase overall production in society and hence make more goods and services available. Similar to the effects from pollution, this also increases the number of goods and services that are available for those who are stimulated to exercise. Furthermore, if more people stay healthy, they are less likely to infect others.

The merit-goods aspect related to celebrating the achievements of national competitors in international championships can also generate externalities. People in general will regard it to be a value of its own to be able to share the pleasure with someone else. Indeed, the 'common sharing' element is usually a part of the celebration and the atmosphere that exists under such circumstances. Having a party completely alone is not much value. A state of national celebration will require that a large number of people to follow the event on TV. The possibility will be reduced if only a minority of the people have the ability to watch the channels that broadcast it. Furthermore, a state of national celebration also requires that the sport and the event really enjoy a widespread recognition by the general public. Hence, guaranteeing that everybody has access to TV programmes from the event represents a prerequisite for such effects to occur. Such impacts also have a momentum dimension. The fact that people enjoy the experience at the same time, for example watching it live on TV, will strengthen the impacts compared to if people only could read about it in newspapers the day after. There are no doubts that the effects can be stronger if each and every one of us is able to watch it live on TV.

These kinds of impacts also fall into the category of *pure public goods*. It is impossible to exclude someone from feeling pride and enjoy the successes of national participants in international competitions. Moreover, the fact that one person is feeling pride does not reduce the possibility for others from enjoying the same (that is the benefit is non-rival). Boardman and Hargreaves Heap (1999) identify a different sort of externality, namely that the broadcasting of popular events might stimulate conversation, so that people have a broader platform for initiating conversations with strangers.

The migration of popular sporting events to pay-TV channels represents a disadvantage for those who cannot afford to subscribe to these channels. Thus, a concern with equity also provides a reason for government intervention. However, the equity argument is insufficient as a single argument for a governmental intervention, since unequal income distribution influences people's ability to purchase all sorts of goods. The sports programmes themselves really must be so important that they should be provided for people who cannot afford to subscribe to channels with restricted penetration.

It will be difficult or impossible to achieve the optimal production level of sport programmes that generate externalities and merit goods without any market regulation. Profit maximising advertising channels will always prioritise sports and events that attract the interest from mass audience. Pay-TV channels will base their activity on programmes that a sufficient number of viewers are willing to pay to watch. Hence, commercial channels always have a motive to undermine the impacts we have discussed above, that relate to merit goods, externalities and public good aspects.

Figure 9.2 illustrates the market failures (efficiency losses) that can occur from charging the viewers of TV sports programmes. The inefficiency that is due to the charging of *public goods* is identical to the triangle $Q_1 ab$. The costs of delivering programmes beyond this level are zero, while the channel charges a fee so that the consumption of programmes is Q_1. This fee drives a gap between the cost of delivering and consumers' assessment of the programmes. Beyond the Q_1 level, additional viewers evaluate the programme higher than the costs of offering it, which indeed is zero on a short-term perspective.

The aggregate demand curve in the figure, $\sum WTP_i$, is summated vertically. This means that it comes from the summation of each and every viewer's individual demand curve. Individual 2's demand curve is put on top of individual 1's demand curve, while individual 3's demand curve is put on top of individual 1 and 2's aggregate demand curve, and so on. The aggregate demand curve, $\sum WTP_i$ is derived by adding the individual demand curves on top of each other.

This principle for deriving the demand curve is different from how the demand curve for private goods is derived, which is based on horizontal summation. The

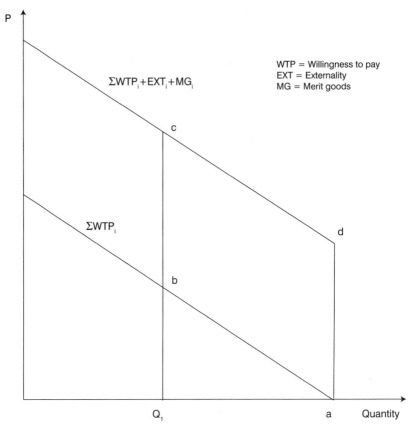

Figure 9.2 *Dead weight loss from charging the viewers*

reason for this is that a private good is of a nature where it is exclusive. This means it can only be consumed by one person. If one person drinks a bottle of Coke, no one else can drink the same bottle. Contrary to this, a pure public good can be consumed by many people simultaneously. Everybody can share it without damaging each other's possibility of consuming the same good. Hence, to assess the value that the consumption of a public good has for society requires that each and every consumer's value is included in the assessment. The principle is in accordance with guidelines from welfare economic theory. The reason for this is the non-rival criterion, which means that a TV viewer does not reduce the ability of others to watch the same programme.

The upper aggregate curve in Figure 9.2, $\Sigma WTP_i + EXT_i + MG_i$, also includes *externalities* and *merit goods*. Hence it covers the total benefits that the programme creates. If the TV company charges the viewers a fee so that the quantity is Q_1, the efficiency loss that will only accrue to the charging of merit goods and externalities is represented by *badc*. The total efficiency loss is identical to the area $Q_1 adc$, which is the two efficiency loss areas added together. This is the loss for society from charging viewers. The measurement of the value of externalities and merit goods is based on vertical summation. This is because both of them have public good characteristics.

THE EUROPEAN LISTED EVENTS REGULATION

In Europe, Listed Events was first introduced as a national regulation in the UK in 1990. It prevented certain sporting events from being shown exclusively on a pay-per-view basis, whilst allowing the events to be shown on non-terrestrial subscription channels. Later the regulation was tightened in the Broadcasting Act 1996, which extended the prohibition from pay-per-view to subscription channels, but without changing the list of events (Cowie and Williams, 1997). The idea was later adopted by the European Commission in the 'Television Without Frontiers' Directive 97/36. The principle in the directive is that each member state can draw up a list of events, national or non-national, that it considers being of major importance for the society. These events should only be allowed to be broadcast on channels with a minimum penetration decided in the respective nations. Among the nations that had passed their own list by 2005 were Austria, France, Germany, Ireland, Italy and the UK, whilst regulations were on their way in other countries. Denmark was among the first nations to invent a list, but withdrew it in 2002. The minimum penetration that is required to be allowed to broadcast events that are on the list varies. The UK requires that channels to have a minimum penetration of 95 per cent, Ireland and Italy 90 per cent, France 85 per cent, Austria 70 per cent, and Germany 67 per cent.

THE AUSTRALIAN ANTI-SIPHONING LIST

The Australian Anti-Siphoning List, which is contained in section 115 of the *Broadcasting Services Act 1992*, empowers the Minister for Communications, Information Technology and the Arts to list in a formal notice what should be available on free-to-air television for viewing by the general public. The first list was gazetted in the Broadcasting Services (Events) Notice No. 1 of 1994. According to the guidelines, its purpose is to protect the access of Australian viewers to events of national importance and cultural significance on free-to-air television by preventing pay-TV operators from siphoning off television coverage of those events before free-to-air broadcasters have had an opportunity to obtain the broadcasting rights. Free-to-air television providers include national broadcasters such as the Australian Broadcasting Corporation (ABC) or Special Broadcasting Services (SBS), as well as the commercial channels, Channel 7, Channel 9 and Channel 10, which can all be watched by the majority of the viewers.

The channels that are allowed to broadcast events on the Anti-Siphoning List must have a minimum penetration of 50 per cent of Australian TV households. Less than one in four Australian households had access to subscription television in 2004. This regulation also allows events to be de-listed if no free-to-air broadcaster is interested in acquiring the broadcast rights, which would allow pay-TV broadcasters to broadcast the event. However, the Anti-Siphoning list is not a list of sporting events reserved solely for free-to-air channels. It does not guarantee them exclusive rights to such events. Pay-TV channels are allowed to acquire such rights, but not exclusively as they also must be held by free-to-air channels that meet the 50 per cent requirement. Furthermore, the regulation does not compel free-to-air broadcasters to acquire the rights to listed events. Neither does it compel them to broadcast events to which they hold rights.

The anti-siphoning provisions were amended in 2001 to allow the automatic de-listing of specified events 1,008 hours (six weeks) before the start of the event. Later, the period has been extended to 2,016 hours (or 12 weeks). The reason for this amendment was to provide adequate time for free-to-air broadcasters to negotiate broadcast rights, whilst at the same time providing a timely window prior to the event, for pay-TV licensees to acquire and promote an event, if a free-to-air broadcaster does not acquire the broadcasting rights.

A comparison between the European and Australian regulations reveals similarities as well as differences. First, the Australian regulation is the most comprehensive of the two. The threshold for being listed is lower than in Europe. As an example, all matches in Australian Rules Football and Rugby League are listed. The equivalence of this would be that the UK Listed Event covered the entire matches in the English Premier League and Rugby Super League; the German list covering all Bundesliga matches as well as domestic leagues in handball; the Italian list covering all Seria A matches and all matches in the domestic leagues in basketball. However, such a pattern is not found in Europe. Indeed, no nation has listed matches in domestic premier leagues, in soccer or in any other team sports. This partly explains why European pay-TV channels have acquired a dominating position in soccer.

As another example, the Anti-Siphoning List includes the Commonwealth Games while the UK regulation has them only on the B-list. This allows pay-TV channels to broadcast live programmes as long as free-to-air channels broadcast delayed highlights. Furthermore, the Anti-Siphoning List covers the entire FIFA's World Cup finals, despite the fact that soccer has a significantly weaker position relative to other sports in Australia than in Europe. Before the 2006 World Cup Soccer finals,, Australia had qualified for the tournament only once, which was the 1974 tournament in West Germany. With the exception of the UK, the European lists only cover the matches of the respective nations and the final, while Germany and Austria also include the opening match and the semi-finals. The Anti-Siphoning List also includes the English FA Cup final, while neither of the European lists covers any foreign cup finals.

The comprehensiveness of the Australian list leaves the impression that the major concerns have been the entertainment aspect and the inefficiency from charging for public goods. This is underpinned by the following statement of the Minister for Communications, Information Technology and the Arts[3]:

> For many Australians, knowing that they can switch on their free-to-air television and watch a football grand final or a Test match is as important as having free access to Australian-made drama or a daily news bulletin.

Hence, preventing efficiency losses that occur from the charging for public goods, such as the triangle identical to Q_1ab in Figure 9.2, seems to be a major rationale behind the Australian regulation.

This is different in the 'European Television Without Frontiers' Directive where the guidelines concentrate more on market failures related to *externalities* and *merit goods*, and not the efficiency loss from charging for public goods. The legitimising of the Austrian list uses the phrase: 'event that is an expression of Austria's cultural, artistic or social identity'. Likewise, the Italian list uses the phrase: 'events that have a particular cultural significance and strengthen the Italian cultural identity'. Furthermore, the UK regulation declares that: 'the event must have a *special national resonance*, not simply of significance to those who ordinarily follow the sport concerned, and is an event that serves to unite the nation; a shared point in the national calendar'. These formulations indicate that the main purpose was not to protect sports fans from being charged when watching their favourite soccer club on TV.

Neither the *Listed Events* nor the *Anti-Siphoning List* indicate that concerns for impact that could improve the health conditions of residents. However, even if such aspects are not mentioned in the regulations they still represent a welfare economic rationale that can support market interventions on such a basis. The fact that Europeans and Australian politicians have not emphasised such effects does not eliminate the welfare economic rationale that exists to stimulate such effects.

Furthermore, it is also worth noting that neither of the two regulations provides any arguments for obtaining a diversity of TV sports. As an example, such ambitions could oblige TV channels to prioritise sports that are popular among minority groups, for instance groups of immigrants.

The fact that the regulations regulate entry to the market also reduces the level of competition. This, in turn, influences the price level compared to a totally unregulated market with free entry and exit. The Anti-Siphoning List does not prevent pay-TV channels acquiring the listed events. However, the fact that pay-TV channels are prohibited from acquiring the rights exclusively reduces their willingness to pay.

Therefore, the regulations have not received overwhelming support from owners of sports rights. The same applies to pay-TV channels, since these are the ones that are hit by the regulations. Contrary to this, free-to-air channels seem to have been more than happy with the regulations, which of course is no surprise as it protects them from competition.

There is a risk that such regulations can end up serving TV channels instead of viewers. It is worth noting that the Anti-Siphoning List covers sports events that that historically have never received free-to-air coverage (Test Match cricket played outside Australia), as well as all events of many sports that historically had only received limited free-to-air coverage (every match of every round in the National Rugby League). In addition, it has also included events that not could be justified as events of national significance (Hong Kong Sevens, Non-Australian matches of all major sports).[4] In 2002, the regulation protected more than 6,400 hours of sports events for free-to-air broadcast. In 2003, however, less than 17 per cent of those hours of events were broadcast live on free-to-air TV, and more than 75 per cent of those hours were not broadcast at all on a free-to-air channel.[5] These examples illustrate the risk of including too many events in such regulations. Similar examples can be found in European markets.

Finally, it also has to be considered critically which TV channels should be allowed to broadcast such events. That is, the minimum penetration required by TV channels to be allowed to broadcast events that are listed. The UK regulation requires 95 per cent and the Irish and Italian 90 per cent. Likewise, other European lists that are suggested, but not yet passed, have similar minimum levels. Table 9.1 presents the most popular TV programmes in some European countries in 2000 and the respective rating figures. The table shows that sports programmes made a considerable impact and accounted for nine of the 16 programmes. The rating figures are only based on measurements of households and hence do not include people who are watching programmes in pubs, restaurants and other public places.

■ **Table 9.1** *Top programmes in European countries, 2000*

Country	Programme	Rating
Austria	News programme	28.4
Belgium	Euro-2000 soccer finals: Belgium vs. Italy	33.8
Denmark	Fiction	32.0
Finland	Documentary	43.0
France	Euro-2000 soccer finals: France vs. Italy (final)	41.7
Germany	Euro-2000 soccer finals: France vs. Italy (final)	25.6
Greece	UEFA CL-match: Man. United vs. Panathinaikos	20.8
Ireland	Game show	35.9
Italy	Euro-2000 soccer finals: France vs. Italy (final)	38.5
Netherlands	Euro-2000 soccer finals: Italy vs. Netherlands (semi-final)	50.0
Norway	Euro-2000 soccer finals: Norway vs. Yugoslavia	46.6
Portugal	Euro-2000 soccer finals: France vs. Portugal	33.9
Spain	UEFA CL-final: Real Madrid vs. Valencia	30.1
Sweden	Entertainment	49.3
Switzerland	News programme	33.2
UK	Soap	33.7

Source: Solberg (2002b)

■ **Table 9.2** *European Listed Events (2005)*

Austria
Summer and Winter Olympics
FIFA World Cup football matches (for men) if the Austrian national team is involved, as well as the opening match, the semi-finals and the final of the World Cup (for men)
European Championship football matches (for men) if the Austrian national team is involved, as well as the opening match, the semi-finals and the final of the football European Championship (for men)
The final of the Austrian Football Cup
FIS World Alpine skiing championships
World Nordic skiing championships
The Vienna Philarmonic Orchestra's New Year concert
The Vienna Opera Ball

France
Summer and Winter Olympics
All competitive French football internationals, home and away
Opening match, semi-finals and final, football World Cup
Semi-finals and final of European football championship
Uefa Cup final, if French club is involved
Champions League final
Final of football's French Cup
Rugby Union's Six Nations tournament
Semi-finals and final of Rugby World Cup
Final of French rugby union's Top 16 tournament
Final of European Rugby Cup, if French club is involved
Finals of French Open tennis championships, men and women, involving a French player
Final and semi-finals of tennis's Davis Cup and Fed Cup, involving French team
French Formula 1 grand prix
Cycling's Tour de France
Cycling's Paris –Roubaix race
Finals of European Basketball Championships, men and women, involving French national team
Finals of the World Basketball Championships, men and women, involving French national team
Finals of European Handball Championships, men and women, involving French national team
Finals of World Handball Championships, men and women, involving French national team
World Athletics Championships

Germany
Summer and Winter Olympics
All European Championship and World Cup matches involving the German national football team, as well as the opening match, the semifinals and finals, irrespective of whether the German team is involved
The semi-finals and final of the German FA Cup
The German national football team's home and away matches
The final of any European football club competition (Champions League, UEFA Cup) involving a German Club

Ireland
Summer Olympics
The All-Ireland Senior Inter-County Football and Hurling Finals
Ireland's home and away qualifying games in the European Football Championship and the FIFA World Cup Tournaments
Ireland's games in the European Football Championship Finals Tournament and the FIFA World Cup Finals Tournament
The opening games, the semi-finals and final of the European Football Championship Finals and the FIFA World Cup Finals Tournament
Ireland's games in the Rugby World Cup Finals Tournament
The Irish Grand National and the Irish Derby
The Nations Cup at the Dublin Horse Show

continued...

■ *Table 9.2* continued

Italy

Summer and Winter Olympics

The Football World Cup Final and all matches involving the Italian national team

The European Football the Italian national team

All matches involving the Italian national football team, at home and away, in official
    competitions

The final and the semi-finals of the Champions' League and the UEFA Cup where an Italian
    team is involved

The Tour of Italy Championship final and all matches involving (Giro d'Italia) cycling
    competition

The Formula One Italian Grand Prix

The San Remo Italian Music Festival

UK

The UK list is somewhat different from what has been approved in the other countries. It
    contains both an A-list and a B-list. The former category follows the same principles
    as in the other countries, but is stricter as it covers all the matches in the World Cup
    soccer finals, not only the matches involving UK teams and the finals. Events on the B-
    list are allowed to be screened exclusively on channels that do not meet the 95 per cent
    penetration, assuming edited highlights or delayed coverage are broadcast on a channel
    with 95 per cent penetration

The A-list includes the following events:

The Olympic Games

The FIFA World Cup Finals Tournament

The FA Cup Final

The Scottish FA Cup Final (in Scotland)

The Grand National

The Derby

The Wimbledon Tennis Finals

The European Football Championship Finals Tournament

The Rugby League Challenge Cup Final

The Rugby World Cup Final

The B-list includes the following events:

Cricket Test Matches played in England;

Non-finals play in the Wimbledon Tournament

All other matches in the Rugby World Cup Finals Tournament

Five Nations Rugby Tournament matches involving home countries

The Commonwealth Games

The World Athletics Championship

The Cricket World Cup – the final, semi-finals and matches involving home nations' teams

The Ryder Cup

The Open Golf Championship

Guidelines:

The guidelines drawn up by the European Commission and the governments in the respective
countries provide some ideas about what kind of impacts the Listed Events try to protect.

The Italian regulation requires that an event of major importance must satisfy (at least) two
of the following four criteria:

    the event and its outcome is of special and widespread interest in Italy, to people other
than those who usually watch this type of event on television;

    the event enjoys a widespread recognition by the general public and has a particular
cultural significance and strengthens the Italian cultural identity;

    the event involves a national team in a specific sporting discipline in a major international
tournament;

    the event has traditionally been broadcast on free television and has enjoyed high viewing
figures in Italy;.

continued...

■ **Table 9.2** *continued*

The guidelines in the Austrian regulation have several similarities with the Italian. It requires the events to be of substantial social interest and at least satisfy two of the following criteria:

the event already commands widespread attention in Austria, particularly as a result in the media;

the event is an expression of Austria's cultural, artistic or social identity;

the event is – particularly because of the involvement of top-level Austrian sportsmen/women – a sporting event of special national significance or commands widespread attention among viewers in Austria owing to its international importance;

the event has previously been broadcast on free-access television.

The UK regulation requires that the event must have a special national resonance, not simply of significance to those who ordinarily follow the sport concerned, and is an event that serves to unite the nation; a shared point in the national calendar. Such an event is likely to fall into one or both of the following categories:

it is a pre-eminent national or international event in the spor;t

it involves the national team or national representatives in the sport concerned.

The German list does not set up any specific criteria, except for the basic criterion; events of major importance for society.

■ **Table 9.3** *Events on the Anti-Siphoning List, 1 Jan. 2006 to 31 Dec. 2010*

Olympic Games	Each event held as part of the Olympic Games..
Commonwealth Games	Each event held as part of the Commonwealth Games
Horse Racing	Each running of the Melbourne Cup organised by the Victoria Racing Club
Australian Rules Football	Each match in the Australian Football League Premiership competition, including the Finals Series
Rugby League Football	Each match in the National Rugby League Premiership competition, including the Finals Series Each match in the National Rugby League State of Origin Series Each international rugby league 'test' match involving the senior Australian representative team selected by the Australian Rugby League, whether played in Australia or overseas
Rugby Union Football	Each international 'test' match involving the senior Australian representative team selected by the Australian Rugby Union, whether played in Australia or overseas Each match in the Rugby World Cup tournament
Cricket	Each 'test' match involving the senior Australian representative team selected by Cricket Australia played in either Australia or the United Kingdom Each one day cricket match involving the senior Australian representative team selected by Cricket Australia played in Australia or the United Kingdom Each one day cricket match involving the senior Australian representative team selected by Cricket Australia played as part of a series in which at least one match of the series is played in Australia. Each World Cup one day cricket match
Soccer	The English Football Association Cup final Each match in FIFA's 2006 World Cup soccer finals
Tennis	Each match in the Australian Open tennis tournament Each match in the Wimbledon (the Lawn Tennis Championships) tournament Each match in the men's and women's singles quarter-finals, semi-finals and finals of the French Open tennis tournament Each match in the men's and women's singles quarter-finals, semi-finals and finals of the United States Open tennis tournament Each match in each tie in the Davis Cup tennis tournament when an Australian representative team is involved
Netball	Each international netball match involving the senior Australian representative team selected by the All Australian Netball Association, whether played in Australia or overseas
Golf	Each round of the Australian Masters tournament Each round of the Australian Open tournament Each round of the United States Masters tournament Each round of the British Open tournament
Motor Sports	Each race in the Fédération Internationale de l'Automobile Formula One World Championship (Grand Prix) held in Australia Each race in the Moto GP held in Australia Each race in the V8 Supercar Championship Series (including the Bathurst 1000) Each race in the Champ Car World Series (IndyCar) held in Australia

For a detailed description of the Anti-Siphoning list, see: http://www.aph.gov.au/library/pubs/BD/2004-05/05bd004.htm

Notes

2 THE DEMAND FOR SPORTS BROADCASTING

1 Share percentage relates to the proportion of people watching rugby league expressed as a percentage of the total amount of people watching television at that time.
2 TVR is the percentage of all people with access to a television, watching the programme.

3 THE STRUCTURE OF SUPPLY

1 British Sky Broadcasting Group plc Annual Report and Accounts 2004.
2 BBC Annual Report and Accounts 2003/4.
3 BBC Statements of Programme Policy 2002/3.
4 http://www.sbs.com.au/sbscorporate/index.html?id=404.
5 http://www.aba.gov.au/tv/content/ozcont/index.htm.
6 http://www.aba.gov.au/tv/content/index.htm.
7 *TV Sports Markets*, vol. 9, no. 3.
8 *TV Sports Markets*, vol. 9, no. 3.
9 *TV Sports Markets*, vol. 8, no. 21.
10 *TV Sports Markets*, vol. 9, no. 5.
11 http://www.tvb.org/rcentral/mediatrendstrack/tvbasics/30_Total_and_TV_Ad_Volume.asp.
12 Broadcasting & Cable, 2003 Industry Profiles 2003.
13 http://www.nielsenmedia.com/whatratingsmean/.
14 Source of data: MediaCom, Norway.
15 Broadcasting & Cable (2002), vol. 135, no. 5, pp. 14–16
16 Interview with Charles Tomkovick, a professor of management and marketing at the University of Wisconsin-Eau Claire, who has been studying Super Bowl advertising by movie companies for five years. The figure refers to a survey carried out by BIGresearch, CIA, January 2005.
17 http://www.aba.gov.au/tv/content/advertising/index.htm.
18 Broadcasting & Cable in Europe – Industry profile, August 2003.
19 http://www.museum.tv/archives/etv/P/htmlP/payperview/payperview.htm.
20 http://www.telenor.com/ir/quarterly_reports/2q02/pdf_xls/2_kvartal_2002eng_godkj.pdf.
21 *TV Sports Markets*, vol. 7, no. 7.

4 THE COST STRUCTURE OF SPORTS BROADCASTING

1 BBC Annual Report and Accounts 2003/4.
2 http://www.kampanje.com/cgi-bin/kampanje/imaker?id=51765.

5 INTEGRATION

1 *TV Sports Markets* (2003), vol. 7, no. 7.
2 http://www.footballeconomy.com/archive/archive_2001_01.htm.
3 http://www.footballeconomy.com/.
4 http://www.visi.com/~sgrantz/xfl.html.
5 http://en.wikipedia.org/wiki/XFL.

6 COMPETITION BETWEEN CHANNELS

1 *Soccer Investor*, 2002 editions.
2 *TV-Sport Markets*, April 2003.
3 *Soccer Investor*, 2002 editions.
4 *Soccer Investor*, 2002 editions.
5 Baskerville Communication Corporations (1997): *Global TV-Sports Rights*, London.
6 http://media.guardian.co.uk/worldcup/story/0,11974,741487,00.html.
7 Desbordes, Michel (2003) 'The relationship between sport and television: the case of the French network TF1 and the World Cup 2002'. Paper presented at the 5th IACE-conference in Neuchatel, Switzerland, May 2003.
8 http://www.telenor.com/ir/quarterly_reports/2q02/pdf_xls/2_kvartal_2002eng_godkj.pdf.
9 http://www.gouldmedia.com/tsr.html.
10 http://www.timesonline.co.uk/article/0,,10369-1577567,00.html.

7 THE PRICING AND SELLING OF TV SPORTS RIGHTS

1 Baskerville Communication Corporation (1997): Global TV Sports Rights.
2 Kagan World Media (1999): European Media Sports Rights.
3 *TV Sports Markets* (2003), vol. 7, no. 7.
4 Rodney Fort's web site: http://users.pullman.com/rodfort/SportsBusiness/BizFrame.htm.
5 http://www.euractiv.com/Article?tcmuri=tcm:29-134541-16&type=News.
6 Japan had a population of 127.5 million in 2006, while France had 60.9 million and the Netherlands 16.5 million. Source: *CIA Factbook*, 2006.
7 Source: Irish Independent, 3 October 2004. Retrieved 07.11.2006 from http://unison.ie/irish_independent/stories.php3?ca=35&si=1261912&issue_id=11502.
8 *China Daily*, 24 August 2005. Retrieved 01.12.2006 from http://china.org.cn/english/sports/139588.htm.
9 http://www.nba.com/schedules/international_nba_tv_schedule.html.
10 http://www.nhl.com/nhlhq/intl/fact_sheet.html.
11 http://www.exchange4media.com/e4m/media_matter/matter_010406.asp
12 ibid

8 THE AUCTIONING OF SPORTS RIGHTS

1 EBU represents 65 member broadcasting organisations in 49 countries, mainly across Europe, but also in the Middle East and North Africa.
2 Horsman, M. (1997) Sky High (UK, Orion Business Books), pp. 97–100.
3 http://media.guardian.co.uk/worldcup/story/0,11974,741487,00.html.
4 Interview with TV2's sport director, Bjørn Taalesen in *Dagens Næringsliv* (a Norwegian business newspaper), 31.10.2000.

9 MARKET INTERVENTION IN SPORTS BROADCASTING

1 *TV Sports Markets* (2005), vol. 9, no. 3.
2 *Daily Post*, 27 May 2005.

References

Andrews, D.L. (2003) Sport and the Transnationalizing Media Corporation, *Journal of Media Economics*, 16(4), 235–51.

Baimbridge, M, Cameron, S. and Dawson, P. (1995) Satellite broadcasting and match attendance: the case of Rugby League, *Applied Economic Letters*, 2, 343–6.

Boardman, A.E. and Hargreaves-Heap, S.P. (1999) Network Externalities and Government Restrictions on Satellite Broadcasting of Key Sporting Events, *Journal of Cultural Economics*, 23(3), 167–81.

Brown, A. (1996) Economics, Public Service Broadcasting and Social Values, *Journal of Media Economics*, 9(1), 3–15.

Brown, W.S. (1995) *Principles of Economics,* St. Paul, MN: West Publishing Company.

Cairns, J., Jennett, N. and Sloane, P.J. (1986) The Economics of Professional Team Sports: A Survey of Theory and Evidence, *Journal of Economic Studies*, 13(1), 3–80.

Carlton, D.W. and Perloff, J.M. (1999) *Modern Industrial Organization* (3rd edn), Boston, MA: Addison Wesley Longman.

Cashmore, E.E. (1994) *And Then There was Television*, London: Routledge.

Collis, D. and Montgomery, C. (1997) *Corporate Strategy: A Resource-Based Approach*, Burr Ridge, IL: Irwin.

Cowie, C. and Williams, M. (1997) The Economics of Sports Rights, *Telecommunication Policy*, 21(7), 619–34.

Deloitte (2004) *Annual Review of Football Finance*, Manchester: Deloitte & Touche.

Deloitte (2005) *Annual Review of Football Finance*, Manchester: Deloitte & Touche.

Deloitte (2006) *Annual Review of Football Finance*, Manchester: Deloitte & Touche.

Desbordes, M. (2003) The Relationship Between Sport and Television: The Case of the French Network TF1 and the World Cup 2002. Paper presented at the 5t. IACE-conference in Neuchatel, Switzerland, May, 2003.

Dixit, A. and Skeath, S. (1999) *Games of Strategy*, New York: W. W. Norton & Company.

Douma, S. and Schreuder, H. (2002) *Economic Approaches to Organizations* (3rd edn), London: Prentice Hall, Pearson Education.

Downward, P. and Dawson, A. (2000) *The Economics of Professional Team Sports*, London: Routledge.

Dunnet, P. (1990) *The World Television Industry – An Economic Analysis*, London and New York: Routledge.

El-Hodri, M. and Quirk, J. (1971) An economic model of a professional sport league, *Journal of Political Economy*, 79, 1302–19.

Fizel, J.L and Bennett, R.W. (1999) The impact of college football telecasts on college footbal attendance, *Social Science Quarterly*, 70(4), 980–8

Forrest, D., Simmonds, R. and Buraimo, B. (2004) Outcome Uncertainty and the Couch Potato Audience, Lancaster University Management School Working Paper No. 2004/047.

Fort, R. (2003) *Sports Economics*, London: Prentice Hall, Pearson Education.

Fort, R. and Quirk, J. (1995) Cross-subsidization, Incentives, and Outcomes in Professional Team Sports Leagues, *Journal of Economic Literature*, XXXIII (September), 1265–99.

Fort, R. and Quirk, J. (2004) Owner Objectives and Competitive Balance, *Journal of Sports Economics*, 5(1), 20–32.

Furubotn, E. and Pejovich, S. (1974) *The Economics of Property Rights*, Cambridge, MA: Ballinger.

Gaustad, T. (2000a) The Economics of Sports Programming, *Nordicom Review*, 21(2), 101–13.

Gaustad, T. (2000b): *Fjernsynssport: Rettighetsspørsmål og rettighetsøkonomiske konsekvenser.* Research report no 12, Oslo: Handelshøyskolen BI.

Gerrard, W. (2000) Media Ownership of Pro Sports Teams: Who are the Winners and Losers?, *Sport Marketing & Sponsorship*, September/October, 199–218.

Gratton, C. and Solberg, H.A. (2004) Sports and Broadcasting: Comparisons between the United States and Europe, In *International Sports Economics Comparisons*, eds R. Fort and J. Fizel, Westport, CT and London: Praeger.

Gratton, C. and Taylor, P. (2000) *The Economics of Sport and Recreation*, London: Spon Press.

Haugland, S.A. (1996) *Samarbeid, allianser og nettverk* (Collaboration, alliances and network), Oslo: Universitetsforlaget.

Haugland, S.A. (2004) *Samarbeid, allianser og nettverk* (Cooperation, alliances and networks), second edition, Oslo: Norwegian University Press.

Hausman, J. and Leonard, G. (1997) Superstars in the National basketball Association: Economic Value and Policy, *Journal of Labor Economics*, 15, 586–624.

Head, J. (1974) *Public Goods and Public Welfare*, Durham, NC: Duke University Press.

Heubeck, T. (2004) The Collective Selling of Broadcasting Rights in Team Sports, German Working Papers in Law and Economics, vol. 2004, Paper 13.

Horsman, M. (1997) *Sky High*, London: Orion Business Books, pp. 97–100.

Johnsen, H. (2001) A Cost Perspective on Televised Sport: The Optimal Economic Utilisation of Sports Media Rights. Paper presented at the 15th Nordic Conference on Media and Communication Research, Reykjavik, 11–13 August.

Kaldor, N. (1950) The Economic Aspects of Advertising, *Review of Economic Studies*, 18, 1–27.

Kanazawa, M. and Funk, J. (2001) Racial Discrimination in Pro Basketball, *Economic Inquiry*, 39, 599–608.

Kesénne, S. (1996) League Management in Professional Team Sport with Win Maximizing Clubs, *European Journal for Sport Management*, 2(2), 14–22.

Kesénne, S. (2004) Competitive Balance and Revenue Sharing: When Rich Clubs Have Poor Teams, *Journal of Sports Economics*, 5(2), 206–12.

Kuhn, H.W. and Tucker, A.W. (eds) (1953) A Value for N-Person Games, in *Contributions to the Theory of Games, Volume II, Annals of Mathematics Studies*, 28, 307–17, Princeton, NJ: Princeton University Press.

Law, A., Harvey, J. and Kemp, S. (2002) The Global Sport Mass Media Oligopoly: The Three Usual Suspects and More, *International Review for the Sociology of Sport*, 37(3–4), 279–302.

Levin , H.J. (1980) *Fact and Fancy in Television Regulation*, New York: Sage.

McAfee, R.P. and McMillan, J. (1987) Auctions and Bidding, *Journal of Economic Literature*, XXV (June), 699–738.

McChesney, R. W. (1989) Media Made Sport: A History of Sports Coverage in the United States, in L.A. Wenner (ed.) *Media, Sports and Society*, London: Sage, pp. 49–69.

McMillan, J. (1991) Bidding for Olympic Broadcast Rights: The Competition Before the Competition, *Negotiation Journal*, July, 255–63.

Merges, R.P. (1995) The Economic Impact of Intellectual Property Rights: An Overview and Guide, *Journal of Cultural Economics*, 19, 103–17.

Meyer, C.B. (1998) Strategiske veivalg og motiver for fusjoner og okjøp (Strategically choose of direction and motives for mergers and acquisitions), in K. Boye and C.B. Meyer, *Cappelen, Fusjoner og oppkjøp* (Mergers and acquisitions), Oslo: Akademisk Forlag.

Monopolies and Mergers Commission (MMC) (1999) *British Sky Broadcasting plc and Manchester United plc: A Report on the Proposed Merger*, London: The Stationery Office.

Musgrave, R. (1958) *The Theory of Public Finance*, London: Macmillan.

Neale, W.C. (1964) The Peculiar Economics of Professional Sports, *Quarterly Journal of Economics*, 78(1), 1–14.

Noll, R., (1974) *Government and the Sports Business*, Washington, DC: Brookings Institution

Noll, R. (1988) *Professional Baketball*, Stanford University Studies in Industrial Economics Paper no. 144, Palo Alto, CA: University of Stanford.

O'Keeffe, L. (1999) The Economic and Financial Effects of the Introduction of Super League in Rugby League, PhD thesis at Sheffield Hallam University.

O'Keeffe, L. (2002) Tradition to Technology – Rugby League and the Road to Murdochisation. Paper presented at the 10 th European Sport Management Congress, 4–7 September, Jyväskylä, Finland.

Pozner, E.A. (1972) Merit Wants and the Theory of Taxation, *Public Finance*, XXXVII(4), 460–73.

Pindyck, R.S. and Rubinfeld, D.L. (2004) *Microeconomics* (6th edn), Upper Saddle River, NJ: Pearson Education.

Quirk, J. and Fort, R. (1997) *PAY DIRT: The Business of Professional Team Sports*, Princeton, NJ: Princeton University Press.

Quirk, J. and Fort, R. (1999) *HARD BALL: The Abuse of Power in Pro Team Sports*, Princeton, NJ: Princeton University Press.

Rasmusen, E. (2001) *Games and Information. An Introduction to Game Theory*, Oxford: Blackwell Publishers.

Reve, T. (1990). *Mimetic Behaviour in Banking* Working Paper 48, Bergen: Center for Applied Research.

Rottenberg, S. (1956) The Baseball Players' Labour Market, *Journal of Political Economy*, 64, 243–58.

Shibli, S. and Coleman, R. (2005) Economic Impact and Place Marketing Evaluation: A Case Study of the World Snooker Championship, *International Journal of Event Management Research*, 1, 13–29.

Shibli, S. and Gratton, C. (1999) Assessing the Public Profile of Major Sports Events: A Case-Study of the European Short Course Swimming Championships, *International Journal of Sports Marketing and Sponsorship*, 1(3), September/October, 278–95.

Slater, J. (1998) Changing Partners: The Relationship Between the Mass Media and the Olympic Games. Paper presented at the Fourth International Symposium for Olympic Research, 1–3 October 1998.

Sloane, P.J. (1971) The Economics of Professional Football: The Football Club as a Utility Maximiser, *Scottish Journal of Political Economy*, 17, 121–45.

Solberg, H.A (2002a) The Economics of Television Sports Rights. Europe and the US – A Comparative Analysis, *Norsk Medietidskrift* (A Norwegian Mediajournal), 10(2), 59–81.

Solberg, H.A. (2002b) Cultural Prescription – The European Commission's Listed Events Regulation – Over Reaction?, *Culture, Sport, Society*, 5(2), 1–28.

Solberg, H.A. and Gratton, C. (2000) The Economics of TV-Sports Rights – The Case of European Soccer, *European Journal for Sport Management*, 7, Special Edition, 69–98.

Solberg, H.A. and Hammervold, R. (2004) Sport Broadcasting: How to Maximize the Rating Figures, *Trends in Communication*, 12(2), 83–100.

Szymanski, S. (2001) Income Inequality, Competitive Valance and the Attractiveness of Team Sports. Some Evidence and a Natural Experiment from English Soccer, *Economic Journal*, 111, F69–84.

Sweezy, P.M. 1939. Demand under Conditions of Oligopoly, *Journal of Political Economy*, 47, 568–73.

Thomas, S.M. and Jolson, M.A (1979) Components of demand for major league baseball, *University of Michigan Business Review*, 31(3) 1–6.

Todreas, T.M. (1999) *Value Creation and Branding in Television's Digital Age*, Wesport, CT: Quorum Books.

Varian, H. (2002) *Intermediate Microeconomics – A Modern Approach* (6th edn), New York: W. W. Norton and Co.

Vrooman, J. (1997) A Unified Theory of Capital and Labor Markets in Major League Baseball, *Southern Economic Journal*, 63(1), 594–619.

Whannel, G. (1992) *Fields in Vision: Television Sport and Cultural Transformation*, London: Routledge.

Williamson, O.E. (1979) Transaction-Cost Economics: The Governance of Contractual Relations, *Journal of Law and Economics*, 22(2), 233–61.

Withers, G. (2002) Economics and Regulation of Broadcasting. Discussion Paper No. 93, Graduate Program in Public Policy, RSSS, Australian National University.

Zhang, J.J. and Smith, S.W. (1997) Impact of broadcasting on the attendance at professional basketball games, *Sports Marketing Quarterly* 6(1), 23–9.

Index